SAVING A CONTINENT
THE UNTOLD STORY OF THE MARSHALL PLAN

Charles L. Mee Jr.

PART ONE

1
THE OPPORTUNITY

IN JANUARY 1947, high above the Mediterranean, in the wild and barren mountains of northern Greece - near Mount Olympus, the legendary home of the gods - ragged, armed gangs of outlaws had managed to harass the Greek government almost to the point of collapse. The outlaws, who called themselves rebels (*antártes*), were holed up throughout the northern and central parts of Greece, along the Piniós River, in the Pindus Mountains - where they fought by night and disappeared during the day. The cities of Greece belonged to the central government, and the countryside belonged to the antártes - a situation that during the next several decades would become the very model of the modern polity in much of the world.

Subhi Sadi, the Middle Eastern representative of the Chase Bank, reported to his home office in New York: "Actually there are two Greeces: cities such as Athens, Piraeus, and Salonica where the government is in control but with the help of strong security forces - especially in the working people's quarters; and the countryside where the government is not in control except where the Armed Forces operate."

The antártes were, by 1947, reduced to subsistence. They had few medicines, no aspirin or sulfa drugs, little salt, cloth, shoes, oil, flour, or cigarettes. But they did have corn bread and goat cheese, and, like guerrilla fighters everywhere, they needed not so much to win as to persist until the will of the governors was exhausted. And the aim of the antártes was aided by general economic conditions in Greece. American diplomatic reports (touchingly classified secret and top secret) mentioned, "Food prices up 4 percent this week, Govt deficit hit new high for last reporting period, imports were trickle, food supplies about exhausted. This has resulted in widespread unrest . . . demands of merchant seamen for 110 percent wage increases, Piraeus dock workers for double present wages, threatened strike textile mill workers."

Britain had long supported the uncertain Greek government. Greece had been Britain's ally during the war, and when the Greek king had had to flee the Nazis, the British took him in. After the war, the British had a natural affinity for the government of Greece, and in the memoranda and cables he sent home, Richard Windle, a British representative to an economic commission in Greece, was constrained to acknowledge that the situation was "sticky."

The antártes had been spawned by the EAM, the National Liberation Front, a large and popular political movement with a membership of about 700,000. Drawn primarily from the working class and the peasants, the EAM was generally leftist, with a somewhat disorganized, largely Communist leadership. During the course of World War II, the EAM had brought together a substantial military force, the ELAS, which had become the most effective guerrilla band in Greece. By the time the Germans had been compelled to withdraw from Greece, in the autumn of 1944, ELAS had come to control most of northern Greece, and EAM, meanwhile, had carried out a mixed program of terror, reform, vendetta, modernization, and slapdash justice that had earned it broad popular support.

Then, in December 1944, government police forces fired on an EAM demonstration in Athens. Civil war threatened. The Russians remained pointedly distant from the Greek Communists. British troops intervened on the side of the government, and the government's forces defeated EAM.

The British gave full support to the government even though British diplomats frankly considered the regime corrupt; for, just as EAM had shown itself ready to engage in vendetta and terror, so too had the government customarily used terror, arrests, beatings, deportation, and murder in order to have its way.

Former EAM/ELAS men retreated to the mountains, and the country did dissolve in civil war. "There is really no state here," an American Foreign Service officer cabled Washington, "in the Western concept. Rather we have a loose hierarchy of individualistic politicians, some worse than others, who are so preoccupied with their own struggle for power that they have no time, even assuming capacity, to develop economic policy."

By January 1947, however, the British were no longer able to support their friends in Greece. The government needed both economic and military aid in order to hold out against the antártes, but the British, so devastated by the Second World War, had no more money or credit or arms to offer. Britain, in the memorable phrase of another young State Department officer, "was like a soldier wounded in war who, now that the fighting was over, was bleeding to death." The empire had begun its collapse. It could no longer take care of its own.

In truth, in the aftermath of the war, nations were in shambles everywhere. Nearly all of Germany and much of Eastern Europe had been devastated. Bridges and roads were gone. Rivers and canals were plugged with sunken barges and fallen bridges. Unexploded bombs and shells lay in the fields. Of those who had survived the war, millions were wounded, sick, or merely dazed, weak, or stunned. The Russians reckoned their war losses at 20 million soldiers and civilians dead. Poland counted its losses at 4.3 million dead, Yugoslavia at 1.7 million. France had lost 600,000, America 400,000, Britain 390,000. Germany had lost 4.2 million, Japan 1.2 million, Italy 410,000. Six million Jews had been killed in Germany.

Many remembered that the desolation of the First World War had led - some said inevitably - to the outbreak of the Second, and the reminders were disquieting. Once again, postwar inflation whipsawed the survivors: cigarettes, coffee, and chocolate were better currencies than Deutsche marks. Prices rose in Italy to thirty-five times their prewar level. The old Hungarian currency was simply abolished when inflation reached 11,000 trillion pengös to the dollar. In the winter of 1946-47, the cold was so severe, in England especially, as to cause a coal shortage, and thus an industrial paralysis. Before the year was over, disastrous harvests all across the continent would leave Europeans hungry, and, in some places, even starving.

Beyond all this daily suffering lay a whole array of invisible destruction. The death and sickness and shattered homes and cities had all been felt at once; only gradually did the wounded nations come to realize that many of their factories, devoted so narrowly to wartime production and left unrepaired during the war, had become obsolete. Skilled workers had been killed, and so work forces were less able than they had been before the war. Food was in short supply and, even as agriculture revived, the fertility of the neglected soil was found to have declined. Raw materials were scarce.

Industry faltered. Trade was undone. Financial crises erupted everywhere. The skills and habits and arrangements of economic activity had been broken. The financial and political relationships among the European powers and their colonies and dependencies were wrecked. The great imperial powers of the nineteenth century, having weakened one another in World War I, had destroyed themselves in World War II.

The awesomeness of this act of self-destruction cannot easily be overstated. The suicide of Europe left the world with a vast power vacuum - and without any world political system to order the relations among nations. In short, the destruction of the old empires left the world in a classical state of anarchy, or chaos.

Destruction and chaos, while they may be painful to those who suffer them, are not necessarily a misfortune for all. To some, chaos is rich with opportunity. If the old empires could no longer hold on to their colonies and satrapies, then someone else might well pick up the shards. Someone else might colonize the colonizers. Someone else might transform Europe and Britain - and the dependencies of Europe and Britain - into an assortment of provinces, possessions, trusts, leaseholds, unequal friendships, or even into a new empire.

At the end of World War II, only two great powers remained strong enough to consider taking over, or materially influencing, Europe - the United States and the Soviet Union. Having recently cooperated to defeat Hitler, and having found that the need for cooperation had vanished when Nazi Germany was defeated, the United States and the Soviet Union had commenced to find fault with each other even before the war had ended. At the Potsdam Conference in the summer of 1945, the major powers had divided Europe into Eastern and Western spheres of influence, but neither side was happy with the bargain it had made, and both sides complained about it. By the spring of 1946, when former British Prime Minister Winston

Churchill announced that the Soviet Union had rung down an "iron curtain across Europe" (along the line to which Churchill, incidentally, had agreed at Potsdam), and so divided the Continent between the free and the enslaved, the two sides were voicing their complaints without modulation. And yet, it was not until another year had passed that it became entirely evident that Europe was weak and becoming daily weaker, that the former European allies and protectorates were in danger of collapse, and that decisive power remained in the hands of only Russia and America. The reasons for cooperation between Russia and America had come to seem entirely negligible, and as the advantages in open competition became irresistible, it seemed pointless even to pretend to seek accommodation.

The question that the Americans and the Russians - or certain of their leaders at any rate - asked themselves under the circumstances was not whether to act, but rather when and where.

How the two great powers would have, or try to have, their way in the world would be determined in part by vast historical forces entirely outside their control; in part by their geographical positions, their natural resources, their climates, their soils, and their crops; it would certainly be determined by their economies and the positions of their armies; in some measure, it would be determined by the backgrounds and expectations, assumptions and idiosyncrasies of the individuals who struggled to shape all these forces to their advantage. Politics is the means by which men and women and nations, given their ordained starting points, determine who shall have his way, and how he shall get it. In this sense, foreign policy is a grand and prolonged revelation of national character.

As for the Americans, who considered themselves to be the victors in the recent war and the custodians of the greatest republic on earth, most of them could hardly help feeling that they were a people of exceptionally fine character. Most felt, as Cecil Rhodes said of his fellow Britons in the balmy days of the nineteenth century, "We happen to be the best people, with the highest ideals of decency and justice and liberty and peace, and the more of the world we inhabit, the better it is for humanity."

Whether or not the Russians felt quite the same way about themselves, they too tended to speak in terms of the favors they wished to bestow on the world. While the Russians explained American behavior as the inevitable expansionist, exploitative end of capitalist development, and the Americans explained Russian behavior as an inexorable Marxist-Leninist conspiracy to conquer the world, both sides went about moving into the world in a way that Thucydides would have understood.

On a gray Friday afternoon, February 21, 1947, in Washington, secretaries and junior State

Department officers in the gloomy old pile known as the State, War, and Navy Building were idling their way toward the weekend. The State Department had actually outgrown this antique gaggle of offices as it was even then outreaching its historically modest duties. As the twentieth century progressed, the department found that it needed increasingly more space, and it was now packing itself up to move out of its old quarters into a new building. Old State, as the accustomed offices were called, was a place of high-ceilinged rooms, carpeted and cream-colored, with carved wainscoting and fireplace mantelpieces. Secretaries, it was true, had to make do with small spaces in the passageways between offices; messengers sat dozing in wooden swivel chairs in the hallways, waiting for their assignments; the heating system made the offices stifling in the winter (as the sun did in summer); yet Old State had a lovable, ramshackle quality to it. Its denizens loved it and were not eager to move, except that the new building would give them even more room for expansion.

In earlier days, even as recently as the twenties, the department had been composed to a great extent of well-born, well-bred, well-schooled, polo-playing East Coast gentlemen, or men who could pass for such. But during the thirties and forties, as America's involvement with the rest of the world grew, the erstwhile handful of clubbable gentlemen had grown into a department of some thousands of necessarily less carefully selected men (and few women). By the end of World War II, the State Department employed fifty-eight ambassadors and ministers, 989 career ministers, counselors, consuls general, consuls, vice-consuls, and other officers, and 11,500 staff officers, accountants, chauffeurs, charwomen, secretaries, cooks, valets, and messengers. As a whole, the group was not quite as old school tie as it had been, although the men at the top still tended to be Ivy Leaguers and their subordinates affected a style that would seem appropriate to the quiet ecstasies of the Mid-Atlantic accent, the embroidered pocket handkerchief, the creak of the heavy leather club chair.

On that memorable Friday, the Secretary of State, George C. Marshall, had left early in the day to go up to Princeton to deliver a speech. Shortly after he left, the private secretary to Lord Inverchapel, the British ambassador to Washington, called. Dean Acheson, the Undersecretary of State, spoke with him. His Majesty's Government, Inverchapel's secretary said, had "a blue piece of paper" for Marshall, and the British wished urgently to deliver it. "A blue piece of paper," as Acheson knew, was trade talk for the most important of diplomatic messages. The paper, Acheson was told, dealt with British aid to Greece.

Acheson understood at once that the British were announcing the end of their empire. The moment had been anticipated for at least several months in the State Department - and by some, certainly by Acheson, eagerly awaited. Since Marshall was gone, the paper could not be delivered to him. And since Acheson was only Undersecretary, he could not receive the British ambassador. Instead, Acheson suggested, with a quick instinct for protocol, that Inverchapel have a member of his staff deliver a carbon copy of the note to a member of Acheson's staff. In this way, the Americans could receive the news, and could also begin the staff work that Marshall would want done before taking any action. The blue paper itself could be delivered officially to Marshall on Monday morning.

Forty-five minutes later, Acheson had copies of not one but two papers - one on Greece and one on Turkey. The Greek paper outlined the situation in that beleaguered country and stated simply that "His Majesty's Government, in view of their own situation, find it impossible to grant further financial assistance to Greece." The paper on Turkey outlined a similar state of economic dislocation there, a similar shortage of funds to support the government's armed forces (although the government was not immediately threatened in Turkey by "bandits" as it was in Greece), and a similar inability of his Majesty's Government to make "any further credits available to Turkey."

The news could not have been delivered to an audience more perfectly prepared to receive it.

Acheson, age fifty-four, had grown up perhaps not so much in America as in an imaginary country of upper-middle-class Anglo-America that coalesced here and there in apparitions of understated comfort along the Eastern seaboard of the United States. His father was an Episcopal clergyman of English descent who had become Bishop of Connecticut. His mother was the daughter of a wealthy Canadian distiller. Acheson was raised in what he called the "Golden Age of childhood" which "reached its apex in the last decade of the nineteenth century and the first few years of the twentieth, before the plunge into the motor age and city life swept away the freedom of children and dogs [and] put them both on leashes. . . . As for the Athens of this golden age, it lay, of course, in the Connecticut Valley, just where the river leaves white fields of shade-grown tobacco, and enters the gorge channeling it past Haddam and Hadlyme. . . . Here a town . . . Middletown . . . flowered briefly when clipper ships dropped anchor there. . . . This boom left imposing houses on High Street at the top of the hill, with its four rows of great elms."

The Achesons lived at the bottom of the hill, in the rectory on Broad Street, elm-shaded too, not far from the white-painted church, the playing field, the livery stable, the blacksmith's shop, Mr. Walsh's harness shop, the row of apple trees near the brick wall of the judge's stable, the escape route up the apple trees to the stable roof, down to the carriage yard and on into the maze of backyards.

"Within the rectory," Acheson recalled, "the foreign element topped the American two to one; in influence, the disparity was far greater. My sister and I were by constitutional right citizens of the United States, while the other five were subjects of the Queen - Empress, Victoria, Defender of the Faith." Cazzie the cook and Maggie the maid were both Irish. Marie Sinclair, called Sin, a Toronto girlhood acquaintance of Acheson's mother who came to help care for the children, was "a loyal British subject." Acheson's father, the son of a Scotch-Irish professional British soldier and an Irish Protestant mother, was a British subject "with deep affection for Ireland." And Acheson's mother, English Canadian, educated at boarding school in England, was monarchist, whose "enthusiasm for the Empire and the Monarch," as Acheson said, "was not diluted by any corrupting contact with Canadian nationalism."

Acheson was raised, then, in a world of bracing standards of self-discipline, assumed privilege, and, remarkably enough, little of what could be called religious feeling. His father was the patriarch of the family, Olympian in his detachment, except on the family vacations, when he was the boon companion, setting the standard for endurance in hiking, hard work in pitching camp, enthusiasm in singing and storytelling. "As a prelate," however, as Acheson recalled, "he was a baffling man, widely read in theology and Christian doctrine, yet rarely speaking of either, privately or in his sermons, which so far as I can remember dealt more with ethics and conduct . . . based on a perception of what was decent and civilized for man inextricably caught up in social relationships."

The Queen's birthday was celebrated every year, though quietly. The Union Jack was raised on the flagpole, and at dinner everyone was given claret (the children's diluted with water) and stood solemnly while Acheson's father said, "the Queen," at which the others all said, "the Queen," and drank their claret - "which was not very good."

Soon enough, too soon for Acheson's taste, he was sent away to Groton, and then to Yale (where he made his way onto crew in his freshman year, and then into Scroll and Key, Delta Kappa Epsilon, and Phi Beta Kappa), and Harvard Law School. Between Groton and Yale, Acheson had begun to cultivate a mustache that finally became both bushy and clipped, both assertive and disciplined, both prickly and precise, so that, by the time he was a young man, when he elevated his chin and cocked his head slightly to one side and arched his bristly left eyebrow, he looked rather like a reincarnation of that great nineteenth-century imperialist, Lord Kitchener of Khartoum.

He had an understandably high regard for his own intelligence and a less thoroughly examined regard for the values, and what he took to be the high standards, of his class. He came to have little regard for public opinion ("not because the people do not know the facts . . . but because they do not know the issues exist") and, in time, to dismiss a tribe of critics, characteristically, as "primitives." His view of the world was not quite theological, and yet he did tend to see the world as divided between the elect and the damned, and to have some sense that a member of America's elect would be more at home with a member of England's elect than with the democratic stew of his own country. Together, these members of the elect would pursue goals that transcended merely democratic values of freedom to engage in one's own purposes. "The individual," said Acheson, "makes the pilgrimage to choose what is good and reject what is evil, to transcend appetites and achieve the aspirations of the spirit." Life, in short, has a higher goal than mere peace and contentment, and such lesser goals may need to be sacrificed to the struggle to attain perfection of the spirit. The ultimate goals of life are not matters of individual free choice; the ultimate goals have been chosen, and the individual must measure up. To the extent that the mass of people do not understand such issues, they will have to be led - even against their ignorant will - by an enlightened elite.

Acheson's career as a young lawyer was imbued with a sense of resolute measuring up. Among his professors at Harvard was Felix Frankfurter, and after he graduated, Acheson was placed - with Frankfurter's blessing - as a private secretary to Louis Brandeis, Associate Justice of the Supreme Court. During the twenties and early thirties, Acheson worked in Washington for the firm of Covington, Burling, and Rublee, where he practiced corporate and international law. In 1933, on the recommendation of Frankfurter and Brandeis, President Roosevelt appointed Acheson Undersecretary of the Treasury. Acheson, however, was not entirely happy in the Roosevelt Administration ("I was always conservative," he later said), and he returned to his law firm in 1934.

When World War II broke out, Acheson emerged again, this time to advocate all-out aid to Britain as the essential line of defense for the United States and, indeed, for Western civilization. "We are faced," Acheson said, "with elemental, immoral and ruthless power. In dealing with it, you can be wrong only once. Remember, I beseech you, that the judgment of nature upon error is death." Roosevelt appointed him Assistant Secretary of State.

During the war, he was particularly useful, because of his background, in economic matters. As time went on, and Secretary of State Cordell Hull was replaced by Edward Stettinius, and Stettinius was replaced after Roosevelt's death by James Byrnes, Acheson established himself as the man who could help a new Secretary of State get to know the department and its bureaucracy. Although he was not uninterested in money, he was always willing to sacrifice his economic interests to his higher aspirations. When General Marshall replaced Byrnes as Secretary, Marshall made it clear that he wanted Acheson to be his deputy chief and manage the department - for an interim period at least, until Marshall could bring in his own staff.

Immediately after the war, Acheson had expressed the belief that the United States and the Soviet Union could accommodate one another in the world. In time, however - with the help of the unfriendly behavior of the Soviet Union - Acheson became disturbed by the Communists. "We have got to understand," he said as early as June 1946, "that all our lives, the danger, the uncertainty, the need for alertness, for effort, for discipline will be upon us." As he said later, speaking of the "distant and shadowy figures in the Kremlin," it was difficult "to believe that so monstrous an evil can exist in a world based upon infinite mercy and justice. But the fact is that it does exist. The fact is that it twists and tortures all our lives."

After the wars in Europe and Asia had ended, and it had become evident that the great European empires had finally eliminated one another, Acheson saw the task before the world as one of rare "enormity." It was, he thought, "just a bit less formidable than that described in the first chapter of Genesis. That was to create a world out of chaos; ours, to create half a world, a free half, out of the same material." It was a worthy enterprise for a clergyman's son; without doubt, it was God's work. And Acheson pursued it with uncommon wit, devotion, and self-discipline. It cannot be said that he pursued it in order to save democracy, which he abhorred, or for the sake of profit, for which he had little passion. Acheson's goal, which he took to be America's goal, was the exalted aim of saving nothing less than Western civilization - or, more precisely, Western, Anglican civilization, the community of his childhood world. Almost without giving it a moment's thought, when Greece collapsed, Acheson reached out to pick up the British Empire as though it had always been his.

Acheson gathered his staff that Friday afternoon in February, and asked them to clear their weekend so that they could work up background studies on Greece and Turkey by Monday morning. What was wanted, as Acheson made clear during the course of the weekend, was not papers considering whether to take any action, but papers considering, under the circumstances, just what actions to take.

And then, having set the department in motion, Acheson phoned Secretary Marshall and the President and explained "what had happened . . ."

2
THE PRESIDENT

IF ACHESON WAS the perfect audience for Lord Inverchapel's message, no more perfect recipient for Acheson's message can be imagined than President Harry S Truman, who had assumed office on the death of Franklin Roosevelt on April 12, 1945. Truman, age sixty-three in 1947, was a man who loved to move, to act, to do, to walk fast, to make decisions, to get on with it. He was a little fellow, a banty rooster of a man, quick to smile, quick to cuss, quick to pick up his shoulders, stand straight, stiffen his lip, and look tough. Dressed characteristically in a double-breasted gray suit, white shirt, polka-dot bow tie, a World War I discharge button in his lapel, a gold Masonic ring on his left hand, gray hair cut short and slicked down, his clear blue eyes framed by steel-rimmed glasses that magnified his eyes arrestingly and lent him an extra edge of attentiveness and spark, he set out shortly after six each morning on a brisk walk (120 regulation Army paces per minute) from the White House up to Dupont Circle or over to the Washington Monument, astonishing passersby with his cheerful greetings, giving pungent off-the-cuff one-liners to the little band of reporters who hustled along with him, announcing to all that he was "fine and dandy," thank you, stopping to shake hands with a street sweeper and compliment the man on his tidiness.

He was pure small-town, a natural man. As his ninety-two-year-old mother said of him, "Harry will get along." Born on a Missouri farm near Kansas City, Truman had been a shy, quiet boy, who wore glasses from the age of eight, read books, and played the piano - all, apparently, at his mother's behest. His father was a loud, profane, aggressive man, a livestock and mule trader. Truman's middle initial, S, has no period after it, because it is not an abbreviation for anything. It is, rather, an expression of the first political compromise of his life: His parents, unable to decide whether to name him for his maternal grandfather Solomon Young or his paternal grandfather Anderson Shippe Truman, gave him the middle name S.

Raised in a disciplined Baptist home, with a brother and a sister, he lived a life that was, by the standards of the Middle West during the time of his boyhood, a bit bookish. He said in later years that he had read every single book in the local library - which sounds like one of those harmless exaggerations a boy will tell his friends and parents. In fact, he must have read a lot of them, and remembered everything he read: As President he had the capacity to amaze an aide or a foreign diplomat or an ambassador's wife with a sudden lengthy disquisition on a piece of little-known history of a Middle Eastern country or on the inland waterways of Europe. He knew a remarkable number of stories of battles and generals and Great Men. His view of history was largely that of the nineteenth-century master of narrative, Thomas Carlyle: that history is shaped by forceful heroes.

He went to public schools, and when it came time for college, he applied to West Point - which was both free and well suited to his developing temperament - but his poor eyesight kept him out.

Denied college, he bumped around from one odd job to another, as a clerk in a drugstore, a timekeeper for a construction crew on the Santa Fe Railroad, a bookkeeper at a bank in Kansas City. When he was twenty-two, an uncle turned over a farm to his father, and Harry went to work on the farm for twelve years, until he was thirty-three years old. It can hardly be said that, by 1917, his career looked like that of a future President of the United States.

Then, when the United States joined in toward the end of World War I, Truman enrolled in the Field Artillery School at Fort Sill, Oklahoma, where he applied himself with terrific concentration. His eagerness was rewarded with the command of an artillery battery - or perhaps a senior officer thought he would take the starch out of Truman by giving him command of "a hard-boiled bunch of Kansas City Irish" who had worn out five previous captains. But in the bespectacled Truman, the battery met its match. Truman took his men through the Saint-Mihiel, Vosges, and Meuse-Argonne offensives and was mustered out a major who knew jujitsu.

Among others whom he met in the Army, he became chums with James Pendergast, the son of Mike Pendergast, a Democratic leader in Jackson County, Missouri, who was in turn the brother of Thomas J. Pendergast - Boss Pendergast of Kansas City. Although Truman went into the haberdashery business with another Army buddy after the war (and lost his shirt), he told Mike Pendergast that he thought politics would be great fun, and soon enough the Pendergasts were putting him up for one small office or another in Jackson County. He won, lost, studied law at night, dropped out of law school, helped set up the Kansas City Automobile

Association - but nonetheless, after it all, at the age of forty, Truman was unemployed and in debt.

He had, meanwhile, married Elizabeth Virginia Wallace, known as Bess, his childhood sweetheart - a marriage that was to prove one of the soundest in America. As a boy he had been shy with girls; as a man he was shy with women; he was, as his biographer Robert Donovan has written, "one of the few soldiers in the American Expeditionary Force who had found the Folies Bergère 'disgusting.'" He believed that the first victory that "great men" won was always "over themselves and their carnal urges." He was, in any case, faithful to Bess: loyalty was to Truman among the greatest of virtues - perhaps, indeed, the first among all - and it began at home.

Loyal, too, to the Pendergasts, taking his political defeats like a good soldier, he was finally given a position as presiding judge of the county court of Jackson County. The presiding judgeship was not a judicial post; it was, rather, an administrative one. Truman was in charge of a chunk of political patronage - and, while he dispensed well-paid work to loyal supporters, he was scrupulously honest himself; he took no kickbacks, and he saw to it that a full day's work was done for a full day's pay.

"I had charge," he said, "of the spending of $60 million for highways and public buildings in Jackson County" during the next eight years. "Nobody ever found anything wrong with that, and it wasn't because they didn't look hard either." Of course, he did dispense an awful lot of work. "We built more miles of paved roads in Jackson County," he bragged, "than any other county in the nation, with two exceptions."

Feeling he had done a good job, Truman asked Boss Pendergast for a more important post. Truman had in mind, so the story goes, an appointment as tax collector. But Pendergast had his own problems: He had been canvassing among the prominent local Democrats for someone he might put up for the Senate and been turned down on all fronts. With almost offhand casualness, he turned to Truman and offered him the nomination. Truman took 90 percent of the vote in Boss Pendergast's western Kansas, lost 90 percent of the vote in eastern Kansas (which was controlled by another machine), and led in the less easily manipulated rural areas. Pendergast sent him to Washington with the advice to work hard, keep his mouth shut till he knew the ropes, and answer his mail. He was known as the Senator from Pendergast.

Delighted to be in the Senate, Truman was a Democratic regular, loyal to his national party leaders, and to his President, and to the President's New Deal legislation - although his own instincts were more conservative, and he thought the President was surrounded, as he said, by the "lunatic fringe" and that his cabinet was a "mudhole" of liberals. Before the Second World War, Truman had been something of an isolationist, and he had even voted for the Neutrality Act when it came before the Senate. But when Roosevelt led the country into war, Truman followed loyally. He did keep his mouth shut, too, except when he heard from some Missouri contractors that they thought they were not getting their fair share of defense work. Truman proposed a Senate investigation. Roosevelt and Senator James F. Byrnes got together and decided to stem criticism by making Truman the head of his own committee to look into war contracts. The Truman Committee went to work at once and helped to regularize the enormous amount of political patronage that the wartime budget generated. Just as in the days when he was presiding judge of Jackson County, Truman never took a kickback. No one ever found anything wrong with the way he conducted business. And a poll of Washington reporters listed him among the ten civilians most helpful to the war effort. It was said that his committee had saved the country billions of dollars.

In 1944, when Roosevelt began to cast about for a vice-presidential candidate to run with him on the Democratic ticket, Truman looked good. He had not had what could be called a distinguished career, but he had shown, first of all, a fine sense of loyalty. Roosevelt had been mildly impressed by his committee and had nothing against him. The bosses liked him. Other candidates might have more apparent stature, but they also had clusters of enemies who might hurt Roosevelt's chances for reelection. Truman had no enemies, and, to the Democratic Party as well as to Roosevelt, the main thing was the President's reelection. As the Democratic convention approached and no clear alternate candidate came forward, Robert Hannegan, Democratic National Chairman, who was, like Truman, a Missouri boy, proposed Truman to bosses Flynn of the Bronx, Kelly of Chicago, Hague of Jersey City, and several others - and they agreed. Truman got it.

When President Roosevelt died, Truman was shocked - as were a lot of others. Though Roosevelt had been ill and exhausted for some time and his death in office was reckoned all but certain, it seems no one quite allowed himself to imagine that Truman would actually become President. Before he was given the vice-presidential nomination, Truman himself had said that there were a million Americans better qualified for it than he was. And when he heard of Roosevelt's death, he lamented to a Senate friend, "I'm not big enough for this job." It was said that Roosevelt, though he had taken Truman onto the Democratic ticket, had never considered the Senator from Pendergast to be of the same class. One of Roosevelt's secretaries declared: "I just can't call that man President."

Some were not amused by the stories that came out of the White House (and would keep coming out about the unrepentant President), about the President's poker games with his old back-slapping, bourbon-drinking chums from Missouri, about how the President would sit down to the piano with a glass of bourbon in hand and play "How Dry I Am," about how the President would take a break now and then to go out on the south lawn to pitch (left-handed) some horseshoes, or how, one evening at dinner, alone in the White House dining room with Mrs. Truman and their daughter, Margaret, the President, in the middle of the dessert course, suddenly flipped a watermelon seed across the polished table at Mrs. Truman and a moment later Bess flipped one back, and then Margaret joined in and the three of them broke into a watermelon-seed fight - the butlers discreetly retreating to the pantry.

Others were delighted with the new President. His modesty was refreshing to many who had begun to find Roosevelt's patrician manner tiresome. Truman's offhand remarks traveled the Washington social circuit quickly - his reference to the men in the State Department as "the striped pants boys," telling his cabinet that when President Lincoln asked his cabinet's advice on the Emancipation Proclamation everyone voted no, except for Lincoln, who voted "aye" and then announced, "The ayes have it." Truman had no false pride.

Soon after he was sworn in, so the story goes, he called former Secretary of Commerce Jesse Jones to give him the good news that "the President" had appointed a friend of Jones's as Federal Loan Administrator. "Did he make that appointment before he died?" asked Jones. "No," said Truman, not in the least flustered, "he made it just now."

Some days he would swim in the White House pool (the breast stroke, with his glasses on). He did twenty-five sit-ups every day. Mrs. Truman would listen to the radio broadcasts of the Washington Senators' games, and sometimes she and Margaret would play Ping-Pong. Before dinner, the President and Mrs. Truman each had one bourbon. "As long as I have been in the White House," he confided to an old friend from the Senate, "I can't help waking at 5 a.m. and hearing the old man at the foot of the stairs calling and telling me to get out and milk the cows."

He was a pragmatist, a middle-of-the-roader, a man who given a job did the best he could, just as the American GIs had done recently in Europe; and he, like the GIs, seemed a living proof that any man could rise to greatness if called on to do so - and then go around at night, before he went to bed in the White House, and wind the clocks and check the doors and windows.

Another group saw in Truman some distinct possibilities. During Roosevelt's long term in office, the executive branch of the government had come to be filled with men of a worldly outlook that harmonized well with that of the urbane President. By the end of the war, these men, whom Truman inherited as his principal advisers, were confirmed, all but instinctive, internationalists. If they had questions about America's involvement with the rest of the world, their questions were not whether America should be a great world power but what their strategy ought to be. Since America's primary competitor after the war was the Soviet Union, talk of grand strategy naturally tended to gravitate toward talk of the appropriate attitude toward the Russians.

Within his circle of advisers, Roosevelt had had both hard-liners and soft-liners, but as the end of the war approached, even some of his more moderate advisers came to believe that the attitude of wartime cooperativeness was being abused by the Russians and that it was, in any case, no longer the most suitable policy for the circumstances that followed the war.

Averell Harriman, Ambassador to the Soviet Union, felt that Roosevelt had simply been too accommodating with Stalin. The way to deal with a bully, Harriman believed, was to be tough in return. Even Roosevelt himself expressed some "little resentment" to Stalin over charges of bad faith the Russians had made against the Americans. Indeed,

Roosevelt grumbled to one visitor, he could not do business with Stalin anymore.

Yet Roosevelt clung officially to an ameliorative diplomacy. He was temperamentally inclined to a diplomacy that held that great nations have naturally divergent, competitive, even hostile aims, and that it is the art of politics to recognize the needs of an opponent and to work to minimize and accommodate differences. The weakness of such a policy, of course, seemed to have been proven just a few years before, when the Western democracies "appeased" Hitler and so led him on to greater and greater boldness. The strength of Roosevelt's policy was that it did not close off options too quickly - that it left open the option of cooperation if it turned out, in fact, that Russian provocations had neither the will nor the resources to back them up, that they were largely bluff; it was a policy tempered so as not to drive an opponent to the very countermeasures of hostility that were feared.

In any case, at Roosevelt's death, those advisers who had advocated a tougher stance toward the Soviet Union stepped forward and found in the new President's temperament a natural ally.

One of Truman's first acts as President was to receive Soviet Foreign Minister Vyacheslav Molotov, who was passing through Washington on his way to a meeting in San Francisco, preliminary to the founding of the United Nations. Harriman had suggested that Truman ought to speak to Molotov cordially about America's disappointment over the way the Soviet Union was bullying Poland and working to install a puppet government - in contravention of the agreements Stalin, Churchill, and Roosevelt had made at the wartime conference at Yalta, which called for the Soviets to respect democratic principles in Eastern Europe, that is to say, to help form a "balanced" government composed of both Polish Communists and Poles who were in exile in London and who were friendly to the West.

Whatever the soft-spoken Harriman may have had in mind, Truman more than delivered the message. The Yalta accords, Truman told Molotov, needed to be honored; the Polish issue was important in the United States.

Indeed, replied Molotov, Poland was important to Russia as well, especially since it was right on Russia's border, and the Russians would be happy to talk to the British and the Americans about Poland.

There was nothing to talk about, said Truman. Stalin had made an agreement; it was only up to him to keep his word.

To be sure, said Molotov, the three governments had established a basis for settling their differences, and the Soviet Union was prepared to talk more on that basis.

Nothing remained to talk about, said Truman; the Russians must simply keep their word.

The two men nattered at each other. Neither accommodated the other. In the end, Molotov, looking "a little ashy," declared, "I have never been talked to like that in my life."

"Carry out your agreements," said Truman, "and you won't get talked to like that."

"I gave him the one-two, right to the jaw," Truman said happily after the meeting. ("I did regret it that Truman went at it so hard," said Harriman, "because his behavior gave Molotov an excuse to tell Stalin that the Roosevelt policy was being abandoned.")

Truman's remarks to Molotov traveled the gossip network with wonderful speed, and all those who had been hanging back from taking a tough line with the Russians commenced to rally around the new President at once.

They praised him for his decisiveness and his forthrightness and his candor. They found in him a refreshing directness, a lack of pretension, a fine boldness. And they buttressed one another - the old hard-liners, the moderates who were changing their minds, some others who found Roosevelt's patrician ways somewhat lofty and grand - and they urged one another on to even tougher talk.

Some of the praise had the faintest suggestion of anxiety about it, and many of Truman's colleagues were frankly perplexed, as Henry Wallace - already on his way to becoming one of Truman's antagonists - confided to his diary in the early days of Truman's presidency: "It almost seemed as though he was eager to decide in advance of thinking." But many Washingtonians were simply relieved at not having to deal any more with FDR's notorious tendency to postpone decisions and leave his options open. As one State Department official said of Truman, "When I saw him today, I had fourteen problems to take up with him and got through them in less than fifteen minutes with a clear directive on every one of them."

While Washingtonians argued with one another over whether the new President was a breath of fresh air or a vulgar comedown from Roosevelt, Sam Rayburn, the canny old Speaker of the House, and an old friend of Truman's, judged the new President to be neither; he was, rather, in Rayburn's eye, just another good fellow from the Middle West who was being both underrated and overrated, depending on the politics of those who judged him, a man out of his depth who would have to keep his wits about him just to survive. Remember, Rayburn told the President, when he got a chance to give him a piece of confidential advice, people "will say you're the greatest man who ever lived in order to make time with you. And you know and I know that it just ain't so."

But as time went on, Truman added to the impression that seemed to work so well for him. He allowed many of the liberal New Dealers to resign from the administration. He let those who suggested America could cooperate with Russia resign as well. He appointed and promoted those who took a tough stance toward the Soviet Union.

Near the end of the war, Truman made the final decision to drop the atomic bomb on Japan. Although it seemed not to be widely known, Truman's advisers were in conflict about the use of the bomb. Some military men said it would save a million American lives. Others simply assumed that, since the bomb had been developed at great expense, it would be used. Momentum was on its side. And yet the President was told, before he made his decision - by General Dwight D. Eisenhower of the Army, General Henry H. Arnold of the Air Force, and by Admiral Ernest J. King of the Navy - that the bomb was not militarily necessary to defeat Japan or to save millions of American soldiers' lives. The Japanese were, in fact, already looking for ways to surrender through diplomatic channels. Truman's adviser and close friend Admiral William D. Leahy went so far as to say the use of the bomb was barbaric. But Truman made the decision to use it, and having made the decision, let it be known that he had never lost a moment's sleep over it.

In another notable departure, Truman was the first President to appoint a military man to the traditionally civilian job of Secretary of State. As one of Truman's aides noted, the appointment of General Marshall actually "startled" Washington: "Several Washington commentators deplored what they called the 'military takeover.' General [Douglas] MacArthur already was exercising supreme authority in Japan and Korea; General Mark Clark was the chief American representative in Austria; General [Lucius] Clay was the key figure in Germany, about to become military governor; General [Walter] Smith was ambassador to Moscow; Admiral Alan G. Kirk was ambassador to Belgium; and now General Marshall had become Secretary of State." Whether such appointments were matters of coincidence or design, whether they simply reflected Truman's old admiration for West Point or not, they gave his administration an aura of aggressiveness.

Between the time he took office in the spring of 1945 and the early months of 1947, what had been a temperament had developed into a policy. Eventually, he would be delighted to have a plaque on his desk that bore the legend "The Buck Stops

Here" and to wage a political campaign whose rallying cry was "Give 'em hell, Harry!"

Still, no sooner had Truman begun to wriggle free of the uncomfortable comparisons with his great predecessor, and begun to establish himself as President in his own right, than he was handed the usual insult to Presidents: His party was defeated in the midterm congressional elections of 1946.

Led by Senator Robert Alphonso Taft of Ohio, the Republicans gave vent to the stored-up irritations of more than a decade: With the war safely won and prosperity safely restored, the Republicans set out after the New Deal big spenders, the champions of budget deficits, the proponents of the United Nations, the friends of Russia, the promoters of internationalism, those who had, in the past few years, poured billions of dollars into foreign aid for Europe, as into a rathole, while the Continental powers were proving they could not get together and cooperate with one another even now when their very survival seemed to depend on it and continued to throw away American dollars not on rebuilding their industries, but on social programs that would never help them become self-supporting again. The Republicans complained, as Robert Donovan has written, of Roosevelt's "arrogant individualism," of an "unconstitutional dictatorship," of "lavish spending," of "socialistic experiments," of "un-American" tendencies, of the need to see to "the restoration of freedom," as Taft said, "and the elimination or reduction of constantly increasing interference with family life and with business by autocratic government bureaus and autocratic labor leaders," and voiced demands to cut the budget, to cut taxes, to cut domestic programs, to ensure that America did not become too involved in costly and possibly dangerous adventures in foreign lands, to avoid foreign entanglements, to restore a modest, limited government to America. And lest anyone doubt that these Republican sentiments were shared by a majority of Americans, the midterm elections demolished the Democrats in Congress. The Republicans gained fifty-six seats in the House, thirteen in the Senate; and critical committee chairmanships passed from the hands of liberal Democrats into those of Southern Democrats and conservative Republicans who determined to wreck Truman and put Taft or another Republican in the White House in 1948.

(It was then, too, that Acheson cemented his close friendship with the President. Truman returned from the campaign trail, chastened, aboard a train that brought him into Washington's Union Station. In Roosevelt's day, as a sign of respect, the entire cabinet had customarily gone down to the station after such an election to welcome the President home. In 1946, the station platform was empty - save for the lone, elegant figure of Undersecretary of State Acheson. Truman never forgot.)

What the President needed, if he were not soon to be swept from office, was some large program that would let him recapture the initiative, something big enough to enable him to gather in all the traditional factions of the Democratic Party and also some middle-of-the-roaders, and at the same time, something that would hamper the Republican phalanx, something that would establish Truman as a world leader like Roosevelt. Perhaps only one issue could so perfectly have satisfied all these divergent needs - and in retrospect it seems to have been remarkably easy to find.

Soon after the President received Acheson's phone call from the State Department, he summoned to his office some of the men on whose advice he had come to rely. At lunch with James Forrestal, the Secretary of the Navy, and several others, the theme was struck at once: British "abdication from the Middle East," said one of the men, bore "obvious implications as to their successors." The competition between America and Russia was to be joined in the mountains of northern Greece.

When Forrestal met with Clark Clifford, one of the President's political strategists, the two men agreed - Forrestal thinking of international politics, Clifford of domestic politics - that the central issue for the Truman Administration was best conceived as "which of the two systems currently offered to the world is to survive." Forrestal, writing in his diary, summed up the understanding of the correct strategy that Truman's cabinet had agreed on: "We should have to recognize it as a fundamental struggle between our kind of society and the Russians' and that the Russians would not respond to anything except power."

As Clifford understood it, the issue fit in well with the requirements of domestic politics, for the Republicans were caught in a peculiar double bind. While they spoke forcefully of their fear of big budgets and foreign entanglements, they had also traditionally, since 1917 at least, as the party of business, spoken vociferously of their fear of communism - and that fear was to prove their political undoing.

In the past, cabinet members had disputed with one another over the appropriate attitude to take toward the Soviet Union, and diplomats had complained - sometimes in the newspapers - of bad faith or provocative actions by one side or the other. The Russians had apparently dug in their troops in the countries of Eastern Europe, after having unceremoniously taken over the governments (but insisted they were demobilizing and respecting democracy), and the Americans had abruptly suspended wartime lend-lease aid to Russia (insisting the agreement had naturally expired). But now the President would take all the guesswork out of the relationship, all the public pretense, all the protestations of cooperative intention. He would not merely make a speech. He would go before Congress and ask to have his words endorsed as an official declaration of sorts.

Every administration needs a theme - not just for the narrow needs of a reelection campaign but also to announce to the Washington bureaucracy and to one's allies what the administration's policy will be, so that friends can rally around and help to work out the implications of policy in a coherent way. The ship of state must set a course, and, in early 1947, the apparent condition of the world, the advice that came to the White House, the political situation of Congress, all seemed to urge the President in the same direction.

And so the declaration for which Truman sought Congress's approval presented the world view out of which his administration would operate. It contained a theme, a coherent set of beliefs, a sales pitch, a policy, a direction, and a political strategy for his administration. It identified America's enemy and declared America's allies, and it staked Truman's claim on history.

3
THE OVAL ROOM

IF TRUMAN'S CABINET had more experience of the international diplomatic scene than the President did, Truman at least knew the domestic political scene and how to talk to congressmen. Within a few days of receiving Acheson's phone call, choosing the most direct course open to him, Truman invited a select group of congressional leaders to attend a briefing, under an atmosphere of the greatest urgency, in the Oval Room (as the Oval Office was then called). Representative Joe Martin, the new Republican Speaker of the House, was there, and Sam Rayburn, who, after the elections of 1946, was now Democratic Minority Leader; also present were Senator Tom Connally, the ranking Democrat on the Senate Foreign Relations Committee, Styles

Bridges, the Republican chairman of the Senate Appropriations Committee, and several others, including Arthur Vandenberg, the Republican Senator from Michigan. Only Senator Taft was conspicuously absent. Acheson said that Taft's absence was "accidental" - although that hardly seems likely.

"I knew," said Acheson, "we were met at Armageddon. We faced the 'leaders of Congress' [Acheson set them apart with quotation marks of the slightest condescension] - all the majority and minority potentates except Senator Taft."

Truman led off with a brisk synopsis of the situation in Greece, filling in the plight of the Greek government, its threat from the guerrillas, and the inability of the British government to continue supporting Greece and Turkey. "I explained to them," Truman recalled, "the position in which the British note on Greece had placed us. The decision of the British Cabinet to withdraw from Greece had not yet been made public, and none of the legislators knew, therefore, how serious a crisis we were suddenly facing." Then, with the sure touch of a man who knew when to ask and when to inform, "I told the group that I had decided to extend aid to Greece and Turkey and that I hoped Congress would provide the means to make this aid timely and sufficient."

Once the President had laid out the intended action, he turned to his Secretary of State to give the details. General George Marshall was a model Secretary of State for the time. He was a military hero who had not fired a shot during the recent war. He had no apparent ambition but to serve others, no ax to grind but to do his duty. His only vice was a weakness for maple sugar candy. His presence in the Oval Room lent the occasion a certain dignity and plausibility.

A man of fine bearing, age sixty-seven, tall, blue-eyed, with silver hair and a pink face, who inspired unreserved respect and warm feelings from his staff, Marshall had, at the same time, something impenetrable about his character. Affectionate yet reserved, attentive yet formal, he remained aloof even with his closest colleagues. He kept his most intimate thoughts to himself. When he took over as Secretary of State, one of the first things he said to Acheson was that he expected complete candor from his subordinates, including the frankest criticism. "I have no feelings," he said, "except those I reserve for Mrs. Marshall."

Marshall had been a shy, sensitive boy, gawky and awkward. His parents - a rather stiff, distant martinet of a father and a warm, affectionate mother - had come from Kentucky. One of their ancestors had been the illustrious Chief Justice of the Supreme Court John Marshall, and the Marshalls considered themselves well-born gentry. The young Marshall grew up with some of the courtliness, and the sense of belonging to history, but without the pretension, of this Southern tradition.

As a boy, he suffered by comparison to an accomplished older brother, suffered from the belief that his father favored his brother, and from his father's apparent belief that George was not terribly bright or gifted. When he was a young man he was sent off to the Virginia Military Institute, an anachronistically traditional military school, where he did badly at first, and suffered under the judgment of the school's commandant - and then finally graduated near the top of his class, having discovered, as he said, the pleasure of giving commands and seeing hundreds of young men move at his word.

He got married at once, to Elizabeth Carter Coles, four years his senior, who had previously dated his brother. When Marshall's brother spoke rudely of the match, Marshall stopped speaking to, or of, his brother - forever. Elizabeth, called Lily, was a beautiful but delicate woman (suffering, as she revealed to Marshall on their wedding night, from a heart condition) who would be a semi-invalid throughout their marriage and unable to have children - facts that Marshall accepted without complaining to others or reproaching his wife, who became profoundly devoted to him.

Because there were so few wars to fight, he was posted from time to time to various schools, where he learned theory, strategy, and patience, and became himself a teacher of young recruits. He served in World War I (and helped to draw up the plans for the Meuse-Argonne offensive), and his peers noticed traits of character that would be observed for the rest of his career: He listened well; he was calm and uncommonly dispassionate; he seemed able to set aside his ego and his feelings entirely; he prized efficiency; he made decisions easily and firmly; he had a conventional mind but a good one; he was a first-rate administrator, a manager; he was unfailingly loyal to his friends and his superiors. He was self-disciplined to such perfection that he seemed relaxed. By May 1919, he had been appointed aide-de-camp to General John J. Pershing, who said of Marshall: "He's a man who understands military."

After World War I, Marshall worked in Washington with Pershing, lobbying Congress on behalf of the military, and so completing his education as one who understood not only military, but also the politics of the military.

Then, in 1927, his wife died - after twenty-five years of marriage. How large a blow this was to Marshall is impossible to judge, since he was able to conceal his feelings from others almost completely. Yet, during the next half-dozen years or so, his career faltered. In 1930, he remarried, his wife the daughter of a clergyman, and his career began to resume a certain shape and purpose. During the New Deal years, he organized a number of Civilian Conservation Corps camps in the South. He was given a number of Army teaching appointments. Even though he chafed under such duties - believing his career would be lost if he were not given positions in which he could command troops - in fact he was becoming one of the Army's foremost mentors of young men, to whose careers he gave - for years afterward - firm, attentive, warm support.

In 1938, when Roosevelt was looking for a new Chief of Staff for the Army, his most vexing problem was a political one: He wanted to build up a vast army very quickly - in the face of enormous opposition from Congress. He needed a Chief of Staff who not only understood military matters, administration, and the Washington bureaucracy - and had the patience to deal with them all - but someone, too, who had a good political sense and a knack of training young men. In those terms, it can be no surprise - although it was a shock at the time – that Roosevelt reached past twenty major generals and fourteen brigadier generals, and on the advice of General Pershing, chose Marshall.

By the autumn of 1941, Marshall was able to turn out 1 million men for Army maneuvers, the largest peacetime maneuvers in American history. By the time the Japanese attacked Pearl Harbor in December, a good many of Marshall's troops had been in training for more than a year. And as the troops were dispatched into the war, they were replaced by a flood of new trainees until, by the end of the war in 1945, Marshall's operation had trained more than 8 million soldiers.

When it came time to choose a general to command the troops in Europe, Marshall was far too valuable an overall administrator to throw into a single theater of war, no matter how important; and so Marshall was asked to stand aside as Dwight Eisenhower was given the glory job. It was, for a military man, a crushing sacrifice, and Marshall bore it with perfect calm.

He lived with his wife in "Quarters Number 1," the Chief of Staff's plain but comfortable red-brick house, with library, drawing room, oval dining room. At home, Marshall and his wife spent most of their time on the enclosed sunporch overlooking large oak trees and gardens. Their breakfast was served there each morning at seven. Marshall was at his desk in the War Department by seven thirty. After lunch, back home on the sunporch with his wife, he rested for fifteen minutes on the chaise longue. Each afternoon, he rode horseback and then took coffee with Mrs. Marshall. And the Marshalls spent most evenings together. Marshall read. Many subjects bored him, but he loved history. He had once said of his years at VMI that he had been a poor student, except in history. "If it was history, that was all right; I could star in history."

He talked to himself constantly, bucking himself up, disciplining himself, keeping himself on the right track. "I cannot allow myself to get angry," he said to Mrs. Marshall. "That would be fatal - it is too exhausting. My brain must be kept clear." On another occasion he said to her, "I cannot afford the luxury of sentiment, mine must be cold logic. Sentiment is for others."

At the end of the war, he had been detailed to China to see whether he could bring peace between the Communist revolutionaries and the collapsing government there; and then, in January 1947, Truman appointed him Secretary of State.

George C. Marshall was, without doubt, the very soul of a just man, impartial, disinterested, somewhat aloof, yet kindly. He was one of those rare men of whose public career it could genuinely be said that he served. He was the perfect embodiment of that extraordinary American species: the pragmatic altruist.

Nonetheless, Marshall was no politician, no salesman, no canny manipulator of congressmen; and now, taking the floor of the Oval Room to present the President's case, he gave, in the words of one of the young State Department men, a "summary and cryptic presentation [that] failed to put it across to his listeners. In fact," said the young man incredulously, "he conveyed the overall impression that aid should be extended to Greece on grounds of loyalty and humanitarianism."

The legislators grumbled and cleared their throats with annoying questions: "How much is this going to cost? . . . What are we letting ourselves in for?"

Acheson understood, as he later recalled, that "my distinguished chief, most unusually and unhappily, flubbed his opening statement. In desperation I whispered to him a request to speak. This was my crisis. For a week I had nurtured it."

"Is this a private fight," Acheson asked Marshall, "or can anyone get into it?"

Marshall and Truman, "equally perturbed," Acheson said, "gave me the floor."

"Our interest in Greece," Acheson declared to the congressmen ominously by way of introduction, "is by no means restricted to humanitarian or friendly impulses. If Greece should dissolve into civil war it is altogether probable that it would emerge as a communist state under Soviet control. Turkey would be surrounded and the Turkish situation . . . would in turn become still more critical.

"Soviet domination," Acheson continued, "might thus extend over the entire Middle East to the borders of India." (The domino theory was announced: If one nation fell, so might the next and then the next.) "The effects of this upon Hungary, Austria, Italy and France cannot be overestimated. It is not alarmist to say that we are faced with the first crisis of a series which might extend Soviet domination to Europe, the Middle East and Asia."

"Never have I spoken," Acheson recalled, "under such a pressing sense that the issue was up to me alone. No time was left for measured appraisal . . . . Like apples in a barrel infected by one rotten one, the corruption of Greece would infect Iran and all to the east. It would also carry infection to Africa through Asia Minor and Egypt, and to Europe through Italy and France. . . . The Soviet Union was playing one of the greatest gambles in history at minimal cost. It did not need to win all the possibilities. Even one or two offered immense gains. We and we alone were in a position to break up the play. These were the stakes that British withdrawal from the eastern Mediterranean offered to an eager and ruthless opponent."

"Only two great powers remained in the world," one of the young State Department men remembered Acheson saying, "the United States and the Soviet Union. We had arrived at a situation unparalleled since ancient times. Not since Rome and Carthage had there been such a polarization of power on this earth. . . . And it was clear that the Soviet Union was aggressive and expanding. For the United States to take steps to strengthen countries threatened with Soviet aggression . . . was to protect not only the security of the United States - it was to protect freedom itself. For if the Soviet Union succeeded in extending its control over two-thirds of the world's surface and three-fourths of its population, there could be no security for the United States, and freedom anywhere in the world would have only a poor chance of survival." What was at stake, Acheson made clear, was nothing less than the very survival of Western civilization itself.

At the end of Acheson's presentation, there was a profound silence in the room. The crucial figure in the President's office at that moment was Arthur Vandenberg. It was said around Washington that Vandenberg was a hopelessly vain man; it was noticed that, as he grew bald, he parted his hair low on one side so that he could comb it up over his head. But more than that: He loved praise, he loved to be on the inside of things, he hoped to make his mark.

Vandenberg had grown up in Grand Rapids, Michigan, the son of a harness manufacturer who went broke in the panic of 1893. When his father lost his business, and his health, and his mother opened a boardinghouse, the young Vandenberg, age nine, started to earn money by delivering packages in the pushcart that remained from his father's business. In the beginning, he delivered shoes. In time, he grew vegetables, delivered newspapers, operated flower and lemonade stands, and ran a stamp-trading business. He worked hard. He graduated from high school at the head of his class. He went to work as a copy boy for the Grand Rapids *Herald,* and worked his way up to a reporter specializing in political news. When a local man named William Alden Smith ran for the Senate in 1907, Vandenberg promoted his candidacy enthusiastically. When Smith won, he turned around and bought the *Grand Rapids Herald* and handed it over to the twenty-two-year-old Vandenberg to edit.

In 1928, after two decades of boosting Republican candidates, Vandenberg was appointed to fill a vacancy in the Senate, where he acquired a reputation for intelligence and a jovial charm. The more cynical of the young men in the State Department traded gossip about how they had successfully played on the Senator's weaknesses, how, if they wanted a piece of legislation to get through Congress, they would be sure to leave room in advance for the addition of "the trademark" or "the price," as it was variously called - that is to say, the "Vandenberg Amendment," which the senator from Michigan would need to add to a piece of legislation before he would support it. Truman too knew how to woo Vandenberg, and always made certain that the senator received special briefings and was made to feel like one of the insiders.

Vandenberg had been an isolationist before the war, but unlike Truman, he had taken a leading role among the isolationists. Then, when war broke out, Vandenberg dropped his isolationism and came increasingly to embrace an internationalist foreign policy and to champion the idea that the formulation of American foreign policy ought to be above partisan politics - that differences ought to be worked out "in the family" so that the country could present a united front to the world. Such a bipartisan attitude toward foreign policy found wide support during the war, although, with the coming of peace, a good many of Vandenberg's Republican colleagues commenced to argue that bipartisanship was no longer appropriate - that foreign policy above all, since it involved the ultimate values and the very survival of the country, needed to be subject to the tug and pull and open debate of a free republic. Vandenberg, however, remained committed to bipartisanship, and to the idea, now that the war was over, that a warlike competition had replaced it, so that wartime rules must continue to apply. And so, if Vandenberg could be brought along with Truman's plans, he would bring others with him - and split the Republican Party in the process.

Vandenberg was impressed with Acheson's speech. Acheson's arguments were compelling and, what was equally important, sounded as though they would be convincing to others. On the one hand, Acheson painted a picture of the nation making a grievous, perhaps fatal, mistake; on the other hand he offered it the opportunity to do something grand, as grand as ancient Greece itself. When the notion was put that way, Vandenberg could hardly refuse.

It was, finally, Vandenberg's rich, smooth voice that broke the silence. "Mr. President," Vandenberg said, "if you will say that to the Congress and to the country, I will support you, and I believe that most of its members will do the same."

The trick was turned. The wedge had been placed into the Republican Party. The President's new policy was set in motion. Truman was pleased as punch. The meeting broke up.

"The job of briefing the press," Acheson said disarmingly, "I took on myself." That evening, to get the bandwagon under way, Acheson called in twenty newspaper reports for an off-the-record background conference. Prominent among the newsmen was James Reston of *The New York Times*. Within several days of Truman's meeting with the congressional leaders, Reston had published the first of many pieces in the *Times* that would speak of the need to oppose Soviet influence in the eastern Mediterranean, the need for the President and the Congress - the one Democratic, the other Republican - to get together on a common policy, the need to consider whether the United States was prepared to take up the burden of ensuring world order that Britain had borne during the nineteenth century.

Hanson Baldwin, a colleague of Reston's on the *Times,* followed Reston's lead and added some flourishes to Reston's rhetoric. The United States, Baldwin wrote, in language reminiscent of Acheson's, "far more than any single factor, is the key to the destiny of tomorrow; we alone may be able to avert the decline of Western civilization, and a reversion to nihilism and the Dark Ages."

4
THE DOCTRINE

ON THE MORNING of February 28, Acheson called a meeting back at the State Department with his departmental officers and other aides. To these young men, as to Acheson, there would never be a more exhilarating time in their lives. When Acheson came to write his memoirs, he would call them *Present at the Creation;* all the men around him shared that sense of momentousness about their actions. Acheson spoke to his aides with "an unusual gravity of manner. . . . Tenseness and controlled excitement grew by the moment . . . as Acheson launched into a full statement of the larger issues, repeating the exposition that had so impressed the legislators." By the end of this presentation, the men around Acheson felt "that they were the most privileged of men, the participants in a drama such as rarely occurs even in the long life of a great nation."

There was, said Acheson, "a great job to be done," and it would have to be done "with great speed. Within a few days it was necessary to draw up in detail a program of economic, military, and technical aid to Greece and Turkey, to draft the necessary enabling legislation, the President's message to Congress . . . and to develop and get under way a program of public information." Tasks were assigned, and the men put to work. Information was assembled; military hardware was assessed; specific dollar figures for economic assistance were totted up.

When Joseph Jones sat down to draft a speech for the President, he found that "a great deal of doctrine and phraseology had come into common usage among the officials concerned during that week of decision." Before he even started to imagine what the President might say, Jones already had: the democratic government of Greece, the extremists and terrorists who opposed it, the Communists who led the extremists, the Soviet-inspired threat to Greece, the falling dominoes across Europe, the Middle East, and Asia, the threat to free governments everywhere, and to Western civilization itself. He also knew that "insofar as possible, mention of the British should be avoided."

At a meeting on March 4, Acheson sat with a dozen aides and sorted through various drafts of the speeches, notes, and other papers and read out paragraphs or sentences that he thought might be useful. Everyone had favorite sentences or phrases; visions of an applauding Congress drifted through the minds of some of the young men as they suggested one sentence or another. Jones sat nearby taking notes, and soon a draft of the speech was sent over to the President.

"The first version was not at all to my liking," Truman recalled. "The writer had filled the speech with all sorts of background data and statistical figures about Greece and made the whole thing sound like an investment prospectus. I returned this draft to Acheson with a note asking for more emphasis on a declaration of general policy."

On March 5, Acheson gathered his speechwriters again, and they worked over the text. Clark Clifford had some favorite sentences to add, such as "This is a serious course upon which we embark. I would not recommend it except that the alternative is more serious" and "The seeds of totalitarian regimes are nurtured by misery and want. They spread and grow in the evil soil of poverty and strife. They reach their full growth when the hope of a people for a better life has died." Acheson at one point leaned back in his chair and mused, "If FDR were alive I think I know what he'd do.

He would make a statement of global policy but confine his request for money right now to Greece and Turkey." The outline of the arguments stayed in place, but the rhetoric was shaped and pointed, and the general nature of the issue - the notion that America needed not simply to save Greece, but to oppose threats to democracy everywhere - was emphasized more clearly.

"It seemed to me half-hearted," Truman said when he saw this revision. "The key sentence, for instance, read, 'I believe that it should be the policy of the United States . . .' I took my pencil, scratched out 'should' and wrote in 'must.' In several other places, I did the same thing. I wanted no hedging in this speech. This was America's answer to the surge of expansion of Communist tyranny. It had to be clear and free of hesitation or double talk."

By March 8, Acheson was passing the draft of the speech around the State Department and the White House - not so much to solicit advice, but rather to give advance notice of the line that the administration was laying down. Some of the officials in the department, when they saw this late draft of the speech, were upset by it: In the course of its redraftings, it had become so extravagant, so global in its claims, so harsh in its warnings. By placing the limited problem of Greece in a universal context, might it not lead to unlimited commitments all over the world? A White House speechwriter wrote a memo to Clifford: "There has been no overt action in the immediate past by the U.S.S.R. which serves as an adequate pretext for 'All-out' speech. The situation in Greece is relatively 'abstract'; there have been other instances . . . where the occasion more adequately justified such a speech." Never mind, Clifford replied; the speech was needed as "the opening gun in a campaign to bring people up to [the] realization that the war isn't over by any means."

Vandenberg, meanwhile, gathered his colleagues in Congress and told them that the President was about to address a joint session of Congress and that although he himself intended to suspend his final judgment until after he had heard the President's speech, he wanted his colleagues to know that they faced "a matter which transcends politics. There is nothing partisan about it. It is national policy of the highest degree."

Excitement grew on Capitol Hill, fed by Acheson's chats with journalists and congressmen. "Many," reported *The New York Times*, "hope the President's message will outline the horizons of the influence in the world that Mr. Truman believes now the United States should attempt to exercise." Editorial writers suggested that the time had come for the United States to take on the responsibilities of world leadership. Representative Charles Eaton, chairman of the House Select Committee on

Foreign Aid, declared the moment to be "the most fateful in the history of our country."

At midday on March 12, the chamber of the House of Representatives was cleared for the President's appearance. The representatives who ordinarily sat in the front rows had to move back to make room for members of the Senate and the President's cabinet. Clerks, secretaries, ex-congressmen, wives and children, movie actors, diplomats, and members of the White House staff jammed the galleries. At 12:45, the Speaker of the House, Joe Martin, called the House to order, and the doorkeeper announced the members of the United States Senate, who were led in and down the center aisle by Senator Vandenberg and the sergeant at arms. As soon as they were seated, the doorkeeper announced the cabinet of the President of the United States, and the members of the cabinet were led in by Undersecretary of State Acheson. (Marshall was traveling.) At 1 p.m., the doorkeeper announced the high point of this studiously commonplace democratic ceremonial: The President of the United States, escorted by a committee of senators and representatives, entered briskly, with a black folder under his arm, and walked with quick, businesslike strides down the aisle to the speaker's rostrum, where he waited for the applause to die away and the members and guests to resume their seats before he opened the black folder. When he spoke, it was thought that his voice was flat and, as an orator's voice, disappointing - but forceful.

"The gravity of the situation which confronts the world today," he said, "necessitates my appearance before a joint session of Congress." Without preliminary niceties, Truman announced the stakes: "The foreign policy," he declared, "and" - something that had not been mentioned before, something to bring the remote Greek crisis right into the room in which Truman's audience sat - "the national security of this country are involved.

"The United States has received from the Greek Government an urgent appeal for financial and economic assistance . . .

"The very existence of the Greek state is today threatened by the terrorist activities of several thousand armed men, led by Communists . . .

"Greece must have assistance if it is to become a self-supporting and self-respecting democracy . . .

"The United States must supply that assistance. . . . There is no other country to which democratic Greece can turn. . . ."

The President did say that the Greek government "has made mistakes. The extension of aid by this country does not mean that the United States condones everything that the Greek Government has done or will do." Essentially, said the President, the United States condemned extremism of the left or of the right. His audience knew who the extremists of the left were: the Communists. In truth, the Greek government itself constituted the extreme right, but the President seemed to suggest that there was some other group of extreme rightists - so that by definition, when the United States backed the existing government of Greece, it was backing "moderates."

"At the present moment in world history," said the President, "nearly every nation must choose between alternative ways of life. The choice is too often not a free one. One way of life is based upon the will of the majority. . . . The second way of life is based upon the will of a minority forcibly imposed upon the majority. It relies upon terror and oppression. . . ."

Having taken the problems in Greece and cast them in global terms, the President was led to a global situation, which soon became known as the Truman Doctrine, a conceptual framework that had such a powerful appeal that it established itself as the ultimate rationale for American foreign policy for the next several decades:

"I believe," said Truman, "that it must be the policy of the United States to support free peoples who are resisting attempted subjugation by armed minorities or by outside pressures."

He meant, with his doctrine, that America would support "free peoples" everywhere. Until that moment, no President had ever declared as policy that the United States would venture outside the confines of the Americas as a matter of common practice in peacetime. The Monroe Doctrine had extended the United States' hegemony - and limited it - to the Americas. The Truman Doctrine announced that America was henceforth a world power, that it recognized no limitations to its interests and would protect its interests everywhere.

He meant, said Truman, to support free peoples by giving them financial aid, but, in addition to funds, "I ask the Congress to authorize the detail of American civilian and military personnel to Greece and Turkey. . . . I recommend that authority also be provided for the instruction and training of selected Greek and Turkish personnel for purposes indicated in this message. . . . This is a serious course upon which we embark."

When the President announced his doctrine, there was no applause; the audience sat in stunned silence. The President's speech had been remarkably aggressive. These senators and representatives and their friends, having just begun to enjoy the pleasures of peace, felt even rudely treated. As the editor of the *San Francisco Chronicle* would write, "It was something like the feeling on the day of Munich. . . . The man in the street began thinking about the taste of brackish water in canteens, and the mud of foxholes, and the smell of the dead, and all those reminders of the recently finished war, and wondering." Diplomats, too, were surprised by Truman's speech. Secretary of State Marshall, who was in Paris on his way to Moscow, was "somewhat startled to see the extent to which the anti-Communist element of the speech was stressed" and cabled Truman to say that the speech "was overstating the case a bit." One of the men in the British Foreign Office was shocked by the "enormous hullabaloo" that surrounded Truman's request for aid to Greece. The sum requested - $400 million - was pin money. Why make such an issue of it? The policy of aid to Greece, the English diplomat observed with some perplexity, "was made to seem hardly less than a declaration of war on the Soviet Union." Clearly, what the President sought was more than a mere few hundred million dollars in aid.

The members of Congress rose, as was their habit, and, at last, applauded the President. But the applause was not enthusiastic. Nor was it accompanied by the usual complement of approving shouts and rebel yells. Rather the applause had, as a young State Department man noted, "a bewildered quality about it." The President looked up into the galleries and shot a fleeting smile at Mrs. Truman and then went straight for the doors, and a vacation in Florida.

5

THE COMPETITION

IN MOSCOW, SECRETARY Marshall set out in a limousine from the American Embassy for a conversation at the Kremlin with Generalissimo Josef Stalin. Marshall and Stalin were to meet, by Stalin's nocturnal standards, early in the evening, at 10 p.m. The embassy limousine, flying the American flag, moved quickly along the Arbat - a street that the new American Ambassador, Walter Bedell Smith, thought was probably the most heavily policed in the world. It was along the Arbat that Russian officials drove between their Kremlin offices and their dachas; a policeman was to be seen every hundred yards, and four policemen were stationed at each intersection. As the limousine, which enjoyed "Kremlin privileges," approached the intersections, all the lights turned green, and the car sped right on through.

Marshall had been in Moscow for almost five weeks for a meeting of the foreign ministers of the United States, the Soviet Union, Britain, and France. Their principal topic was, as it had been since the end of the war, just how to treat Germany. Germany's division into four zones at the end of the war - each zone occupied by one of the four Allied powers - had given the German industrial heartland, which lay in the west, to Britain, France, and America. The agrarian east fell into Russia's zone. The Russians, having come out of the war damaged by German invasions, hoped to repair some of the damage by taking industrial equipment out of Germany as war reparations. Unfortunately, that wish conflicted with the thoughts of the Western powers: that Germany itself was in ruins and that if Germany did not revive, then the very center of the European economy would remain ruined, and so the European and the world economies would remain chaotic. If the Russians took reparations, revival of the West could not occur. But the Russians felt that if they could not take reparations, revival of the Soviet Union could not occur.

In retrospect, it appears that neither side was right. Germany was not as devastated as it looked. Beneath a surface that appeared to be the very essence of disaster, only its fuels and transportation were truly devastated. Eighty percent of its industrial capacity in the American and French zones had survived the war. Indeed, German industry had expanded during the war. It could probably have recovered and provided reparations at the same time.

In 1947, however, a genuine impasse appeared to exist, and neither side was eager to relent. The Russians insisted that they had gotten firm assurances at Yalta that they would get $10 billion worth of reparations. The British and Americans insisted that it was clear that Germany must recover first, before it could pay reparations. Britain and America were pouring aid into Germany: They had no intention of seeing aid go in one door and out the other.

For Britain, these issues had recently taken on even greater urgency. As in Greece and Turkey, so too in Germany: The British did not have the resources to support others. German occupation had become an intolerable burden on the British, and they needed agreement at once to rebuild the German economy to take the strain off Britain. As a partial measure, they had already appealed to the United States to merge the American and British zones into a new dual-occupation unit called Bizonia. But even that was a stopgap measure, and if the British could not get the Russians to go along too, at least they wanted the French to join the other two Western powers to rebuild Germany.

The French, on the other hand, were not so enthusiastic about revitalizing Germany. The French, after all, had suffered at the hands of the Germans in two world wars in the twentieth century. France and Germany had been in competition, whether violent or not, for longer than anyone could remember. Both countries wanted, at the least, to "lead" Europe if not dominate it, and the end of the Second World War had given France a wonderful opportunity to hold Germany down, and let it rise up slowly, only after France had finally established itself as the leading continental power.

Among other things, the French wanted ownership or partial administrative control of the great centers of German mining and heavy industry - the regions of the Ruhr, the Rhineland, and the Saar. Until France had at least those advantages, the French refused to agree to any plan for German economic unification or recovery. If Germany had been casually split into four zones after the war, perhaps that was not such a misfortune; perhaps it would be a fine thing to keep the Germans split. Such a policy had been enormously popular with the French after World War I. Then, the French had hoped to shatter Germany into as many pieces as it had had in the nineteenth century before Otto von Bismarck had united it into such a powerful, and dangerous, force on the Continent. Now, at the end of World War II, the French worked tirelessly to keep Germany from being entirely revived - and even to secure its own importance in Europe by remaining somewhat independent of the world's two great powers, to play both sides against the middle and so be left the key power on the Continent, to remain neutral, conducting a policy "between east and west," to be *la France seule.*

The impasse, then, was not a simple matter of Russian-American conflict. Indeed, the man in charge of the American occupation zone, General Lucius Clay, consistently blamed the French more than the Russians for obstructing plans for Germany. The French dealt, said one American in Moscow, with "Byzantine complexity."

Nonetheless, however vexingly complicated the international situation might be, it could be simplified. The United States and Britain could find a common ground in uniting against the Soviet Union and forcing the French, thereby, to join them. It was a time-tested technique - to identify a single, common foe and, sweeping aside all complications, to unite against it. A belief in the evil designs of the Soviet Union was becoming irresistible on many practical, as well as moral, grounds.

At the main gate of the Kremlin, Marshall's limousine was met by a pilot car and, as an alarm bell rang, the two cars passed through the gate in the massive stone wall and on into the Kremlin courtyard, past the Kremlin Museum, past the Hall of Soviets (formerly czarist ballrooms), past the Greek Orthodox churches and the bell tower, and directly up to the inner building in which Stalin had his offices. At the entrance, as Ambassador Smith noted was customary, stood an usher "in the Kremlin uniform of dark gray with inconspicuous red braiding on the collar and cuffs. Standing with him was a tall officer with the gold shoulder boards of a colonel, very soldierly in his olive drab tunic with red braiding, dark blue breeches with red stripes, and high soft black leather boots . . . [and] a belted pistol in a black leather holster."

An elevator took the visitors to the third floor, where they walked down a long, narrow corridor. The entrance to Stalin's office lay through a high double door, "covered with dark green, padded and quilted leather, which opens into a succession of reception rooms" and, at last, into "a paneled conference room." There, at the far end of the conference room, stood Stalin, Molotov, and Stalin's interpreter.

Stalin, a tyrant who held half the world in thrall, whose ruthlessness had been proven over and over again in his rise to power and his staying there, who snuffed out life without regret or apparent second thought, was a disarmingly frail man in the flesh: small, paunchy, pasty-faced, neither apparently ill nor well, somewhat awkward - still the same shock of white hair and the walrus mustache, his left arm withered from a childhood illness or accident and drawn up stiffly at his side, his face pockmarked, teeth bad, his manner calm, slow, self-assured. And he was a man, too, of remarkable charm; Truman, when he met Stalin, liked him, as most politicians did.

He was sixty-nine years old in 1947. He had been in power for twenty-five years. For most of those twenty-five years, he had been accustomed to holding his meetings at night, which often ran through the night and into the dawn, and sleeping during the day. He was largely cut off from daily life in Russia, rarely venturing out of his closely guarded, nocturnal meetings with his ministers and the heads of state or officials of foreign nations. Cut off as he was, he ruled with as complete a mastery as any politician ever had, a phenomenal feat that would seem to give the lie to the notion that politicians need to be in touch with the real world in order to dominate it.

Few could doubt at the end of the Second World War that Stalin's Soviet Union presented a formidable opponent for the United States. That Russia would become such a power in the world had been foreseen as long ago as the 1830s by Alexis de Tocqueville, who said, in a famous passage from *Democracy in America,* that even then, "There are on earth today two great peoples, who, from different points of departure, seem to be advancing toward the same end. They are the Anglo-Americans and the Russians. . . . All the other peoples appear to have attained approximately their natural limits, and to have nothing left but to conserve their positions; but these two are growing. . . . To attain his end, the first depends on the interest of the individual person, and allows the force and intelligence of individuals to act freely, without directing them. The second in some way concentrates all the power of society in one man. The one has liberty as the chief way of doing things; the other servitude. Their points of departure are divergent; nevertheless, each seems summoned by a secret design of providence to hold in his hands, some day, the destinies of half the world."

By 1947, the Soviet Union had come to realize nearly all the ancient ambitions that the czars had for so long harbored. Russia, having been invaded over the centuries by the Germans, by the French, by the Poles, by the Swedes, by the Tartars and the Magyars and the Penchenegs, by the Kharkovs and the Avars and the Bulgars and the Huns, had at last laid claim to a whole buffer zone of Eastern European nations, moved in its armies, secured its positions, installed friendly governments, and squashed any hint of revolt against the Soviet Union. Russia had indeed advanced far into the heart of Europe - or, as Churchill liked to say, the borders of Asia had been advanced to the Elbe.

Most American policymakers had long since accepted the view that the world was divided into two spheres of influence. Such an assumption was taken for granted in the State Department briefing book that Truman had carried with him to the Potsdam Conference. The question was: How much more was Russia determined to take? Were the Russians about to advance their armies all the way to the Atlantic Ocean? It was said at the time that the Soviet Union had an army of fully 208 divisions. "Russia's armies and air force," said *U.S. News & World Report,* "are in a position to pour across Europe and into Asia almost at will."

In retrospect, according to recent American intelligence estimates, the situation does not seem to have been quite so simple. In fact, the Russians had no more than 175 divisions - which were, at full strength, only three-quarters the size of an American division, and of which only a third were at full strength by Russian standards. Of these, only thirty were occupying Eastern Europe. Assuming some would have had to stay behind to maintain occupation forces, no more than twenty-five divisions might have been sent west. With a possible twelve divisions held in strategic reserve, the Soviets might have had as many as 700,000 to 800,000 troops ready to move west. For a successful offensive, most military strategists believe they need to outnumber defensive troops three to one. The Western European countries - Britain, France, Belgium, Norway, the Netherlands, and Denmark - along with American occupation troops, numbered 800,000. As a backup, the West had the atomic bomb.

To support an invasion of the West, Russian transport would have had to move over roads and rail networks still devastated by war, to cross bridges that were seriously damaged or nonexistent, and to rely on a communications system that was primitive by Western standards. Stalin was no more able to take Western Europe than Western armies were able to reconquer the countries Russia occupied. The war had actually achieved a true stalemate between Russia and America.

Although not all Washingtonians interpreted this information in the same way, an American intelligence report of November 1945 concluded that Russia would be incapable of any war for another fifteen years. In August 1946, intelligence sources intercepted a personal communication from Marshal Georgi Zhukov to the Russian foreign minister saying that his armies were not prepared to fight a war.

At the same time (contrary, again, to what is commonly thought), the Soviet Union began to demobilize its armies as early as June 1945 and continued on into 1949. In Czechoslovakia, the Russians withdrew nearly all their troops. In 1946, Western intelligence put Soviet troop strength in

Czechoslovakia at a mere 5,000; by 1948, it was down to only 500. Evidently, Stalin needed men back home after the war to rebuild Russia.

Entire cities had been leveled, among them Kharkov, Kiev, and Minsk. Leningrad, under siege by the Germans for two years, had been reduced, as Walter Laqueur has written, to "a mere shadow of the beautiful and active city it had once been." Steel production was down to 50 percent of the prewar level, agricultural production was at 60 percent - this among a people who had never reached the levels of prosperity common to Western Europe before the war. Food rations were exceptionally low. As in Europe, drought had struck the Soviet Union in 1946 and 1947. Tractors and other machinery were scarce, and peasants "had to sow and harvest by hand," as Laqueur wrote, "and sometimes even put themselves to harness." The Soviet Union was not a country bursting with health, ready to spill over into the world out of a sheer excess of power and wealth.

Politically, too, it is not clear that Stalin was on the offensive in the first years after the war. As ambitious as he was, as committed to world conquest as he might have been, he was evidently not eager to see many Communist parties succeed in Western Europe - where other Communist leaders might emerge to rival his own leadership of the world Communist movement. An external Communist movement that he could not control was more a threat than a boon.

Having bitten off a whole tier of Eastern Europe, uncertain that he could hold and control even that with his own army and economy ravaged by the war, it appears, in retrospect at least, that Stalin had all he could handle in the years right after the war, and that his policy, having moved Russia into that part of Europe that the czars had historically hungered for as a buffer zone between themselves and Western Europe, Stalin meant to be absolutely intransigent, but not any more expansionist.

Indeed, Stalin seems, in 1947, with his country weakened and his position insecure, to have been almost all bluff. Unfortunately, not least of all for Stalin himself - who, among other things, could ill afford an arms race - his bluff was terribly convincing. He was, after all, one of the truly evil men of the twentieth century. His elimination of political enemies within Russia, in the purges of the 1930s, with their jailings, tortures, show trials, exiles, and executions, produced a spectacle of tyranny that vies with the standards of inhumanity at any time or place. In all, the Stalinist purges may have claimed as many as 20 million victims. He made it easier than most politicians to expect the worst of him.

Marshall opened the pleasantries by remarking that he remembered seeing Stalin last at the Teheran

Conference in 1943, when they had talked briefly about amphibious operations. "Yes," said Stalin amiably, "the second front" - a reference to the Allied invasion of Europe, which Stalin had made clear he thought Marshall, whom he admired, should command.

"You look just the same as when I saw you last time," said Stalin, "but I am just an old man."

They sat down at the large table: Marshall, Smith, and their interpreter, Charles Bohlen; Stalin, Molotov, and their interpreter. Behind Stalin hung portraits of the great Russian marshals of the Napoleonic Wars, Suvorov and Kutuzov, who had fought off the most terrible invasions Russia had ever suffered. Molotov kept silent. Marshall spoke. Stalin doodled, in red ink, on a pad. Stalin had the habit, according to Smith, of drawing little lopsided hearts, with question marks in the middle, although on this occasion he was drawing the head of a wolf. His face, as usual during such conversations, was expressionless. He did not look at Marshall directly as the Secretary spoke but kept his head turned aside, taking a puff from time to time on his long Russian cigarette, and turning only now and then to glance directly into the Secretary's eyes.

Molotov sat silently. He was, Ambassador Smith recalled, a "correct and courteous" man but "repellingly colorless." Even "when attempting to be humorous, he appears stiff." Molotov was one of the few major figures in the revolution of 1917 to have survived as long as he had - to the age of fifty-seven, and still in the Russian government. The son of a shopkeeper, he went away to school at the age of twelve and, by the time he was fifteen, had already joined a students' Marxist group and taken part in the revolution of 1905. While still a teenager, he was arrested by the czarist police and deported to Vologda in northern European Russia. It was during his years of exile (and escapes and fresh arrests) that he took the pseudonym Molotov ("hammer").

His instinct for survival and his steady advancement in a world of enemies was highly refined. By 1925, at the age of thirty-five, he was a member of the Politburo, the youngest member ever to have a place there. By 1930, he was Premier and was concerned principally with the management of domestic programs in the industrial and agricultural phases of the Five-Year Plans for economic advancement. In 1939, as the Kremlin leaders anticipated some role for Russia in World War II, Molotov was appointed Commissar for Foreign Affairs. Because of his apparently limitless capacity for intransigence, his ability simply to outsit all other foreign ministers, he was known as a man with a cast-iron bottom.

"The Secretary," according to the notes that Bohlen scribbled down during the conversation, "said he wished to tell Stalin that he was very concerned and somewhat depressed at the extent and depth of misunderstandings and differences which had been revealed at this conference. He said he intended to speak frankly . . . since that was the way he had been trained as a soldier and he was no diplomat." As far as America was concerned, "there had been a serious and steady deterioration in public regard toward the Soviet Union . . . due in large measure to the fact that many communications had been sent to the Soviet Government with no answer being received and that this was a most unusual practice."

Molotov whispered something to Stalin.

As for the issues discussed at the conference, the United States was "seriously concerned" at the idea of a restored and unified German government, which the Russians favored. The United States felt that such a German government would constitute "a real danger for the peace of the world." The United States was coming around to the thought that a divided Germany was not a bad idea - in a political sense - although a unified economic plan was still necessary.

As far as reparations were concerned, Marshall said that the charge had been made that the United States had taken $10 billion worth of reparations from its zone, as though that might justify the Russians taking a similar amount in reparations.

In fact, said Marshall, the United States may have taken between $20 and $30 million worth; he had personally signed a memo to this effect, and expected, since he had given his word, that that would be believed.

Stalin replied, as was his habit in such diplomatic conversations, very quietly, in a tone that was at once cordial and unyielding. In conversation, as Ambassador Smith said, "the length and sequence of his remarks made me feel that either he has a remarkable memory and great power of concentration, or that the points . . . had been anticipated."

About the Soviet government not responding in a timely fashion to notes from the American government, "there was occasional sloppiness in the operation of the Soviet government." The Russians had suffered heavy losses in the war; "they were only learning every day how badly they had been hurt." Nonetheless (here he mentioned the subject about which Molotov had whispered to him), "with regard to Soviet delays in replying to your representations on various subjects, I would remind Mr. Marshall that more than two years ago the Soviet government made a request of the United States for a final credit, and that to date no reply or acknowledgment has ever been received . . . and this possibly was due to sloppiness on the part of the United States government."

Smith passed a note to Molotov. Molotov glanced at it; it said Smith had replied to this point personally the previous year. Molotov whispered to Stalin.

Stalin corrected himself, tempering his objection somewhat, saying that perhaps a year was a long time to wait for a reply. The point remained: the United States had not been quick to help its ally.

"As to the German government," said Stalin, the Russians too "were against a strong centralized German government and they no less, and perhaps even more than anyone, did not wish to see Germany rise again as an aggressive power." Yet, only if Germany were unified, Stalin seemed to believe, could the Russians draw reparations from all Germany - including the industrial west. And so, he said, he did not see how economic unity was possible without political unity. The Germans would need to be kept down, but they needed to be unified nonetheless.

Finally, as for reparations, at present, with Germany divided into zones, the Soviet Union was able to take a total "of barely $2 million. . . . This was insignificant and much too small." At Yalta, said Stalin, where he had suggested $10 billion, Roosevelt had said he thought that was a "very small" amount. Now, "there was apparently a different point of view, and that was to take no more reparations than had already been taken. This the Soviet Union could not accept. . . . The

United States and England might be willing to give up reparations; the Soviet Union could not. Their people, who had suffered more than any other people, would not agree. . . . While reparations might not be popular in the United States and England, $10 billion of reparations were very popular in the Soviet Union."

Nonetheless, Stalin said, turning abruptly mellow, as for the Conference of Foreign Ministers that was now drawing to a close in Moscow, he did not think "the situation was so tragic. . . . After all, these were only the first skirmishes and brushes of reconnaissance forces on this question. Differences had occurred before on other questions, and as a rule after people had exhausted themselves in dispute they then recognized the necessity of compromise." Stalin thought that compromises were possible on all the main questions. It was necessary, he said, "to have patience and not become depressed."

When Stalin had finished speaking, Marshall replied briefly, saying that he appreciated the frankness of the Generalissimo and would "consider it carefully. He was encouraged by [Stalin's] last words and he only hoped Generalissimo Stalin was right.

"Stalin assured the Secretary that his closing remarks were correct."

The meeting was adjourned at eleven thirty, and Marshall, Smith, and Bohlen made their way back up the Arbat to the American Embassy.

The larger Conference of Foreign Ministers was given its formal ending not long afterward, in a dinner at the Kremlin, in the hall of Catherine the Great. A good many of the Kremlin insiders were there: Stalin, of course; Molotov, sporting a new, dark blue suit; Georgi Malenkov, General Secretary of the Communist Party, wearing the old party uniform of tunic with turned-down collar; Nikolai Voznesensky, smiling and lifting his glass in the direction of any Westerner whose eye he caught; Andrei Zhdanov, Russia's chief propagandist, a usually bubbling storyteller, now ailing, eating nothing but a bowl of clear soup.

The usual toasts were exchanged, but the atmosphere was otherwise quiet, and dinner did not last an hour. After dinner, Stalin led his guests away from the possibility of conversation, down a curving flight of blue-carpeted stairs to a movie theater, where they watched a film of a Russian folk tale called *The Stone*. The theater seats were set out in pairs, and by each pair of seats was a small table with a box of chocolates, glasses, and a double magnum of champagne.

"We were home by midnight," Ambassador Smith recorded with some surprise, "probably a record for entertainment at the Kremlin."

The whole meeting between Marshall and Stalin seemed very odd to Ambassador Smith, although he could not say just why. But surely the most remarkable aspect of the encounter was that it hardly qualified as an encounter at all. Disagreements were stated but not gone into; no proposals for settlement were offered; no difference was negotiated; no common feelings were brought up to provide grounds for cooperation. Such simple statements of position usually occur at the beginning of a conference, and the subsequent meetings then search for compromises and grounds for settlement. But these statements came at the end of the conference: They summarized what the two sides would not resolve. Perhaps Stalin meant what he said, that these were just the opening skirmishes of an argument; but, in truth, the argument had been going on for several years. It was not to be settled. The two sides would not agree. What was being stated in these early years after the war were the grounds for divorce. At first, as the two sides gradually worked their way out of the old wartime alliance, the grounds were stated imprecisely, awkwardly, hazily; in time, they would be stated clearly and sharply. Meanwhile - no doubt partly out of honest conviction, and partly out of the need for appearances - each side tried to avoid being blamed for the breakup.

"We can say without hesitation," *Pravda* declared at the end of the meetings, "that the Conference marked the beginning of the solution of the German problem."

Marshall, on the other hand, concluded that Stalin's cordiality proved nothing but that he wanted to lull the West. Evidently the Russians were happy to smile, to wait, to negotiate, to string the Western powers along until Britain's burdens did bring down the United Kingdom, and Germany did go bankrupt, and the Continent did collapse into economic ruin. America needed to act, to act at once, and unilaterally.

Back home from Moscow, Marshall gave a radio address to the nation: The recovery of Europe, he said, "has been far slower than had been expected. Disintegrating forces are becoming evident. The patient is sinking while the doctors deliberate . . . action cannot await compromise through exhaustion."

"Moscow represents," as one of Marshall's advisers concluded, ". . . the culmination of a trend away from Yalta, away from the position held, at least by American representatives at Yalta, that a sufficient community of interest existed between east and west to permit agreement on certain basic principles of international organization."

"The lengthy Moscow Conference," mused French Foreign Minister Georges Bidault, "was drawn out by endless festivities, frozen amusements, formal parties and sumptuous banquets where most of the time was taken up in toasts [which] . . . marked the end of an era."

6
THE HOME FRONT

IT IS COMMONPLACE to say that domestic politics often determine foreign policy; it is less often noticed that the way a nation behaves in the world has a lamentable tendency to come home - which is, without doubt, the principal self-interested reason to conduct a civil foreign policy. The battle that Washington waged with the Soviet Union was snapped up at home - with little sense of diplomatic restraint - and sent factions of leftists, rightists, pro-and anti-Communists flying at each other, and abandoning those who had thought of themselves as moderates to an absurd sort of political no-man's land.

Among those on the left, oddly enough, stood Henry Wallace, another Midwestern boy with a suspicion of highfalutin rhetoric, former Secretary of Agriculture, former Vice-President of the United States, former Secretary of Commerce - now, suddenly, newly defined as a radical leftist. A genial-looking, fifty-nine-year-old man with a rumpled face and a hick's haircut - parted far over to the left with a high pompadour in front - Wallace had been Secretary of Agriculture as early as 1920, in President Warren Harding's cabinet, and had established a reputation as an inventive and clear-minded bureaucrat - churning out ideas on farm relief, soil conservation, and other administrative matters: one of the very few men to escape the Harding years with his reputation actually enhanced. In the late twenties, Wallace switched from the Republican Party to the Democratic, and in 1933, Roosevelt appointed him Secretary of Agriculture once again. Gradually, Wallace eased away somewhat from his farming constituency and became, more generally, a champion of American liberalism and the New Deal. His new politics won him the vice-presidency in 1940, and then as time went on and the Democratic bosses grew tired of his idealistic platitudes, it cost him the job: In 1944, Truman replaced him as Vice-President, and Wallace was nudged back into the cabinet as Secretary of Commerce.

After the war, Wallace was left increasingly alone as the country's leading Rooseveltian spokesman for reform at home and cooperation abroad.

He thought that American foreign policy was becoming under Truman increasingly bellicose, and increasingly an excuse to confuse and rout domestic political opponents and to scuttle liberal, New Deal reforms.

He reached the breaking point with Truman in September 1946 when he gave a speech in New York, in Madison Square Garden. Before he delivered the speech, he thought it might arouse some controversy, so he went over it with Truman. Truman gave it the OK, and Wallace delivered it. America must find, said Wallace, some middle ground in international relations, some way to maintain amicable relations with the Soviet Union. He criticized Russia for its repression, and he took a swipe at "namby-pamby pacifism" in the United States. But, overall, he said, "the tougher we get, the tougher the Russians will get." American policy, he said, had certain excesses built into it - a fact he blamed on the British, and on the Republicans.

The speech was bad enough in its implicit criticisms of Truman's policies, but then someone - Truman thought Wallace himself - leaked a letter that Wallace had written the President several months before. In that letter, now printed in papers across the country, Wallace said he thought the Russians had some genuine reasons for feeling insecure: American military expenditures "make it appear either (1) that we are preparing ourselves to win the war which we regard as inevitable or (2) that we are trying to build up a predominance of force to intimidate the rest of mankind." What the United States should really do was offer Russia economic aid and open up trade, to "help clear away the fog of political misunderstanding."

Instead, the United States was increasing Russia's fears enormously, with the way Americans were talking about the atomic bomb. "Would we have been enthusiastic if the Russians had a monopoly of atomic energy and offered to share the information with us at some indefinite time in the future at their discretion if we agreed now not to try to make the bomb and give them information on our secret resources of uranium and thorium?"

As for the money that America was spending on arms, there was "no lasting security in armaments." Nuclear weapons in particular provided America nothing but "security against invasion after all our cities and perhaps 40 million of our city population have been destroyed by atomic weapons." Nothing in Wallace's letter, it seemed, took account of any reasons Americans might have to be suspicious of Stalin. As hard as Wallace might have labored to be evenhanded, he seemed to Truman (as the President wrote in his diary), "a pacifist 100 percent . . . a 'dreamer' . . . The German-American Bund under Fritz Kuhn was not half so dangerous." Altogether the President thought Wallace was "a cat bastard." Within a few days, Truman asked for Wallace's resignation.

Nothing stopped Wallace from talking, however. After Truman's speech announcing the Truman Doctrine, Wallace spoke up within twenty-four hours. The doctrine, he said, was simply "betraying the great tradition of America," was really "the best salesman communism ever had," would absolutely plunge America into a "reckless adventure," and would assuredly guarantee a "century of fear." Truman's policy of stopping Russian advances wherever they seemed to be occurring would require the United States to jump ceaselessly from one place to another to "police Russia's every border" - a feat clearly beyond the resources of any country, a policy foredoomed to failure.

What Wallace said was certainly worth hearing, and yet the more he talked the less formidable he became. As Acheson noted with real pleasure, "We were fortunate in our enemies." As Wallace attracted more and more followers from the extreme left wing, he looked like nothing so much as a Communist himself. The more he spoke on behalf of his point of view, the more he discredited it.

From the political right, meanwhile, the President was savaged by a group led by Senator Robert Taft. Pear-shaped, bespectacled, fifty-eight years old and balding, with his hair firmly slicked down on his head, the son of President William Howard Taft, Senator Taft impressed his colleagues as a diligent but boring man, principled to the point of fossilization, aloof to the point of coldness. As Vandenberg was the leading Republican spokesman on foreign affairs, Taft was the leading Republican on domestic matters - and when the two men differed, as they often did, Vandenberg an internationalist, Taft an isolationist, Vandenberg a friend of Democrats, Taft a steely conservative, both men harboring their own presidential ambitions, they would square off, as Truman said, "just like two roosters." Taft had voted against most of the New Deal. In 1941, when Britain turned to the United States for aid to fight Germany, Taft voted against the Lend-Lease Act, which allowed the President to supply arms to any country whose defense might seem vital to America. To grant such powers to the Executive, said Taft, would "give the President power to carry on a kind of undeclared war."

When Pearl Harbor was attacked, Taft voted to enter World War II, but as soon as the war ended, his instincts to limit American foreign ventures returned. He wanted the government to be limited in size and in powers, and he understood that a venturesome foreign policy would cause the federal government to grow enormously.

During the war, said Taft, Americans maintained that "no nation had the right to remain neutral." That same attitude, he said, seemed to have lingered on with bad effect. "Our whole attitude in the world" after the end of the European war, Taft said, "including the use of the atomic bomb at Hiroshima and Nagasaki, seems to me a departure from the principles of fair and equal treatment which has made America respected throughout the world before this Second World War. Today we are cordially hated in many countries."

Furthermore, Taft declared, in "recent foreign policy" Americans seemed still to be "affected by principles of expediency and supposed necessity," and had largely abandoned the principle of justice. The United States had "drifted into the acceptance of the idea that the world is to be ruled by the power and policy of the great nations and a police force established by them rather than by international law." The Truman Administration, Taft said, had lost sight of the fact that policemen are merely incidental to the law; policemen without law threatened to become tyrants or creators of anarchy.

One of Senator Taft's protégés in the House of Representatives lambasted the Truman Doctrine with equal fervor. "I believe," said Representative George Bender of Ohio, "that the White House program is a reaffirmation of the nineteenth century belief in power politics. . . . It is a program which points to a new policy of interventionism in Europe as a corollary to our Monroe Doctrine in South America. Let there be no mistake about the far-reaching implications of this plan. Once we have taken the historic step of sending financial aid, military experts and loans to Greece and Turkey, we shall be irrevocably committed to a course of action from which it will be impossible to withdraw. More and larger demands will follow. Greater needs will arise throughout the many areas of friction in the world."

In fact, Bender said (in a later speech, after he had warmed up), he opposed any congressional appropriation of funds for military collaboration with "the petty and not so petty dictators of South America," along with much else of the administration's programs which seemed "part of the whole Truman doctrine of drawing off the resources of the United States in support of every reactionary government in the world."

Yet, at the same time that Taft and his political allies were calling for a traditionally modest federal government, they also found it hard to deal with the consequences of modesty. The Democrats, said Taft, had "pursued a policy of appeasing Russia, a policy which has sacrificed throughout Eastern Europe and Asia the freedom of many nations and millions of people." To Taft, the agreements that Roosevelt had made at Yalta, and Truman at Potsdam, to recognize a Soviet sphere of influence in Eastern Europe, had been a shameful and unnecessary capitulation to Stalin. Never mind that Churchill had been party to the deal, that Churchill had even outlined its terms in a meeting with Stalin in Moscow in the autumn of 1944. Never mind that Stalin had as a quid pro quo recognized a Western sphere of influence taking in all of Western Europe, Canada, South America, Central America. And never mind, finally, after the war, that the West could not recapture Eastern Europe short of a war that only the smallest minority thought could be won or that could be won only if the United States were willing to use atomic weapons to utterly subdue the Soviet Union and then, presumably, occupy it. Taft insisted that Truman had acquiesced in a sell-out, in appeasement, in a sacrifice of millions of people and many nations.

Moreover, not even Wallace and Taft constituted all of Truman's domestic political problems of the moment. Rather more bizarrely, the President had also been placed on notice by the House Committee on Un-American Activities that his administration was on trial.

HUAC, as it was called, was not a new committee. Between 1919 and 1935, members of Congress had occasionally stirred themselves to inquire into the possibility of a Communist menace destroying

America from within. On four separate occasions, the activities of Communists in the United States had been the subject of formal investigations, which, in general, and in spite of a waxing and waning vogue for communism in America, failed to turn up much information of interest.

By 1938, however, the toll taken by the Depression and the rumblings of war in Europe had aroused sufficient anxiety that Congress passed legislation to require agents of foreign organizations to register with the federal government. Another congressional committee was formed and, in May 1938, charged to investigate what Congress referred to, somewhat vaguely, in its enabling legislation as "un-American activities." Although the committee might have been expected to slip gradually from notice, as its predecessors had done, it was led by an energetic chairman, Martin Dies of Texas, who lashed into Communists and Fascists and other subversives with such abandon as to become a famous figure. In 1945, the Dies committee was given tenure as the House Committee on Un-American Activities and - the Fascists having been beaten in the war - devoted itself entirely to destroying Communists.

Over the years, the Dies committee had already found the work of rooting out Communists to be, among other things, politically useful. Dies disliked the New Deal, and the New Deal, predictably enough, had attracted a lot of liberals onto the federal payroll. As the bureaucracy of the New Deal expanded rapidly, and drew reformers and socialists and anti-Fascists and even Communists to Washington along with the liberals, and as the speed of hiring overtook the care of screening, Dies increasingly found that he was able to turn up suspicious-seeming people on President Roosevelt's payroll. These people - presumably boring from within, stealing secrets, betraying diplomatic and military plans - could be used to discredit the New Deal.

These same people, or others like them, could be supposed as well to be employed still by President Truman, and could be used to discredit his administration too. Especially after the congressional elections in the fall of 1946, Republican calls for a "house-cleaning" in the Democratic administration sounded faintly alarming. The issue, whatever its real merits, had become mischievously useful. The Republicans seized on it as a means to hold the Democratic President in check, to badger him with hints and charges that his ideas and appointees were not entirely loyal to America.

In truth, as Truman's presidency developed, for all the support that he gathered from those who were feeling expansionist and internationalist, he was being attacked at the same time from left, right, and even center - by Wallace on the left, Taft and HUAC on the right, and, in the center, by large numbers of the American people, who were tired of war and wary of policies that might lead to war. What the President's opponents on the right had not quite anticipated, however, was that they helped to create an issue that Truman himself could grasp and turn against everyone.

Although Truman disliked "parlor pinks" and "Reds" as much as the next fellow, he was not personally much impressed by the notion of internal subversion. "People are much wrought up about the Communist 'bugaboo,'" he wrote to a former governor of Pennsylvania, "but I am of the opinion that the country is perfectly safe so far as Communism is concerned - we have far too many sane people. Our Government is made for the welfare of the people and I don't believe there will ever come a time when anyone will really want to overturn it."

Nonetheless, the President did need to take the weapon out of the hands of others, and there were men in his administration who were eager to root out some Communists. Over at the Department of the Navy, Secretary Forrestal frankly wondered whether Americans whose religious beliefs imbued them with pacifist tendencies, and Americans who tended to be isolationists - whose views so conveniently suited the Communists - were not, in fact, a serious threat to national security. Over at the Federal Bureau of Investigation, Director J. Edgar Hoover worried about the Communist propaganda that emanated from apparently legitimate organizations that were, in actual fact, merely "fronts" for the Communists. Many perfectly decent American folks, not Communists at all, were nonetheless dangerous to American security simply because they were overly tolerant of Communists, "soft" on communism, "dupes" of the Communists, or, worse, "fellow travelers."

Such sentiments had a good deal of support from organizations around the country, from the American Legion to the U.S. Chamber of Commerce. Francis Cardinal Spellman of New York led an anti-Communist Catholic movement, saying, "Every Communist is a potential enemy of the U.S. and only the bat-blind can fail to be aware of the Communist invasion of our country."

Over at the Department of Justice, Attorney General Tom Clark had a list that he had inherited from a wartime security program. Ninety-one organizations were on the Attorney General's list of possible Communist, fascist, totalitarian, or just plain "subversive" outfits, and the United States needed, Clark felt, to combat "the rising tide of totalitarianism . . . coming to our shores" that was reflected in his list. In mid-March, he encouraged Hoover to appear before a House committee to outline the dangers of communism in America.

The Communist Party, said Hoover, was "a fifth column if ever there was one." Its goal was, plainly stated, "the overthrow of our government." Its allegiance was "to Russia, not the United States." Ever since President Truman had called for aid to Greece and Turkey, "the Communists, opposing the plan, had been mobilizing, promoting mass meetings, sending telegrams and letters to exert pressure on Congress." Hoover had a way of dealing with it, however - or at least a way of ensuring that none of these Communists got inside the government itself to bore from within, steal secrets, sap the strength of America at its vitals. He intended to conduct a full background investigation on any federal employee for whom a preliminary check of FBI files showed "derogatory information."

"I have been pleased," Hoover had said on another recent occasion, "to observe that the Communist attempts to penetrate the American Legion have met with failure. Eternal vigilance will continue to keep your ranks free of shifty, double-crossing Communist destructionists. We are rapidly reaching the time when loyal Americans must be willing to stand up and be counted. . . . The Communist Party . . . has for its purpose the shackling of America and its conversion to the Godless, Communist way of life. . . . We, of this generation, have faced two great menaces in America - Fascism and Communism. Both are materialistic; both are totalitarian; both are anti-religious; both are degrading and inhuman." Hoover, in fact, alarmed the President. Truman was afraid that Hoover's tendencies would lead the FBI to set up a "Gestapo."

From inside the administration and from without, the President was being harassed by witch-hunters, and so at last he responded. Never one to use half measures, he responded vigorously. Nine days after his Truman Doctrine speech, the President announced that he was setting up, by executive order, an Employee Loyalty Review Board that would ensure against "infiltration of disloyal persons" into the government. Any person who sought a government job would be put through a loyalty check; any person currently employed would be subject to his superior's review for loyalty.

Henceforth, anyone who did not measure up to the Executive's standards of loyalty could be considered a threat to national security. The order naturally covered anyone who might be a Communist or might be construed as working for the Communists or even as a Communist sympathizer, even, in its broadest, vaguest suggestion, anyone who opposed American (anti-Communist) foreign policy.

Without doubt, Truman had deflected the anti-Communist threat from himself. Indeed, happily, he had done even more: He had gone far toward annihilating Wallace and Taft and his other political opponents with it. Unfortunately, he had done it in a way so extreme, in a way that so inflamed the issue, that in time he seemed to have become as much the captive as the master of his own policy.

7
A CHANGE OF TACTICS

TRUMAN'S OLD FRIEND Winston Churchill - the grand old man of World War II, whose eloquence as wartime Prime Minister of Great Britain had sustained not only his fellow Britons, but people everywhere in their most anguished hours, members of the Resistance in Europe, refugees hiding out underground in farmhouses and nunneries, who heard Churchill's voice on the radio, referring contemptuously to Hitler as "Colonel Schicklgruber," promising to fight on the beaches, in the fields and in the streets, declaring when his American allies entered the war, "This is not the end, nor is it even the beginning of the end, but it is the end of the beginning," the man who was turned out of office at the conclusion of the war at age seventy, played out, exhausted by the awful ordeal - came loyally out of retirement in the spring of 1947 to give his support to his companion-in-peace, the new President of the United States. As the war had drawn to a close and Churchill had foreseen the inevitable decimation of the British Empire, he had come to pin his hopes on an Anglo-American union, on the United States sustaining Britain - perhaps even in a way that would allow Britain to lead the Continent. Now, as Truman made his move in Greece, Churchill did his duty and threw his support behind the President. "If my father had been an American citizen instead of my mother," Churchill wrote in his splendid, cascading King James prose in an essay for *Life* magazine, "I should have hesitated a long time before I got mixed up with Europe and Asia and that sort of thing. . . . But I should also have memories and comprehension of what had happened in the last thirty years or more . . . . I might well have come to the conclusion that the United States has no choice but to lead or fall . . . . Britain and the British Commonwealth as a whole will welcome the establishment of American power in the Middle East and will give her potent aid by every means. Americans should not hesitate to march forward unswervingly upon the path to which Destiny has called them. . . . United . . . we may save freedom, civilization and democracy - and perhaps even roll away the curse of war forever from mankind."

Life was doing its bit for Truman too. Its publisher, Henry Luce, had, after all, declared the twentieth century to be "the American Century," in which America would become "the sanctuary of the ideals of civilization . . . the powerhouse from which the ideals spread throughout the world and do their mysterious work of lifting the life of mankind from the levels of the beasts to what the Psalmist called a little lower than the angels."

On Capitol Hill too, the Truman Doctrine swept toward what appeared to be a terrific victory in Congress. On April 22, a bill that approved aid to Greece and Turkey passed the Senate by a resounding majority of sixty-seven to twenty-three, and on May 8, it passed the House by 289 to 107.

Yet, to those who looked closely at the vote, the apparent victory was, in fact, very unsettling. The vote had been grudging, slow in coming. It had been so difficult to keep on course, so hard to shepherd through to passage, that it had in the end to be reckoned a near escape from defeat.

As the congressmen began to learn, Greece had not been a "crisis" at all. The State Department had known for months what was happening in Greece and that the British had been looking for a chance to ease out of their commitments there. A loan from the Export-Import Bank had gone to Greece as early as January 1946, and become an occasion for the British and the Greeks to talk at length about the need to bring more American aid to Greece. In September 1946, the British had been told directly by then Secretary of State Byrnes that if the British would continue military aid to Greece, America would provide economic aid. In December, the Greek Prime Minister had visited Washington, meeting with Truman and Acheson about aid. The "crisis," a good many congressmen complained, had been trumped up just to railroad Congress into passing the bill.

Congressman Francis Case was sufficiently upset to write the President: "At least seventy-five members, I judge, would have voted against final passage, myself included, had it not been that we thought it would be like pulling the rug out from under you and Secretary of State Marshall in the positions you had taken at Moscow."

From abroad, the reaction was not enthusiastic either. While diplomats had been complaining about the Russians for some time, Truman's speech was the first officially announced break with the Soviets, and it had been taken without any real consultation with the Allies. In addition, Truman's blanket attack on Communists was an attack on two of the largest political parties in Europe - both of which were participating in free, democratic elections in France and Italy.

Charles Kindleberger, a young man in the State Department, noted in a memo for his files, "The

Truman Doctrine was making heavy weather of it, both on Capitol Hill and in the country as a whole." As Kindleberger analyzed it, the Truman Doctrine's "negative, retaliatory, counter-punching features were disliked. Its implications for economic and ultimately military warfare were regretted." And so, once again, "the Department was in a panic as to what to do in Greece. Slapping together an anti-Russian policy to take over the British policing role there, was too much for the country to swallow. It gagged. . . . The Truman Doctrine was no great shakes."

In short, if Truman wanted to put together some sort of internationalist foreign policy for his administration he would need something less tough, something more in keeping with traditional American longings for peace, generosity of spirit, and the ideals of the early Republic, something more in keeping with the American character, as it was seen, just after the war, both at home and abroad.

In fact, even as the Truman Doctrine was bogging down amidst the misgivings of congressmen, State Department officials were sorting through memoranda, background reports, area studies, charts and graphs, cables from abroad, minutes of conferences, and documents with appendices and annexes to see how they could flesh out the Truman Doctrine, to see to it that it was a coherent policy.

The men at State had not lost their enthusiasm for internationalism at all. Acheson formed the Ad Hoc Committee, charged with studying the Greek and Turkish problems to see what "situations elsewhere in the world . . . may require analogous financial, technical, and military aid on our part."

As the committee members scoured the department's files, they were, indeed, able to sweep up a list of countries in addition to Greece and Turkey that might need some economic and military aid under the terms enunciated in the Truman Doctrine. They noticed especially Iran, Italy, France, Korea, Austria, and Hungary. Some other countries, the committee found, had less urgent needs that might, nonetheless, develop into critical requirements at some later date: Great Britain, Belgium, Luxembourg, the Netherlands, the Philippines, Portugal, Czechoslovakia, and Poland. Piecemeal assistance might be needed in Canada, the Latin American republics, and China. Indeed, hardly any country could fail to qualify.

Without even trying, the Ad Hoc Committee was able to gather in a good bit of the world under the rubric of economic need. The committee was able to find projected shortages of bread grains, fats and oils, protein and sugar, and to foresee critical coal deficiencies in much of Europe, an acute shortage of nitrogenous fertilizer, a worrisome potential shortage in European steel production, a need for tractors, construction equipment, freight cars, and mining machinery.

The State Department could not quite string all of these facts into a statement of policy, but the thought of the suffering that afflicted Europe moved a number of department officials to insist, without having given it much thought, that the United States should extend some form of charity. These charitable instincts proved contagious, and in time, few in the department were unaffected by them. Journalists and newspaper editors - impractical people, generally - had long been urging some sort of generosity on the part of the United States toward its allies. But no one, or not enough people, had yet been able to see any usefulness in the idea.

Gradually, however, the advantages of charity began to creep into policy discussions in the department. Roosevelt's economic advisers had not been unimpressed with the notion that it had been the war, and not the New Deal, that brought the United States out of the Great Depression. Between 1940 and 1944, industrial production had risen by 90 percent, agricultural production had risen by 20 percent, and the total gross national product by 60 percent. In 1940, the national debt had been $61 billion; by 1945, it was $253 billion. In 1940, government spending had been $9 billion; by 1945, it was $253 billion. In 1940, government spending had been $20 billion; by 1945, it was $98 billion. By the war's end, Americans enjoyed unprecedented levels of employment and income, and economists in Washington were concerned that the end of the war would bring rapid demobilization of the armed forces, drastic cuts in public spending, slackening demands, production surpluses, and heavy unemployment. Some economists worried that exports - which had risen to as high as $15 billion a year and brought enormous prosperity to the nation - might drop back to their prewar levels of only $3 billion, simply because foreign nations did not have the wealth to purchase goods from America. The world suffered, it was said, from a "dollar shortage"; foreign countries had used up their dollars in purchasing American goods. With their mines and factories destroyed, they could not produce anything to earn more dollars; they could no longer purchase American goods; and so, American exports would inevitably decline and the American economy would shrink rapidly.

By early 1946, industrial production in America was off by 30 percent, and unemployment had risen from .5 million to 2.7 million. Some said unemployment would reach 8 million, some said 10 million. It appeared that economic collapse was possible in America, because of the economic collapse of Europe.

As it turned out, the danger passed. By the middle of 1946, the economy reversed itself again - and in retrospect it appears that the economy needed no further assistance to continue its growth. Unemployment eased: No one, it seems, had quite noticed that the women and boys who had joined the labor force during the war simply went home or back to school, and left jobs open for the returning soldiers. But still, the anxieties persisted in 1946 and 1947. Germany was still in ruins, and Alfred Sloane, the chairman of General Motors, pointed out that Germany had always been, and was still, the "spark plug" of the European economy. If Germany were allowed to collapse, Europe would follow; and if Europe collapsed, America would follow.

Of course, it was no easy matter for the United States to turn around and treat its erstwhile German enemy generously. A good number of Americans could be expected to oppose such a measure - as did Stalin, for his reasons, and the French, for theirs. In truth, the solution to the German problem that would best suit the French - to bury it in the solution of some other problem, to slip it in as part of a larger plan that would ensure that as Germany was rebuilt, it was also held down, that it would be let up only after it had been knit into a balance of power that could contain it - was suited to domestic American politics as well.

Great Britain, meanwhile, presented another, certainly equally engrossing, array of challenges.

The British Empire was ended, to be sure. On March 24, Viscount Mountbatten, in whose veins flowed the blood of Victoria, first Empress of India, was to be seen in solemn ceremony - in naval uniform, his chest resplendent with medals and gold braid, holding a copy of the Holy Bible in his right hand, his gaze firm, clear, and somewhat condescending - as he was sworn in as the last Viceroy of India, sent to New Delhi to turn over to the Indians the government of their own country. With the loss of India, the Jewel of the Empire, the principal treasure that remained of the Empire was the shell of the great commercial system that had channeled enormous wealth back to England: the Commonwealth trading bloc, or the sterling bloc as it was called - a network of commercial arrangements, or system of "Imperial Preference," that enabled the nations of the Commonwealth to trade with one another on terms extraordinarily more favorable than those that were offered to other countries. The system of Imperial Preference made Britain one of the largest trading nations in the world. Before the war, Britain and North America together accounted for half of all the world's trade. Now, given Britain's weakened position, if the United States could take over the sterling bloc, America would remain as the sole Capitalist Great Power.

Understandably, the British were reluctant to give up this last treasure of the empire. It would not be an easy matter for the United States to push Britain over the brink. It did seem, however, that it might be possible, once Great Britain got itself into a tight enough spot, to extend it a helping hand, to support it, and, finally, to embrace it.

The man whose principal responsibility it was to think of such things was the Undersecretary of State for Economic Affairs, William Clayton. He was a huge man, six feet six inches tall, big-boned, square-jawed, blue-eyed, with a gaze level, cold, and somewhat abstracted, as though he did not focus personally on any other. He parted his white hair on the left, which gave him a slightly less severe mien than he had had as a young man, when he had parted his hair precisely in the middle.

At the bridge table, he sat erect - he neither drank nor smoked - and played with a firm determination to discover the location of all fifty-two cards. He neither bluffed nor engaged in any idle banter. He was unfailingly polite and became even more polite when angered. He was noted for his self-control, precision, patience, soft-spokenness, efficiency, and chivalry to women. He was never known to go through a door before another. He invariably opened the car door for his wife and his four daughters. Aside from bridge, his only other form of relaxation was horseback riding. In the early days of his marriage, he bought two Kentucky riding horses so that he and Mrs. Clayton could ride together before breakfast. For a week, Mrs. Clayton rose at 5 a.m. each morning to go for a canter with her husband. After a week, she quit because Clayton, lost in thought, invariably rode out ahead alone.

Clayton was sixty-seven years old, born in Mississippi in 1880. His father had been a cotton buyer, and Will dropped out of school at the age of thirteen to go to work as a court clerk. He studied shorthand at night, and ever after - to the surprise and frequent consternation of others - he carried a pocketful of index cards on which he kept notes, and sometimes verbatim transcripts, of his business conversations. At the age of fifteen, he left home to seek his fortune, and he worked his way up in the cotton business so rapidly that by 1904, he had formed his own company with his brother-in-law, Frank Anderson. By the time of the First World War, Anderson, Clayton & Company was the largest cotton-trading company in the world. In the thirties, while his competitors complained of New Deal restrictions on cotton acreage, Clayton moved his operations to foreign countries where he would not be hampered by such regulations; he built fourteen cotton-oil mills and seventy-five cotton gins in Brazil, Mexico, Argentina, Peru, Paraguay, and Egypt. In 1940, by which time Anderson, Clayton had sales of more than $200 million and controlled 15 percent of the total world cotton crop, Clayton was asked to join the government to help with the procurement of strategic materials. In 1947, whatever the economic realities for the nation as a whole might have seemed, or actually been, Clayton had concluded from firsthand experience that America needed to move forcefully into the world, to buck up foreign economic systems, solve the "dollar shortage," and get American exports fueled up. American cotton was in rather long supply in 1947, and if foreign markets were to collapse, it would be certain economic disaster for Anderson, Clayton & Company.

"Let us admit right off," said Clayton, "that our objective has as its background the needs and interests of the people of the United States. We need markets - big markets - in which to buy and sell." The essential condition, Clayton said (with an eye on the sterling bloc), was multilateral trade - markets open to all, not closed to anyone by bilateral agreements or hindered by high tariffs or any other barriers to trade. If, in such a market, the advantage would just happen to go to the strongest enterprises and nations, well, so be it: that, after all, was what free enterprise was.

What free enterprise was too, as Clayton knew so well, was not merely the avoidance of depression, not merely the staving off of unemployment, not merely staying even, but expanding, getting bigger and bigger. Others might argue whether foreign markets were necessary just to avoid bad times; Clayton was after better times.

Thus Acheson's men, and Clayton, and young Charles Kindleberger, and some few others floundered toward some new policy - one that would allow the United States to assume the role of an international power without arousing the opposition of Americans themselves, that would seem, above all, generous and not harsh, soft and not hard, that would solve the German problem, and the French problem, and the British problem, and Will Clayton's problem, something more economical than military - something that would knit all these complexities into a single, coherent theory and a serviceable prescription for action. Most of the pieces for such a construct had been identified; what was still needed was someone who had the clarity of thought and the command of rhetoric to take all this jumble of potentially useful stuff and put it together in a single interoffice memo.

8
THE POLICY

GEORGE FROST KENNAN had been admitted late to Princeton, and so, when he arrived on the campus in the autumn of 1921, he was given, as he remembered, "the last furnished room in the most remote of those gloomy rooming houses far off campus to which, at that time, late-coming freshmen were relegated." He was only sixteen years old, a year younger than his classmates, "hopelessly and crudely Midwestern" - a Wisconsin boy - and he could not find just the right way to approach boys from the East. He could not get the casual tone just right. Shy, awkward, unable to ask the insiders how things were done, unable to afford the avocations at which others spent their free hours, he remained the perpetual outsider.

He was the son of Kossuth and Florence James Kennan, the descendants of Scotch-Irish farm people who started out in the Northeast in the 1700s and moved west - "rugged and angular people," as Kennan said, "not always attractive . . . the outstanding characteristic of all of them was an obdurate, tight-lipped independence, a reluctance to become involved with other people . . . a fighting clear of every form of association that might limit one's freedom of individual choice."

When Kennan came to write his *Memoirs,* he did not mention his mother. His father, he said, was "a shy, lonely, and not very happy person." He chose, as someone for whom he could feel deep kinship, his father's father's cousin, who was also named George Kennan, and who had been a student of czarist Russia and the author, among other things, of a book entitled *Siberia and the Exile System.* With this distant cousin as an inspiration, and with the encouragement of a high school teacher, Kennan had gone to Princeton.

He left college, he said, "as obscurely as I had entered it," assessing himself "a dreamer, feeble of will, and something of a sissy in personal relations. I had inherited a detestation of scenes which I can only put down as a congenital weakness of the family." He felt he did have, however, a clear and open intellect, and "a high sensitivity to atmosphere and to other people's worlds of thought." He was already, even at this early age, one of those men for whom thinking ahead was a greater pleasure than living in the present, that is to say, a man destined to become a theorist.

On graduation from Princeton, he went directly into the Foreign Service, and was sent almost at once to Switzerland and then to Germany, to Estonia, to Latvia, to Lithuania, back to Germany for training as a Russian specialist, and finally to Russia. Having felt, as a youngster and a young man, that he was an outsider, as an adult he became, in fact, a wandering exile. If he was at home anywhere, it was not so much in a place as in a language. In Estonia, with an impoverished émigré Ukrainian teacher, Kennan conceived a love "for this great Russian language - rich, pithy, musical, sometimes tender, sometimes earthy and brutal, sometimes classically severe." To his love of the language, Kennan added a love of the Russian landscape, of the Russian light, of the famous "white nights" of the far north, that erotic half-light that lasts from sunset to sunrise, "a condition of nature under the spell of which all human emotions and situations seemed to take on a heightened poignancy, mystery, and promise."

His fondness for the land and the people was matched by a personal anguish about their leaders. In the twenties, he had been stricken by the "persecution and 'liquidation as a class'" of entire groups of people. The thought that a government could annihilate whole classes of people absolutely chilled Kennan. Then, in the early thirties, in Moscow, Kennan was stunned first by the murder of Sergei Kirov, a rival of Stalin's. As more and more of Stalin's rivals or suspected rivals disappeared, or were sent to Siberia, or were murdered - finally, as Kennan began to suspect, numbering in the hundreds of thousands and then the millions - he was appalled.

"Troubled by ulcers," as one historian wrote of him, "with an expression that seemed somewhat ascetic," Kennan struck many of his peers as "arrogant, high-strung, ambitious, and very bright." An evaluation report that was filed on him in the early thirties described him as having an "excellent mind, supple and penetrating, and well balanced, save perhaps for a tendency . . . to entertain intellectual concepts rather emotionally."

He married in 1931 (to a Norwegian woman named Annelise Soerensen) and had four children and evidently enjoyed his family life. His circle of friends tended to include a good number of White Russians and other exiles and émigrés and diplomatic travelers who, like Kennan, no longer had a country that felt much like home. "I was no longer a part of what I had once been a part of," Kennan wrote of this time, "no longer, in fact, a part of anything at all. It was not just that I had left the world of my boyhood, although this too was true; it was also that this world had left me . . . . Increasingly, now, I would not be a part of my country."

Kennan cultivated a polished manner. He was a plain-looking young man, six feet tall and slender, with an open, clean-shaven, pleasant face, blue eyes, a high forehead, and awkwardly large ears. He preferred understated dress, well-tailored gray suits, simple silk ties. He enjoyed his ability to move among the upper classes in Europe and elsewhere, and he relished his own fairly detached, Olympian view of geopolitics.

The world was best seen, in Kennan's view, without extravagant hopes or greed or fear, and with a certain tough-minded and cool realism, as a balance among powers and their various spheres of interest. The job of the professional diplomat was to juggle and adjust and rearrange the relationships among the elements that made that balance, i.e., the elements of power - military, economic, political. The aim was the avoidance of violence. The need was to be tactful but tough, to be neither gullible nor hostile.

In Kennan's analysis, conflict between Russia and America was inevitable, but war was not. The only difficulty with Kennan's view was that it lacked a certain excitement. Calm, reasoned, even-handed, expressed in superbly balanced, exquisitely honed, pellucid prose, Kennan's view was destined to ensure its author's continued obscurity as a valued junior Foreign Service officer who would never be invited into the innermost councils of state. His advice might be good, but it was not useful. It did not provide the rationale for dynamic political expansion; it did not offer a framework and rationalization for terrific economic expansion; it did not place America at the head of a great moral crusade. It was an admirable view, but it did not have any zip.

Whether or not he consciously realized his plight at the time, he suffered from it. His chance to break out of it came in the winter of 1946. He was lying abed in Moscow with symptoms of a cold, sinus trouble, and a toothache. He was running a fever. A cable arrived from Washington asking whether the Moscow embassy could explain why the Russians were showing some hesitation about joining the World Bank and the International Monetary Fund. It was a simple question - relayed from the Treasury Department by the State Department - one that could have been answered easily and without much fanfare, since the Russians simply did not consider it in their interests to join in such arrangements. But Kennan saw the question as an opportunity for him to explain Russia once and for all to the people back in Washington. His superior officer was away, and it fell to him to reply to the request for information. "The more I thought about this message," he recalled, "the more it seemed obvious that this was 'it.' . . . . It was no good trying to brush the question off with a couple of routine sentences . . . . Here was a case where nothing but the whole truth would do. They had asked for it. Now, by God, they would have it."

He could not, he said, answer questions "so intricate, so delicate, so strange to our form of thought" in a simple, brief message. He would need to fill in some background so that the behavior of the Russian leaders could be understood. And with that, he launched into an 8,000-word cable that constituted a primer of Russian history and a prospectus of American foreign policy for the next several decades. To his notions of balance-of-power politics, he added a bit of his old hatred of Russia's leaders, a dash of ideological fervor, a lashing of fear, and a call to arms - and, casting it all in his fine prose, he gave the folks back home something they could use, something that ravished the insiders back in Washington.

The Soviet leaders, said Kennan, still feel that they live in an antagonistic "capitalist encirclement," with which "in the long run there can be no permanent peaceful coexistence." Thus, the Soviet leaders are determined to advance the strength of the Soviet Union, to deepen and exploit differences among capitalist powers, and to use "democratic-progressive" elements abroad to bring pressure against capitalist countries.

The Soviet party line, however, does not arise out of a simple objective assessment of real advantages to be gained in the outside world but rather "from basic inner-Russian necessities," that is to say, it is a "neurotic view of world affairs" that arises from a "traditional and instinctive Russian sense of insecurity." Originally, this was the "insecurity of a peaceful agricultural people trying to live on vast exposed plain in neighborhood of fierce nomadic peoples." But, more recently, the Russian rulers "have invariably sensed that their rule was relatively archaic in form, fragile and artificial in its psychological foundation and unable to stand comparisons with western countries."

It was no mistake that Marxism took root in such a country, for "in this dogma, with its basic altruism of purpose [the Russian rulers] found justification for their instinctive fear of outside world, for the dictatorship without which they did not know how to rule, for cruelties they did not dare not to inflict, for sacrifices they felt bound to demand. In the name of Marxism they sacrificed every single ethical value in their methods and tactics. Today they cannot dispense with it. It is the fig leaf of their moral and intellectual respectability. Without it they would stand before history, at best, as only the last of that long succession of cruel and wasteful Russian rulers who have relentlessly forced their country on to ever new heights of military power in order to guarantee external security for their internally weak regimes."

In pursuit of its aims, Kennan said, the Soviet Union would employ: friendly political parties in other nations that would give communism the appearance of an open, bona fide political movement; an underground that would do the real work of the Soviets; associations of workers, youths, women, social organizations, liberal magazines and publishing houses that could be easily penetrated by Communist operatives; international labor organizations; friendly governments in such places as Yugoslavia, Iran, and China. These groups and their agents would try "to disrupt national self-confidence, to hamstring measures of national defense, to increase social and industrial unrest, to stimulate all forms of disunity," to remove from office any politicians - or entire governments - that oppose the Soviet Union, to set the major Western powers against one another, and to "work toward the destruction of all forms of personal independence, economic, political, or moral." In short, these were tactics that, in the years since 1947, seem to have become common to too many nations.

The United States faced, Kennan said, "a political force committed fanatically to the belief that with U.S. there can be no permanent modus vivendi, that it is desirable and necessary that the internal harmony of our society be disrupted, our traditional way of life be destroyed, and the international authority of our state be broken."

Kennan had written the cable in reply to an inquiry from the Treasury Department, but he gave a copy of it to the naval attaché in Moscow, who relayed it to the Chief of Naval Operations in Washington, who relayed it at last to the Secretary of the Navy, James Forrestal. Forrestal asked his aides to find out more about the author of the cable; meanwhile, the Secretary had several hundred copies of it run off and made it required reading for the top officers under his jurisdiction. Kennan's advice had at last become useful.

Forrestal had recently organized the War College in Washington - a center for the study of geopolitics and strategy - and he put in a request to have Kennan detailed at once to lecture on world affairs to 100 select military and diplomatic officers. By the time Kennan arrived back in Washington, he was a celebrity among the cognoscenti. Lunches were organized at the Pentagon so that senators could come by and talk to Kennan.

Among Kennan's other odd jobs was to comment, as Forrestal asked him to do, on a paper that had been written for the Secretary of the Navy about Marxism and Soviet power. "It was a good paper," as Kennan later recalled it. "With parts of it I could agree; other parts were simply not put the way I would have put them." And so, once again, Kennan sat down to compose a long reply to a short question. His reply took the form of a paper for Forrestal called "The Sources of Soviet Conduct." In it, Kennan outlined a way of dealing with the problem that he had described in his cable from Moscow.

The Soviet Union, for all its fearsome appearance, said Kennan, also had some interesting weaknesses. For one thing, he said, "the process of political consolidation has never been completed and the men in the Kremlin have continued to be predominantly absorbed with the struggle to secure and make absolute the power which they seized in November 1917." For another thing, "the Soviet achievement has been carried out at a terrible cost in human life and human hopes and energies. It has necessitated the use of forced labor on a scale unprecedented in modern times under conditions of peace. It has involved the neglect or abuse of other phases of Soviet economic life, particularly agriculture, consumers' goods production, housing and transportation." The war took a tremendous toll, and withal, "we have in Russia today a population which is physically and spiritually tired. . . . There are limits to the physical and nervous strength of people themselves. These limits are absolute ones and are binding even for the cruelest dictatorship."

Above all, said Kennan, in part because of the real limits on Soviet power, in part because of its ideological belief in ultimate victory, the Soviet Union could be surprisingly rational, "sensitive to contrary force," and "flexible in its reaction to political realities." Thus, said Kennan, the United States ought to commit itself to a "long-term, patient but firm and vigilant containment of Russian expansive tendencies." This containment of the Soviet Union could be achieved through "the adroit and vigilant application of counterforce at a series of constantly shifting geographical and political points," or, as he said elsewhere, "at every point where they show signs of encroaching upon the interest of a peaceful world."

Kennan thought, later said that he thought, that he was recommending a moderate means of dealing with the Soviet Union where others were being more warlike. He meant, he said, to oppose a political challenge with a political challenge. (Not that Kennan was entirely averse to backing up his notions of containment with tough measures. Several months later he would forward a paper to Secretary Forrestal about the "possible establishment of a guerrilla warfare corps and a guerrilla warfare school within our new defense establishment." He did not think, Kennan told Forrestal in his covering note, "that the American people would ever approve of policies which relied fundamentally on [underground] . . . methods. . . . I do feel, however, that there are cases where it might be essential to our security that we fight fire with fire.") Yet, once again whether he wished it or not, his bright phrases were picked up without all of his qualifications and touted around Washington with enthusiasm. The notion of "containment" began to take on more and more the appearance of a "doctrine," and the techniques used to apply it were not long limited to political ones.

The Moscow cable, as Kennan later recalled, had "changed my career and my life . . . my official loneliness came in fact to an end. . . . My reputation was made. My voice now carried." He had become, at last, an insider's insider, or, as *The New York Times* dubbed him, "America's global planner." His talent - which was more than considerable - was his ability to take hold of a notion and see all its parts in relation to one another; he could grasp both broad generalities and minute specifics, and relate them all to one another in a forceful, lucid, seamless prose that commanded belief and respect.

Not long after Kennan arrived in Washington, Forrestal sent him over to Marshall, and Marshall suggested to Kennan that the State Department needed a Policy Planning Staff composed of a group of bright young men without operational responsibilities who would serve as a "brain trust" to consider long-range ideas for foreign policy. Kennan was to become the head of this staff as soon as he could break away from his duties at the War College.

Marshall had returned from his meeting with Stalin freshly determined that the United States must shape up a coherent program, and act. He called Kennan to his office at once. As Kennan recalled it, Marshall was brief, to the point: Europe was in a mess. Something would have to be done. If he [Marshall] did not take the initiative, others would. Others, particularly people in Congress, would start coming up with ideas of their own about what ought to be done for Europe. He would then be forced on the defensive. He was determined to avoid this if he possibly could. . . . "I had a limited time (I cannot remember whether it was ten days or two weeks; I remember only that it was brief) in which to give him my recommendations. . . . He then added characteristically . . . that he had only one bit of advice for me: 'Avoid trivia.'"

Kennan quickly assembled a group that included his friend Charles Bohlen, age forty-three, who had been in the Foreign Service for eighteen years and, like Kennan, was a specialist in Russian affairs; Carlton Savage, age forty-nine, who had been in the department for twenty years and was chosen to become the executive secretary of the new Planning Staff; John Davies, age thirty-nine, an old China hand who had more recently been assigned to Moscow; Joseph Johnson, former professor of history, more recently chief of the Division of International Security Affairs; Burton Berry, age forty-six, a nineteen-year veteran in the Foreign Service, most recently on assignment in Eastern Europe; James Angell, age forty-nine, a professor of economics from Columbia University; George McGhee, age thirty-five, a former Rhodes scholar, most recently serving as special assistant to Will Clayton.

In the beginning, as Carlton Savage recalled, "We met almost every day. . . . We met very, very rapidly, very, very frequently . . . very informally. Quite often [Kennan} would have drafts of his for us to go over, and . . . we'd just go over them and . . . suggest changes and discuss things . . . the original drafts were nearly always made by Kennan . . . he was always open-minded for other people's views."

"We'd all gather around the table," another of the Planning Staff members recalled, "and George would start talking. And . . . very often none of us would say a word, but we'd just be looking at him. And he, by watching us, seemed to know just what we were thinking . . . he could tell a person's slant . . . toward a particular subject by bouncing ideas off him and noticing the angle at which they bounced . . . . Rather often he wouldn't have to ask; he'd say, oh yes, you mean so-and-so, don't you? And there'd be a nod, and on he'd go, changing his course to take account of this other factor he may have, for the moment, overlooked."

Soon enough, the Policy Planning Staff commenced to turn out memos - brief considerations at first of one issue or another, and then, as time went on, longer, more thoroughly reasoned papers. Eventually, these considerations were all compiled for a report ("Certain Aspects of the European Recovery Problem from the United States Standpoint") that was given to Secretary Marshall.

The condition of the world was best characterized, as the Planning Staff saw it, by "the physical and psychic exhaustion of people everywhere; the feelings of disillusionment, insecurity and apathy occasioned by the developments of the post-hostilities period and particularly by the tendency toward division of the continent between east and west; the destruction and depreciation of physical plant and equipment; the depletion of financial reserves, particularly in foreign exchange and external assets; social and economic dislocation, including the breakdown of the prewar institutional patterns and the destruction of the machinery of economic intercourse; the prolonged delay in adjusting German economy to production for peaceful purposes."

Given this situation, it was possible the Soviet Union would take advantage of Europe's plight. The economic, political, social, and psychological crisis in Europe made European society a possible prey to the Russians. But the way to guard against such possible threat was not, in the view of the Planning Staff, to combat "communism as such but to [ensure] the restoration of the economic health and vigor of European society," to combat the economic maladjustment "which makes European society vulnerable to exploitation by any and all totalitarian movements."

The Planning Staff was not actually deeply impressed with the fears of a real European economic collapse and consequent American economic disaster. Although the report spoke of economic collapse and economic remedies, in fact, said Kennan, "we must recognize that much of the value of a European recovery program will lie not so much in its direct economic effects, which are difficult to calculate with any degree of accuracy, as in its psychological and political by-products."

If it were merely a matter of economics, then Europe could simply rely on extensions of loans and grants-in-aid from the United States directly, from the Export-Import Bank, the International Bank, and International Monetary Fund, and from private investments. America had been extending aid in one form or another throughout World War II and after. And, although it might be a struggle to pass more foreign aid bills through a budget-minded Congress without a good, strong pitch, "further U.S. aid to Europe," as the Planning Staff said in this report, "would not in itself constitute any basic change in U.S. foreign policy." Rather, the essential goal of a fresh approach to economic aid to Europe ought to be to knit the Continent together into a single entity in such a way that the United States would be left, welcome, at its center. Or, as Acheson's Ad Hoc Committee had concluded: "The broad purpose of U.S. aid and assistance is to extend in terms of the U.S. national interest the objective recently enunciated by the President for Greece and Turkey, by supporting economic stability and orderly political processes, opposing the spread of chaos and extremism, preventing advancement of Communist influence and use of armed minorities, and orienting other foreign nations toward the U.S. . . . In addition, the U.S. will probably continue to undertake to alleviate starvation and suffering as such where this action is consistent with U.S. interests."

Such a knitting together in a single program of recovery would have the additional domestic political advantage of overwhelming congressional opponents of wasteful European "welfare" payments with a large plan of presumed ultimate profit to America.

As for Germany, and for the Americans who were still embittered toward the Germans, and the French who still feared German militarism, "to talk about the recovery of Europe," said Kennan in a supplementary memo, "and to oppose the recovery of Germany is nonsense. People can have both or they can have neither." Either Germany could be brought into a general European community, or the United States would have to make Germany "a self-supporting competitor to the neighboring countries of Europe" and forget helping anyone else - by whom he meant, specifically, the French. "This is the real choice for people like the French, and they may as well be brought to recognize it now."

As for Great Britain: "If Britain cannot really be placed on her feet by means such as those outlined in this report," said Kennan's covering memo, "then she would appear to have no future, as an independent nation, except in a dismantling of almost her entire defense and imperial establishment, in attempting to achieve the status of a greater Denmark or Sweden. . . . If Britain cannot adjust herself to her present situation . . . then we will inevitably have to choose between the broad alternatives of abandoning her strategically and politically . . . or of taking her in as an integral part of our own American-Canadian community."

The policy outlined by the Planning Staff had at least one potential stumbling block: If aid were to be extended generously to all those nations that had been devastated by the war, what would prevent Russia and its satellites from joining the program and wrecking its principal intentions? This uncomfortable possibility was addressed in the very first of the Planning Staff's papers: "An effort would first be made to advance the project . . . in such a form that the Russian satellite countries would either exclude themselves by unwillingness to accept the proposed conditions or agree to abandon the exclusive orientation of their economies," that is to say, agree to turn from Russia to the West. Since that possibility was remote, Kennan's more realistic idea was that the policy could be announced as one generously open to all - but constructed in such a way that the Russians and their satellites would have to refuse.

Altogether, then, Kennan and his Policy Planning Staff produced a superb report, drawing together all of the worries and expectations, assumptions and aspirations that had been tossed about in the State Department during the past months: the fear of communism, the need for an anti-Communist program, the political usefulness of exploiting anti-Communist sentiments, the electoral requirements of the President, the economic fears of Will Clayton and others who thought as he did, the dreams of the Anglophiles such as Acheson and balance-of-power theorists such as Kennan himself, the greedy and the power-seekers, the altruists and humanitarians, those who wished to rebuild Germany and those who feared Germany, those who wished to help Britain and those who wished to take over Britain's sterling bloc. And what was most wonderful of all was that the new policy could be summed up in a single word: containment.

The new policy called for the containment of Russian expansionism, for rebuilding and containing Germany at the same time, for rebuilding and containing France and England, for rebuilding and containing a whole array of economic relationships in such a way that the United States could exercise influence over them all. Furthermore, and crucially, the policy was not militaristic: It aroused no dread of war, it had no sound of harshness; it was a policy of generous self-interest, one that responded to the call of duty, one that called upon Americans to give themselves once more to their deepest beliefs in liberty and justice, and to the cherished ideals of Western civilization.

As an extra, but by no means negligible, bonus, the policy would also - by bringing economic and political stability to Europe and saving the governments there from a crisis of confidence or collapse - keep in power those classes that had traditionally ruled on the Continent and with whom Americans had become accustomed to doing business.

The policy was not entirely unlike the idea that Julius Caesar hit upon at the end of the Gallic Wars, which were fought over much the same European battleground 2,000 years before. At the end of his account of the wars, Caesar wrote of himself, "So he made their condition of subjection more tolerable by addressing the tribal governments in complimentary terms, refraining from the imposition of any fresh burdens, and bestowing rich presents upon the principal citizens. By these means, it was easy to induce a people exhausted by so many defeats to live at peace."

9
THE SPEECH

A S USUAL, THE State Department was leaking so badly in the spring of 1947 that it had become difficult to tell a scoop from a plant. As usual too, it was Richard Strout, who wrote the TRB column for the *New Republic,* who sensed what the important stories were.

"A major shift in emphasis," Strout wrote as early as May 5, "has taken place in State Department strategy toward Russia. . . . It is the thesis that the USA must build up and revitalize Western Europe as the best answer to Communist infiltration. . . . In a sense, State Department strategists have now come around, in part at least, to the point a good many 'visionaries' have been urging all along - that one way of combating communism is to give Western Europe a full dinner pail."

Several days after Strout's column appeared in the *New Republic*, Dean Acheson fetched up in Cleveland, Mississippi, at "a great pow-wow," as he called it, of progressive farmers, members of the Delta Council. Truman had been scheduled to speak before the council, but a local political squabble threatened to draw him in, force him to take sides, and embarrass him, so he asked the council if they would like to have Attorney General Tom Clark instead. But Clark was turned down, so Truman offered Acheson, and promised a major speech on foreign affairs.

When Acheson answered the summons to the White House, he was surprised and complimented by Truman's request. Of course he would go, he said, "but it's a hell of a come-down from the President to the Undersecretary." The two men considered what might constitute a major foreign policy address. Acheson suggested "the disintegration of Europe," and Truman liked the idea. As Acheson later recalled it, "What I wanted to do was not to put forward a solution or a plan, but to state the problem and the facts. To do this would . . . shock the country . . . and both the Administration and the Congress - into facing a growing crisis. Did the President agree to this being done? To my doing it? I was an eager volunteer and the time was short." The proposal sounded perfect. Truman agreed.

The setting for the speech was as fine as anything Hollywood could have contrived. Deep in Mississippi delta country, where the cattle fed in knee-deep grass and clover, on the grounds of the Cleveland teachers' college, where picnic tables had been set up under the trees, in a little gymnasium, Acheson took off his jacket - just as though he were a politician - rolled up his sleeves, and talked of the world, of international affairs. He did not read from the text he had brought with him; he had memorized it, and he delivered it with spellbinding effect in his fundamentalist patrician manner.

"You who live and work in this rich agricultural region must derive a certain satisfaction from the fact that the greatest affairs of state never get very far from the soil." When Secretary Marshall returned from Moscow, said Acheson, he talked of food and fuel, their relation to industrial production, and the relation of industrial production to the great issues of peace or anarchy. "Here," said Acheson, "are some of the basic facts of life with which we are primarily concerned today in the conduct of foreign relations."

And with that, Acheson launched into the construct that had become the mutually shared sense of reality back at the State Department: "physical destruction or economic dislocation, or both" in

Europe; an inability - because of obstructionism coming from Moscow - to get Germany, one of the greatest workshops of Europe, back on its feet; the "acts of God," the droughts and harsh winters that had swept northern Europe and England; the enormous strength of the American economy, so enormous as to be positively disorienting to the world's economy, having drawn so much of the world's currency to the United States as to leave much of the rest of the world without the funds to buy any more from America.

Unless, said Acheson, "the various countries of the world get on their feet and become self-supporting there can be no political or economic stability in the world. . . . Without outside aid, the process of recovery in many countries would take so long as to give rise to hopelessness and despair. In these conditions, freedom and democracy and the independence of nations could not long survive."

To be sure, said Acheson, much of the world's deficit was already being financed by loans and grants-in-aid from the United States, the Export-Import Bank, the International Bank, the International Monetary Fund, the loan to Great Britain, and by private investments. Why, then, was anything more, or different, necessary? Because, said Acheson, "it is still far short of what the people of the world need if they are to eat enough to maintain their physical strength and at the same time carry on essential measures of reconstruction and become self-supporting." Further financing, he said, would be necessary.

In addition, the American government was going to require the extension of certain of the President's wartime powers - controls over the sale, transportation, and distribution of certain commodities such as wheat and coal and steel, the power to coordinate the reconstruction of Germany, to alter international trade and tariff agreements, and to regulate more comprehensively the whole balance of trade between America and foreign countries, and so, in some measure, control the domestic production of goods and services that are related to exports and imports.

Someone had commented, said Acheson, that it was remarkable that a blizzard in Europe could have so upset the whole world economic system. "I think we will all agree that something more than a blizzard has caused Europe's current difficulties. But last winter's blizzard did show up the extremely narrow margins of human and national subsistence which prevail in the world today, margins so narrow that a blizzard can threaten populations with starvation and nations with bankruptcy and loss of independence. Not only do human beings and nations exist in narrow economic margins, but also human dignity, human freedom, and democratic institutions."

Acheson was enormously pleased with himself and with his speech - but, as it turned out, hardly anyone else noticed it. The speech got more coverage in Europe than in America, although even in Europe the newspaper editors could not be certain whether Acheson spoke with any authority or was merely expressing some personal sentiments. James Reston of *The New York Times*, however, got onto Acheson about the speech: "Is this a new policy that you are enunciating or is it just a bit of private kite-flying?"

"You know this town better than I do," Acheson replied, with the self-confidence of a man who had already cleared his speech with the President, "Foreign policy is made in the White House - you must ask the President."

And so, at his next press conference, Truman was asked whether Acheson's speech represented administration policy. "Yes," said Truman, it did.

Yet no one seemed to notice. Nor did anyone quite notice the other members of the administration who began to find ways of working similar notions into speeches. Not even Ben Cohen, the former Roosevelt brain-truster, could attract attention when he began to mention specific dollar amounts in San Francisco; talk of $5 or $6 or $7 billion a year for three or four years began to leak out. During the past year, the State Department had been toying with figures and generally kept returning to an estimated overall European deficit of about $18 billion. Not even Alben Barkley, the Vice-President of the United States (who loved to tell the story of the boy who grew up to be elected Vice-President and was never heard from again), could get much attention for the idea. "Alben," said Acheson, "was not to be outdone and he said it was $8 billion." Acheson himself preferred not to speak of dollar amounts. "I just made this decision," as he later recalled, "to keep the talk general . . . because we were not going to get into a position of being asked, 'What place do you have in mind?' Either you don't know, in which case you make a fool of yourself, or, if you begin mentioning places, they are going to be on your doorstep - 'Thank you very much. I'll take it in twenties.'"

After all these tests, if the policy were to catch fire it needed someone to announce it who could command some real attention and respect.

General Marshall secured a copy of Acheson's speech and turned it over to Joseph Jones, who had worked on the Truman Doctrine speech, with the instruction to work up something that the Secretary of State might himself deliver, something that would "hit the same line."

Meanwhile, on May 19, Will Clayton returned from a jaunt to Europe and gave his colleagues a jolt. Over lunch at the Metropolitan Club, Clayton spoke alarmingly of the breakdown in the European economy. If anything, he said, the department had underestimated the seriousness of the situation. What worried him most of all was that "the people on the farms could not get anything in the cities worth trading their food for, and . . . there was no confidence in currencies. So the farmers were feeding food to cattle - what they didn't consume themselves - and the city workers were not getting enough to eat." Silence fell over the luncheon table.

That afternoon, Clayton returned to his office and dashed off a memo: "Europe is steadily deteriorating. The political position reflects the economic. . . . Millions of people in the cities are slowly starving. . . . *Only until the end of this year* can England and France meet the . . . deficits out of their fast dwindling reserves of gold and dollars. Italy can't go that long. . . . Without further prompt and substantial aid from the United States, economic, social and political disintegration will overwhelm Europe . . . the immediate effects on our domestic economy would be disastrous: markets for our surplus production gone, unemployment, depression, a heavily unbalanced budget on the background of a mountainous war debt. *These things must not happen.* . . . Europe must have from us, as a grant, $6 or $7 billion worth of goods a year for three years."

Clayton's memo got to Marshall on May 27. Late in the afternoon of May 28, Marshall's secretary,

Carl Hummelsine, took a stack of papers in to the Secretary for his signature and asked him whether he wished to confirm a tentative commitment he had made to address the graduating class at Harvard College on June 5. Yes, the Secretary said, seemingly casually, Hummelsine might wire his acceptance. The next day, Marshall called Charles Bohlen into his office and asked him to work up a speech, using Kennan's material and - although his Policy Planning Staff was not overly impressed by it - some of the rhetoric from Clayton's recent memorandum.

Having decided to deliver the speech that would at last commit the Secretary of State, and so the administration, to this new policy, Marshall turned his attention to several last-minute considerations.

Based upon the newspaper reaction to Acheson's Mississippi speech, it was clear to Marshall and the administration generally that the proposals about to be made would not be unwelcome in Europe. In any case, as Marshall later said, "Little consideration was given to the European reaction to our proposal, since it was believed that they were sufficiently desperate to accept any reasonable offer of U.S. aid." The difficulty was to get it past the domestic political opposition. As it seemed to Marshall and others, the Truman Doctrine had so chilled American opinion that any more schemes for international involvement would have a tough go of it, and not only with Taft and his close friends. Americans generally felt they had given plenty of foreign aid; these were the people, after all, who had just elected a Congress full of Republicans. These were the people who had not quite noticed the speeches of Acheson, Cohen, and Barkley.

"The greatest fear," Marshall later recalled, "was of an adverse reaction from the Midwest - from Bert McCormick and the *Chicago Tribune*. Originally, I had planned to accept a degree from the University of Michigan in order to spring the 'plan' in the heartland of expected opposition. But this ceremony was cancelled because details of the plan could not be worked out in time." At the same time, some of the administration's political strategists had begun to think it might be best just to slip the plan out quietly and not stir up the opposition.

On the last Sunday in May, Reston almost blew it in the *Times*. He had been talking to Acheson and others in the State Department and had finally cottoned onto the broad hints. His story appeared on page 1 of the *Times:* Consideration was being given to a new aid program for Europe - a four-year program, involving $16 billion. It was a serious leak: The *Times* was regarded as an office bulletin of the insiders, and such stories had to be considered authoritative. Yet, once again, the news was largely ignored.

The speech that was finally constructed for Marshall was a fine piece of work. In the event Americans finally noticed it, it would appeal to their sense of generosity, their fear of communism, and their interest in a strong American economy, and profits. So that Americans would be further persuaded to embark on the program, the speech asked the Europeans to ask the Americans for aid. Europe would have to court America.

And, to make certain from the very outset that the Europeans did not just come along one at a time for handouts, the speech said that the Europeans would have to get together first among themselves, knit themselves together, and then come to America with a single request. There would be no piecemeal aid, no bilateral agreements - only a package deal.

In the event that the speech was picked up by leftists in America and, more especially, in Europe, it specifically did not exclude Russia or Eastern Europe in its invitation to the banquet. Charles Bohlen was particularly tickled by that part. "The Marshall approach," as he later recalled, "was directed against no country or creed but against hunger, chaos, etc." And so, when the Russians could not bring themselves to join it, "what we succeeded in doing was to identify Communism and the Soviet Union with the evils of misery, hunger, chaos, etc."

Finally, to make entirely certain that the speech would not stir up the Middle West, Marshall gave strict orders to the State Department press section that they were to give no publicity to his speech. Truman, who remained above the fray in all this, giving his generals their heads, intervened only to lend a nice political touch at the finish. He called a press conference for June 5, the day Marshall was to speak at Harvard, and worked up some announcements that would grab the headlines in the American newspapers.

Then, to make certain that the Europeans did not miss the announcement under all this careful camouflage, Acheson consented to have a drink with some English journalists on June 2.

He had arranged to meet with Leonard Miall of the BBC, René MacColl of the *Daily Express,* and Malcolm Muggeridge of the *Daily Telegraph* for lunch in a private room at the United Nations Club. As it happened, Acheson was suffering from a bad hangover and, as he set out for lunch, he said to his press aide Lincoln White, "If these Limeys offer me sherry, I shall puke."

Muggeridge, waiting with his British colleagues for Acheson to arrive at the club, said, "Now, we won't have this horrible bad American habit of having strong liquor before, we shall have some good wine with lunch or we shall just have some sherry before lunch."

Acheson arrived.

"Would you like to have some sherry?" Muggeridge asked.

"No," said Acheson firmly. "I think I'd like a dry martini."

And so they sat down to lunch and to chat, and inevitably Acheson's speech in Mississippi was mentioned. Was the speech an expression of a new American policy or Acheson's own idea?

Acheson replied circumspectly, narrating just how the speech had come to be made, how Truman had been scheduled to make a speech, then could not, and had asked Acheson to substitute for him.

Now, said Acheson, the next step needed to come from the European side, because "the administration has rather oversold its case in terms of asking for further money for a scheme to shore up the collapsing economy of some European country or other." He talked of the money that had gone out through the United Nations rehabilitation fund, of British and French and Italian loans and other schemes for which he had "been up to Congress to plead," and said that he could not go again. Now, he said, "there must be some kind of a cooperative and dramatic move from the European side in order to capture the imagination of Congress," which was "in a very economical frame of mind." The Congress was dominated by Republicans, who had been elected "on an economy plea platform."

Acheson, in his memoirs, making certain that he got credit for the deft planting of his story, recalled that he then told the British journalists about the speech Marshall was about to make at Harvard. In fact, according to Miall's recollection, Acheson was more deft than he recalled: He did not mention Marshall's speech at all.

Miall, at the time, was filling in as a commentator on a radio show called "American Commentary," which was broadcast directly to London, and which was avidly listened to by British politicians. Miall thought, as he left the luncheon, that he could do no better than to devote a program to his conversation with Acheson - without attribution, of course - emphasizing that the Americans seemed to be trying to launch a new policy but needed the British to pick up on it and promote it.

Miall's program was scheduled for June 5. On June 4, he happened to be speaking with the press officer at the British Embassy, who had received an advance copy of Marshall's Harvard speech.

"Have you seen the speech that General Marshall is delivering at Harvard?" the press officer asked Miall.

"No, I haven't."

"Well, if I were you I would have a look at it. It is very interesting stuff."

Although Marshall had instructed the State Department press office not to give the speech publicity in the United States, a copy was available for the asking when Miall dropped by the department. But the transcript was singularly understated. "There were none of the trappings of it being an important speech," Miall recalled. "There were none of the double spacing and things by which you recognize that this was a very important *démarche*. However, as I read it that night . . . after I got home [I] suddenly realized that here was chapter and verse for everything that I was trying to say without attribution in this piece that was based on the lunch with Acheson. And so I sat up and rewrote the thing entirely."

The next morning, Miall phoned his BBC editor, Tony Wigan, in London.

MIALL: Hello, Tony. I'd like to explain to you about this position about the Marshall news. I don't know whether you've got a text yet.

WIGAN: I haven't seen it myself.

MIALL: What is happening is that Marshall is making a speech at Harvard . . . Now it is an extremely important speech, and he comes out flatly for this great continental plan of help to Europe.

WIGAN: The full staff and things, you mean?

MIALL: Well, that's sort of the idea. What he wants is for Europe to formulate some sort of a plan together and then there will be big stuff forthcoming from here.

WIGAN: Yes, is it being broadcast?

MIALL: . . . I don't think it is desperately important to us whether it is or not because his voice is so poor. He is not a good broadcaster and I doubt if it is a good idea to have it in his voice. . . .

WIGAN: Yes.

MIALL: . . . so I'll have to . . . [deliver it in my own voice].

WIGAN: I see.

MIALL: . . . all right, let me do this which - I'd better call it "Marshall's Overture." . . .

VOICE: Give ten seconds cue, Mr. Miall, will you?

MIALL: I will give you the ordinary ten seconds cue. I've just got to sort out where I begin it. All right, all right, Miss Williams, I'll go ahead in ten seconds from now.

"I need not tell you, gentlemen," said Secretary of State Marshall to the graduating class at Harvard College, "that the world situation is very serious. That must be apparent to all intelligent people

. . . . For the past ten years, conditions have been highly abnormal. The feverish preparation for war and the more feverish maintenance of the war effort engulfed all aspects of national economies. Machinery has fallen into disrepair or is entirely obsolete. Under the arbitrary and destructive Nazi rule, virtually every possible enterprise was geared into the German war machine. Longstanding commercial ties, private institutions, banks, insurance companies . . ."

He stood on the steps of Memorial Church in Harvard Yard (T. S. Eliot, who was also receiving an honorary degree that day, sat nearby) under a natural canopy of maple, beech, and hickory trees, within a double quadrangle of ivy-covered buildings that had been built in different times and styles - one or two from every century of America's existence.

The people to whom Marshall addressed his remarks were hardly a cross section of Americans: Egalitarianism was on its way to Harvard after the war, but it had not yet arrived. These were the more fortunate and privileged, the more prosperous and comfortable of Americans, although, in some ways, they were representative of the larger middle class from which they came. The men - the fathers of the graduates - seemed a sober lot, with their firm handshakes, direct gazes, double-breasted suits, and rep striped silk ties, their air of confidence and self-assurance. These were the members of the last generation of bankers and businessmen who would do their business at home and, if they could, take their vacations abroad - unlike their sons, so many of whom would do their business abroad and take their vacations at home. These were the men who produced half of the world's product. These were the men who had tipped the balance in favor of the Allied powers who had won the war. Whether they had fought as soldiers or stayed home to produce the technological and economic power that sustained the vast military enterprise, they were proud of their share in the victory - an emotion that is not, as they would live to see, an inevitable by-product of war. Having shared in the victory and felt their strength, they were not naturally given to timidity or hesitation after the war. The war had, perhaps, made them a trifle simple-minded, if only temporarily - a trifle given to thinking in terms of absolute good and evil, of absolutely clear alternatives, of black and white, of the virtue of fast, hard decisions, strong actions, of sticking to one's guns. Unlike their allies, whose own homelands had so recently been devastated by war, the Americans could not easily summon up an understanding of irony, of the limits attending the behavior of nations, of the heartbreaking complexity and mystery of human motives. To their European allies, they could seem naive, excessively optimistic at times, at times overbearing, bumptious, self-consciously masculine, boosterish, loud. And yet they could also seem charming, forthright, generous, open, outgoing.

The women who accompanied the men appeared to reflect other facets of the same American sensibility in their briskly tailored suits, broad at the shoulders and nipped in at the waist, with straight skirts that fell just below the knee, in their broad-brimmed hats with flowers or feathers in the crowns (or simple black bonnets accented at the forehead with a flower the size of a pineapple). They looked bright and well-scrubbed, weighed five or ten pounds more than their daughters would eventually consider chic. Their necklines were high, the collars secured by a tasteful pin or brooch. Their hair was pulled back from their faces, lending them an appearance of confidence, openness, freshness.

Back home, many of these men and women were living in a truly extraordinary piece of recent domestic architecture: the ranch house - open to all the world with its big "picture windows," unbarred, exposed, defenseless, as though there were nothing in all the world to fear. The front and back doors were left unlocked, and in the driveway, the keys were left in the car. With trim front lawns and airy screened porches and collie dogs running free, there may never have been another such period of domestic tranquility in all history - nor a period in which there was such a widely shared belief in an American ideal of abundance and fairness and democracy, of opportunity and possibility, of openness and confidence, of justness and good intention toward the world and a trust in the national leaders elected to represent those ideals.

"The breakdown of the business structure of Europe during the war was complete . . ." Marshall said to his Harvard audience. "The farmer has always produced the foodstuffs to exchange with the city dweller for the other necessities of life. This division of labor is the basis of modern civilization. At the present time, it is threatened with breakdown . . . . The truth of the matter is that Europe's requirements for the next three or four years . . . are so much greater than her present ability to pay that she must have substantial additional help or face economic, social, and political deterioration of a very grave character."

Such a dreadful event could lead to "disturbances" abroad. But not only that: "The consequences to the economy of the United States should be apparent to all."

What Marshall suggested to allay these prospects was a policy of aid to Europe - and to all the world. "Our policy," he said, "is directed not against any country or doctrine but against hunger, poverty, desperation, and chaos." Everyone was welcome to join this great effort of recovery - although, to be sure, any government that sought "to perpetuate human misery in order to profit there . . . will encounter the opposition of the United States."

Such a policy could not work on a piecemeal basis, however. "Any assistance that this Government may render in the future should provide a cure rather than a mere palliative," and so, "Before the United States Government can proceed much further . . . there must be some agreement among the countries of Europe as to the requirements of the situation. . . . The initiative, I think, must come from Europe." And the program would need to be "a joint one, agreed to by a number, if not all, European nations."

The plan would be for Europe to determine its own needs, design its own program for recovery, and then come to the United States with a single request. Of course, said Marshall, the United States would be willing, as the Europeans considered just what their needs might be, to offer "friendly aid in the drafting of a European program."

"With foresight, and a willingness on the part of our people to face up to the vast responsibility which history has clearly placed upon our country," Marshall concluded with a studied anticlimactic effect, "the difficulties I have outlined can and will be overcome."

MIALL: That's the end of that piece.

WIGAN: That's fine, Leonard. That sounds good.

PART TWO

10
LONDON

B Y CHANCE, ERNEST Bevin, the Foreign Secretary of Great Britain, was sitting by his radio that evening - although what he heard so excited him that, in later years, he thought he had heard Miall's broadcast when he woke up in the morning, and he thought he had heard, not Miall, but Marshall speaking to him.

"I remember that morning," Bevin later told an attentive group of journalists, "with a little wireless set alongside the bed just turning on the news and there came this report of the Harvard speech. I assure you, gentlemen, it was like a lifeline to sinking men. It seemed to bring hope where there was none. The generosity of it was beyond my belief. It expressed a mutual thing. It said, 'Try and help yourselves, and we will try to see what we can do. Try and do the thing collectively, and we will see what we can put into the pool.' I think you can understand why, therefore, we responded with such alacrity and why we grabbed the lifeline with both hands, as it were."

The next morning, Bevin was the first to arrive at the Foreign Office - a great stone galleon of a building overlooking St. James's Park. Opened by Prime Minister Disraeli in 1868, the year that Basutoland was taken into the empire, the mighty, mongrel structure had something of the Italian about it, something of the Byzantine, a touch of ancient Greece and Rome, and a little bit of England. Its public entrances, through cobblestone courtyards, were triumphant affairs, leading into a reception lobby paved in mosaic, up a grand staircase carpeted in plum and flanked by alabaster statues under frescoes celebrating the beginnings, the growth, and the apotheosis of the British Empire by way of allegorical heroes and naked women and babes, along corridors of imposing mahogany-paneled doors, to the first suite of offices: the India Office, which was decked out in souvenirs of ivory and silver, bits of statuary, and other artifacts that were the natural spoils, or detritus, of empire.

Bevin himself, of course, did not enter by this public passage but rather by way of a little door below the building's poopdeck, right near St. James's Park and just a few steps from the Prime Minister's residence at 10 Downing Street, which sits like a small cottage or bit of driftwood in the wake of the Foreign Office. Just inside the Foreign Secretary's private entrance is an elevator, which, because Bevin had a bad heart - the "old ticker," he called it - had been slowed down to a particularly stately pace.

The Foreign Secretary rose to an office of impressive proportions, sixty feet from doorway to glistening windows looking back over the park, with its glistening pond speckled with ducks, geese, and forlorn pelicans fed by passersby, and surrounded by deeply green, clipped lawns with banks of marigolds and pink geraniums. Certainly, as Bevin looked out over St. James's Park, or out of the windows on the other wall of his office, the windows overlooking the Horse Guards parade where the red-coated, silver-helmeted Life Guards trooped the colors out past the Admiralty Building and down the Mall to Buckingham Palace, or when he ducked out to see the Prime Minister at 10 Downing Street, it would have taken an extraordinary act of imagination to perceive the dissolution of the empire amidst such a display of wealth, power, grandeur, and quiet civility.

When he arrived at the Foreign Office that morning, his enthusiasm for what he had heard on the radio was met at once with the bland imperturbability of the professional British diplomat.

Sir William Strang, the Permanent Undersecretary, who was, perhaps, just in the least unmoved by Bevin's bubbliness, expressed the opinion that the Foreign Office ought not be precipitous but should instruct the embassy in Washington to inquire at the State Department about just what the Secretary of State might have in mind, if anything.

Bevin was (as Lady Diana Cooper said of him) "massive, rude, and strong as a Stonehenge cromlech . . . as tilled, as fertile, and generous as his English fields. Proud of his lowliness and of his achievements, he loved his fellow-men with as much fervour as he admired himself."

"He talked," said Strang, ". . . as though he were the government in person." But even so, Strang was not able to remain indifferent to Bevin's good cheer for long. "He made his *début* as Secretary of State for Foreign Affairs," as Strang recalled, "at the Potsdam Conference. . . . On his first appearance in the conference room, after greetings and while he was waiting for the proceedings to begin, he took me by the arm and walked slowly to and fro singing the 'Red Flag' very quietly under his breath, and when he had finished, he turned and gave me a broad wink."

Bevin was born in a village in the west of England on the edge of Exmoor Forest in 1881 (he was sixty-six years old in the spring of 1947). His father had been a farm laborer, at a time of utter agricultural poverty in England. His mother, a deeply religious, independent, and politically radical woman, worked at domestic jobs and was the village midwife. His father was dead at the time of his birth; his mother died when he was six, and so Bevin went to live with his sister, a domestic servant.

At the age of eleven, Bevin needed to commence supporting himself. He left school and went to work as a farm boy. At age thirteen, he left the farm and went to the city of Bristol, where he was employed as a kitchen boy, a grocery errand boy, a hotel porter, a streetcar conductor, and a dray-horse driver. At the age of eighteen, he found a career that he was able to settle into for the next eleven years: For eighteen shillings (about $4) a week, plus commissions, he went the rounds of Bristol with a horse and cart selling mineral water.

In Bristol, too, he found his way - through church groups - into the Bristol Socialist Society. He was, from the beginning, angrily opposed to the Communist groups who kept trying to break up the socialist movement, or take it over.

In 1910, Bevin became a founder of the Bristol Carmen's branch of the Dock, Wharf, Riverside, and General Laborers' Union. By 1915, at age thirty-four, he had risen to become the national organizer for the British Dock Workers Union. He was an extraordinarily forceful, persuasive, and energetic arguer. In 1920, he persuaded his fellow union members to take their case for higher wages to a newly established court of arbitration, of which the workers were extremely suspicious. The shipowners hired a battery of lawyers to argue their case. Bevin took it on himself to argue the workers' case, which he presented in an argument of eleven hours, over the course of two and a half days. At one point, hearing a distinguished Cambridge economist tell of how a family could live comfortably on a budget of £3.17s. a week, Bevin went out into the East End and bought a family dinner on the economist's budget, cooked it, divided it into the five portions to accommodate the average size of a dockworker's family, and brought it into court. He called a worker to the stand and presented him with one of the plates.

"Now, Joe," said Bevin, "suppose you had just come home from work, and your good wife should set this dinner before you, what would you say?"

"I'd, I'd," Joe stammered, turning red. "Oh, for God's sake, Ernie!"

"Mr. Bevin," the judge intervened, "the record may show that the witness would express his disappointment and disapproval."

Then, with one of the shipowners on the stand, Bevin was able to establish that a British dockworker, on the diet the Cambridge economist had allowed him, was expected to handle as much as seventy-one tons of cargo a day.

"And do you know the average haulage for a dray horse for a week?" asked Bevin.

"No."

"Fifty tons."

Bevin won his case and won a good measure of fame too. In time, he acquired enemies as well. He helped organize the massive general strike in 1926, a fiasco that had to be called off after five days, leaving bitterness and suspicion on both sides for some years. He was ruthless with older men in the labor movement and shoved them aside mercilessly. Nor was he overly tolerant of democratic processes in union politics, in which he preferred to bully members into a consensus rather than engage in reasoned discourse. Once, when one of his opponents was referred to as "his own worst enemy," Bevin was quick to chime in, "Not while I'm alive, he ain't." In spite, or because of, these tendencies, he continued to rise rapidly in English politics.

In the thirties, he was among the first to oppose Hitler and Mussolini. They had ruined the labor movements in their countries, and that was enough for Bevin. In 1940, when Churchill became Prime Minister, he reached across party lines to form a coalition government and asked Bevin to take over the Ministry of Labour. Then, in 1945, when the wartime coalition government was dissolved, and the Labour Party was given a large electoral majority, and Churchill left the prime ministership, Bevin popped up again, as Foreign Minister in Clement Attlee's cabinet.

Bevin was the shape of a beach ball, and he wore owlish glasses over a great lump of a nose. His vest buttons looked as if they might pop. Buttoning up his suit jacket was out of the question. He spoke well enough to large groups, but he was at his best, his most relaxed and his most persuasive, in small groups. "His penmanship," said Strang, "was unskillful and he wrote with difficulty. Not for him the long and carefully drafted minutes by which a Curzon or an Austen Chamberlain would convey their instructions to their subordinates." But those who worked for him hardly minded: "Half an hour of talk in his room was worth any number of written minutes, and we never hesitated to wait upon him: We could count on the kindliest and most patient reception. Perhaps we sometimes presumed a little too much upon his tolerance." Once, Strang recalled, an aide had only just left Bevin's office when another question came up, and the young man burst into Bevin's office again. "Ha," said Bevin, "the ink is hardly dry on the words out of me mouth, and here you are again!"

Bevin's qualities - his ability to empathize his way into any situation, his interest in turning a question over and over to see its various implications and possibilities, his lack of snobbery, his patience, his ability to wait interminably until the moment seemed right to strike, or to respond instantaneously if the situation required it, his ability to argue relentlessly, to negotiate persistently, and finally to recognize, as Strang put it, that the objective of foreign relations "is not so much victory as a tolerable settlement" - made him an uncommonly able Foreign Minister, and one to whom many of his colleagues referred affectionately - behind his back - as "Uncle Ernie." He enjoyed such confidence from the Prime Minister, from trade union members, and, in large measure, from the British public, that what he said could indeed be taken to be, or to soon become, British foreign policy.

He took over the Foreign Office at a time when he had no choice but to conduct an orderly withdrawal for Great Britain from its imperial commitments. To withdraw, and yet maintain as much as possible, he sensed he could do no better than to have a powerful ally in the world - to use, insofar as he could, to balance against such traditional competitors as France, and to lean on, finally, in an hour of need. His fear, in 1947, was not so much that he and his country would be absorbed by the United States as that the United States would not recognize the role that he thought it must now play in the world. In truth, his commitment to the building of an international community was so powerful he did not find it difficult to imagine doing his bit in a community led by the United States (although his partiality for America had already caused some of his fellow Britons to regard him simply as America's toady). And so, when he heard Miall's broadcast from America, he did not hesitate a moment to, as he said, grab Marshall's offer with both hands.

Should the Foreign Office inquire of the State Department what Marshall might have meant by his address? "Look 'ere, Bill," said Bevin (perhaps the only man in the Foreign Office to call Lord Strang "Bill," certainly the only one to say "Look 'ere" to him), "we know what he *said*. If you ask questions, you'll get answers you don't want. Our problem is what *we do,* not what *he meant.*"

Before Marshall had a chance to take it back, Bevin accepted it - whatever it was. He dashed out of the Foreign Office, to see Prime Minister Attlee. Attlee, as an American newspaper correspondent once said of him, "could get on a London bus without anybody noticing," and yet he was "an exceptionally strong and much underrated Prime Minister." Bevin loved "little Clem," as he called the Prime Minister, and all but ate him up. Foreign affairs, said Bevin, "are the province of the Foreign Secretary. It is in my view a mistake for a Prime Minister to intervene personally except in exceptional circumstances." Or, as Bevin also said, "If you've got a good dog you don't bark yourself."

Attlee evidently agreed. He agreed, too, to the course of action Bevin meant to follow on Marshall's offer. Bevin cabled Paris at once, to instruct the British ambassador there to get in touch with the French Foreign Secretary, Georges Bidault. Bevin would like to come to Paris to talk to Bidault about Marshall's speech. He would arrive on June 17 if that was agreeable to Bidault. (Bidault, however much he may have been abashed to see Bevin so quickly seize the initiative, could hardly refuse.)

Bevin cabled Washington, instructing Archie Inverchapel to inform General Marshall that, "in pursuit of the intention to cooperate with the French in studying the new American approach to Europe adumbrated in your recent speech at Harvard, he proposes to take the initiative by visiting Paris early next week."

From Paris, the American ambassador cabled Marshall in Washington: "Bidault tells me that he is not too happy about Bevin coming here at this juncture because his visit is being interpreted here as a desire on Bevin's part to steal the show." Although, as the American ambassador had to admit, the truth was simply that "Bidault wanted to steal the show."

11
PARIS

O N TUESDAY AFTERNOON, June 17, Bevin stepped off the plane at Le Bourget airport and headed for a meeting with a covey of experts at the British Embassy in Paris. Sir Edmund Hall-Patch, Deputy Undersecretary in charge of economic affairs, led the group of advisers. Sir David Waley of the Treasury was present, along with Mr. Roll of the Ministry of Food, Mr. Brook of the Ministry of Fuel and Power, Mr. Lintott of the Board of Trade, and a dozen others. "But," as one of them said, "if you had asked . . . me what we were going to do in Paris, we couldn't have said."

In fact, although Bevin surrounded himself with a group of experts of various sorts, he was not at all interested in details just yet. He was moving with terrific velocity on the essential issue of initiative. And the French, meanwhile, were scrambling to keep up, having fired off cables to the United States and to the Soviet Union to try to recapture some sense of primacy in the face of Bevin's assault.

In the interest of pursuing their policy of remaining neutral between America and Russia, of balancing the two major powers against one another and leaving France to lead Europe, the French had come up with a postwar recovery program of their own. Called the Monnet Plan - named for Jean Monnet, the French businessman and gentleman farmer who had done much to develop it - the French program intended simply to have France absorb Germany's industrial base.

The coal mines and steel mills of the Ruhr and the Rhineland and the Saar would provide the foundation for France to raise, within a few years, its industrial production to 150 percent of its prewar level. Steel production would be doubled; electric power would be doubled; transport and machine industries would be raised to 150 percent and 160 percent, respectively, of prewar levels; a machine-tool industry would be built. France would be the bulwark of democracy in Europe. Such was the Monnet Plan - which the Americans and the British would need either to sabotage or to absorb into some larger plan.

Bevin went instantly into a staff meeting at the British Embassy to tell his men what line to take with the French at dinner that evening. First, he said, in case the British Foreign Office men had not yet caught on, the Marshall proposal was of the highest importance. As soon as the talks with the French were over, he would get in touch with the Russians and with other governments. Was there some danger that the smaller nations of Europe might feel abused because they had not been sufficiently "brought into the picture?" There was; but "the prime essential is speed."

Bevin brought with him a document - embodying the views of the British government - that would provide a basis for discussions with the French that evening. (Whoever drew up the first working papers, as Bevin knew, set the framework for conversation.) He proposed to discuss the Marshall offer on a "functional" basis, establishing with the French, first of all, and then with other governments, "the fundamental necessities of economic life of which Europe was at present short": food, coal, steel, textiles, agricultural requirements, and transport. In Bevin's view, "food must have first priority because production depended on it." Workers could not work well if they were not fed well.

To be sure, Bevin's list of priorities corresponded with Britain's particular set of needs. But what really impressed Bevin's colleagues was how quickly, and surely, Bevin moved to establish a framework for the Marshall Plan. First, said the Foreign Secretary, came food; next - this neatly set French priorities upside down - mining machinery ("which would assist coal output which, in turn, would assist steel output"). What Bevin had in mind, he said, was "a process like stoking up the fire in the morning." Certainly none of the other men sitting with him in Paris had a more certain grasp of just what was necessary to get workers started working productively, just which steps followed logically from one to the other in order to produce something.

Complexities were introduced at once. Mr. Lintott, of the Board of Trade, felt protective of British transport. If Britain were asked to release some of her transport equipment for Europe, he said, it would be "awkward," because Britain needed such goods for export to hard-currency countries, such as Argentina, for its own balance of trade. Bevin sacrificed transport equipment without a moment's hesitation: If Britain were to lead, Britain must appear unselfish, must hope to achieve its own goals within the larger common good. It was far more important, said Bevin, to assist in general European recovery, so that Europe could produce goods for herself.

Mr. Feavearyear, of the Ministry of Food, feared that an improvement in European standards would mean a reduction in standards at home - that the adoption of common goals would lead to a leveling effect.

Bevin replied at once that he had "no idea of reducing the United Kingdom standard." On the contrary, he intended to "raise it." Nonetheless, he said, setting aside selfish concerns once again, make no mistake, "self-help must be the first principle; afterwards we could reasonably depend on the U.S.A."

Before the meeting broke up, Bevin instructed his advisers that he wanted them to think toward setting up two committees: an executive steering committee that would set policy (that is to say, a small committee of foreign ministers who would hash out the politics of the matter) and a set of ad hoc working committees of experts that would handle the details of economic data and needs. In the end, the aim had to be "to produce a plan for presentation to the United States" quickly - by the end of the summer - "and it must appeal to businessmen, not only idealists, and convince the former that the proposals were not a request for charity but a good investment."

With that, the British received the French for dinner: Paul Ramadier, President of the Council of Ministers, Georges Bidault, Minister of Foreign

Affairs, René Massigli, French Ambassador to London, Hervé Alphand, Director General of Economic Affairs, Maurice Couve de Murville, Director General of Political Affairs, Jean Monnet, and several others.

Ramadier, as Will Clayton once said, "was a simple old man, genuine. You didn't see any 'gold lace' about him, none of that sort of thing." He was five feet ten inches tall, with a shock of graying hair, a little white goatee, and perfectly round spectacles. Fifty-nine years old, a lawyer with a diploma in advanced studies in literature, he liked, in his spare time, to translate Greek and Latin texts. When the Germans had conquered France, and the collaborationist Vichy government was installed, Ramadier had joined the Resistance, in which, because of his gentle manner, he was given the code name "Violette." Then when Charles de Gaulle's Provisional Government in exile, in Algiers, returned to Paris after the war, Ramadier joined the cabinet as Minister of Supplies.

As a bureaucrat, he had proven himself to be stunningly unimpressive, a dreadful bungler given to speaking in large, waffling platitudes; but, as a survivor, his skills could not be doubted.

When the first government of the Fourth French Republic was constituted in January 1947, Ramadier was named Premier - and it must almost have seemed a bizarre punishment for his loyal patriotism. France was shattered after the war into political fragments - each party battle-hardened by the war, sick of compromises, prepared to fight to the end for the (various) ideals for which they had all just risked their lives. Ramadier had the extremely delicate task of forming a coalition government out of the Communists, the Socialists, the leftist Republican Unionists, the Independent Republicans, and the MRP, or Mouvement Républicain Populaire.

Internally, two large political factions leaned in opposite directions: On the left, the Communist Party - one of the strongest Communist parties in Western Europe - threatened to bring the government down if it disdained the Soviet Union. On the right, one of the grand heroes of World War II, General Charles de Gaulle ("immensely tall, remote, infinitely courteous, rather gloomy," as an American journalist found him at the moment), insisted on a grand, independent France leading Europe - with the friendly assistance of the United States. It was up to Ramadier to keep these two large factions in balance - just as, externally, he needed to play the major powers against one another - and, by finesse, to survive.

By the end of January, Ramadier had put together a cabinet composed of nine Socialists (Ramadier's own party), five Communists, five Republican Unionists, two Independent Republicans, and five members of the MRP, including, among that moderate-to-conservative group, Georges Bidault as Foreign Minister. Almost at once, the cabinet faced crisis after crisis and repeated, cliff-hanging votes of confidence. Strikes plagued France, and the workers who did not strike demanded wage increases and threatened to strike. A wheat shortage led Ramadier to declare that France would probably have to remain on a short bread ration for two years.

Food riots broke out; 80,000 dockworkers went on strike; railroad workers went on strike. Communists led many of the strikes (and were opposed by agents of the American Federation of Labor, working with the State Department).

The Communists, far from finding advantage in these troubles, managed to bring great discredit on themselves - to make it seem that they were only unpatriotic spoilers, to make it more difficult for the government to side with Russia in international matters, to make it seem even more urgent for the French government to drop its neutralist stance and grab, "with both hands," at American aid.

The American Embassy sent a stream of anxious cables back to Washington: If the French economy were not put back together, the Communists would soon be able to bring on a cabinet crisis and a new election, and, under the circumstances, the Communists would probably gain more cabinet posts. The influence of the Communists would then extend beyond economic matters to include questions of foreign affairs as well. Ultimately, "their influence within the government would constitute a veto over the conduct of foreign affairs insuring that France does not align itself in major foreign policy issues with the U.S. and Great Britain."

In the view of the Americans in Paris, the French people would stay with the present government or go toward the left, depending upon which politicians could deliver, or seem to deliver, economic stability and well-being. Economic aid was needed in France and needed soon, both to shore up the French economy and, more especially, to shore up the friendly French government of Ramadier and Bidault.

Washington got the point. In fact, already in May, cables had gone out from the State Department to the American embassies in Italy and France: If the ministers who dominated the cabinets in those two countries wanted to have any economic aid to help their countries (and to keep them in office), they would need to understand that they had to "correct the present situation" first - that is to say, would have to purge their cabinets of Communists. It would not be too much to say that the State Department purchased non-Communist cabinets: Both the French and the Italians took the hint at once; both reorganized their cabinets and managed to force the Communists out. Within hours of the reorganization in France, to make certain that the moral of the story was not lost on anyone, John McCloy, president of the World Bank, announced that a large loan was to be granted to the French government.

The man who was charged with threading his way through this minefield of dashed ambitions, war-tempered convictions, dreams of grandeur, threats and bribery, and finding some way for France to flourish in the world, was Foreign Minister Georges Bidault - a small, fine-boned, delicate man, with his hair carefully slicked down and a crisp white handkerchief tucked neatly into the breast pocket of his gray double-breasted suit, a man who carried himself with an air of civil melancholy. He was the son of middle-class parents. His mother had died when he was only two, and his father was turned so dour by the event that the boy grew up in an austere, chilly home. At age ten, a bookish child, he was sent off to a Jesuit school in northern Italy. After service in World War I, he entered the Sorbonne, graduated with the highest honors, and went on to become a history instructor at the Lycée Louis-le-Grand, one of France's most distinguished secondary schools.

While he was still teaching, he also served as foreign editor and columnist for a Catholic daily newspaper, *L'Aube*. The paper's circulation was modest, never more than 20,000, but it was disproportionately influential among certain French intellectuals, and Bidault came to be regarded as one of France's more eloquent analysts of foreign affairs.

He joined the French Army at the beginning of the Second World War, was captured, imprisoned, and then set free. He joined the underground at once - teaching during the day, working for the Resistance at night. Three times a week he published the underground newspaper, *Bulletin de la France combattante.* Under orders from de Gaulle's government in exile, he took part in organizing the several principal anti-Nazi factions (the Resistance, labor groups, and political parties) into a single organization, of which, in the summer of 1943, he became a leader.

As a principal member of the underground government, he donned a disguise (he removed his glasses, grew a mustache, and wore a hat) and took up residence in a maid's room on the Left Bank, and so managed to elude the fervent searches of the Germans and establish himself as one of the most courageous men in Europe.

When de Gaulle's Provisional Government returned to Paris from Algiers, Bidault was named Foreign Minister at once, and he commenced to declare, almost at once, a policy that was both traditionally French and suited to the politics of France at the time: a policy of Gallic independence. France would establish good relations with both Russia and America, he said; France could never "belong only to the West." France would resist acceding to the division of Europe; France would not become the captive of any one side. "If people talk about the 'West' in connection with France, it is because geographically France belongs to the West, but she is equally in the world."

By the spring of 1947, however, Bidault had become less and less sanguine about a truly evenhanded policy between East and West. Rather, something more complicated and unusual suggested itself to French politicians: to commit to the West, but to continue to talk of the internal Communist menace as something that required them to stay independent - to balance external political forces with internal political forces, and so, somehow, remain the masters of their own fate.

After their dinner at the British Embassy, as Bevin recorded in a memo for the files, he and Ramadier and Bidault had "a useful informal discussion." The first order of business, Bevin said, was "the urgency of taking the initiative and of preparing a report at a very early date" to give to the United States. (The French could not have agreed more.) Second, said Bevin, it was essential "to avoid the impression of bypassing the United Nations" - while at the same time, of course, bypassing it. If the matter were left in the United Nations, certain countries (Russia remained nameless) might be able to obstruct the plan. (The French thoroughly agreed.) Third, it would be necessary to set up a special steering committee and then some ad hoc working committees. (The French agreed.)

Ramadier's first thought, when Bevin had finished speaking, was to say that the French regarded it as essential, "because of the internal political situation in France, that before any definite decisions were taken between us, the Russians should be given the opportunity of joining in our deliberations." (Bevin did not disagree.)

The essentials having been established, Bevin, Ramadier, and Bidault parted for the night.

That evening, newspaper reporters and editors, knowing nothing, were in a frenzy. The Communist papers were on the attack: Pierre Courtade, in *L'Humanité*, wrote that the French government was "proceeding exactly as if they wish to prove to the world that it is the USSR which is preventing the implementation of the Marshall Plan on a European scale and thus necessitating its restriction to a western plan. Thus, we must view with reserve the current proposals which would appear to involve cutting Europe in two and leaving France powerless before the intrigues of a subtle and dangerous imperialism." *Franc-Tireur* took a cynical position: America had to have the Marshall Plan in order to avoid an economic crisis at home, so France would be doing America a favor by taking money - and ought to drive a hard bargain. Newspapers on the far right were embarrassingly cordial to Bevin's appearance in Paris. *Epoque* foresaw a "coherent European political economy." *L'Aurore* welcomed "happy days in united Europe."

The next morning, when Bevin met again with his own delegation to prepare for a meeting with the French, he was still anxious about French intentions toward the Russians. Did his colleagues think, asked Bevin, that the French would be ready "to go ahead with an Anglo-French plan and face criticism from Communist and Left Wing quarters?" The British ambassador, Duff Cooper, replied with cool, almost bored, assurance that "Ramadier would find it much more difficult to reject [Bevin's] suggestions than to act without the Russians; he could meet any criticism by the very fact of having *asked* Russia to be sponsoring power." Whatever the French might prefer, the precariousness of the position of the coalition government would force it to take any economic aid it could get: Ramadier and Bidault had to deliver to their people; and as for their need to make an honest effort to consider Communist opinion, they could naturally lie.

Thus reassured, Bevin led his delegation over to the French Foreign Ministry at the Quai d'Orsay. If the British Foreign Office in London immediately called up visions of empire, the Quai d'Orsay was a constant reminder that the French had often fallen on hard times. The Ministry of Foreign Affairs was an imposing edifice, to be sure, with its large, airy windows splashed across the façade overlooking the Seine, its pilastered and porticoed entrances, its gilded and frescoed interiors, its chairs and table legs dripping with flourishes of gold vegetation; and yet it was, too, all second-rate-wedding-cake architecture, imitative stuff, designed by Lacornée in 1845, in the trough between the grandeur of the old monarchy and the sweep of Baron Haussmann's modern Paris. The ministers of the first government of the Fourth French Republic seemed not so much buoyed up by the building as dwarfed by it. Bidault, in any event, according to the British ambassador, simply looked glum and uncomfortable sitting behind his grandiose desk in his cavernous and sparsely furnished office.

Even so, when the British came to call at the Quai d'Orsay, Bidault, having the British on his home ground for the first time, took the initiative. First he summarized the points on which the two governments appeared to agree, based on their conversation of the previous evening. Next, he raised what he considered the most important subsequent issue: "the question of an invitation to the Russians." He wished to make it clear that he and Ramadier felt that "progress on any other basis than that of a prior invitation to the Russians would be impossible."

Bevin raised no objection; he agreed at once.

Bidault then went on to test how far he could go by suggesting that he and Bevin travel to Moscow to meet Molotov.

"I said," Bevin recalled, trapping Bidault rather neatly, "that I was willing to discuss the form and nature of the invitation, but that I must have a prior assurance that if the Soviet reply to such an invitation were negative or noncommittal, the British and French governments would proceed to set up the committees charged with the task of preparing a plan."

Bidault, remembering the pride of France, said that he "did not intend to subordinate the action" that the French government might take to "the attitude of Russia." The main concern of the French government, he said, practicing his foreign/domestic juggling act on Bevin, "was to disarm domestic criticism."

Bevin was satisfied. He had gotten a commitment from Bidault that France would go along with Britain, whatever Russia did. On the matter of going to Moscow, however, Bevin too had his pride: "I said that I was not prepared to go to Moscow merely to court a rebuff." (Far better to bring Molotov to Paris and give *him* a rebuff.)

In the end, the British and French agreed to issue an invitation to Molotov in two forms. In their press release, they would simply suggest a meeting, leaving open the issue of the place. In their private message to Molotov, they would suggest that they preferred London or Paris but would be agreeable to meeting Molotov halfway if necessary.

As for the rest of the message, the diplomats labored on the wording to make certain that Molotov would not be given the impression that the French and the British had gone ahead and decided anything at all on their own, but were waiting for Molotov before even responding to Marshall's offer.

Then the French Minister of Information, a M. Bourdan, wrecked the careful impression of waiting for Russia that the diplomats had struggled to create. At midday, Bourdan announced that Bevin and Bidault had agreed to create a European Economic Commission, and that they were inviting the Russians to join them, if the Russians wanted to. All the diplomats, on both sides, were sent into a flurry. To rescue Bourdan's *faux pas,* they decided to issue an official communiqué at once, to correct the reports that had already appeared in the press. Since, however, it was discourteous to issue a press communiqué before the official message had been delivered to the Russians, the diplomats decided to hand a personal copy to the Soviet chargé d'affaires in Paris and telegraph copies of the message to the British and French ambassadors in Moscow for delivery to the Kremlin. Then all the diplomats had to do was wait for the Soviet chargé d'affaires, who was not in his office, and did not return until evening - from what he claimed, apologetically, and with the aplomb of a Parisian, was "an afternoon in the country."

All in all, Bevin's visit to Paris delighted him: he had taken the initiative, held the initiative, and begun already to force the French to turn against Russia. By the time he got back to the embassy for dinner, his mood was ebullient. Dinner, said Duff Cooper, went quite well. The Foreign Secretary was a happy man. "Bevin talked and talked, and we all listened."

12
FRIENDLY AID

KENNAN, IN HIS memos and reports, insisted from the first that the Europeans, not the Americans, would have to design the Marshall Plan. It seemed to Kennan that this would be crucial so that the Europeans would not feel they were being pushed around. Others in the State Department picked up the idea with the thought that Congress, and Americans generally, would be better disposed toward the Marshall Plan if they felt it was not just a State Department scheme but a cry for aid from Europe. Above all, strategically, if Europeans designed the plan, the burden would be on them to knit themselves together.

Marshall, in his Harvard speech, had said emphatically that the initiative must come from

Europe, that it would be "neither fitting nor efficacious" for America to draw up a program: "This is the business of the Europeans." America would simply provide the wherewithal for a European plan - though America would be prepared to offer "friendly aid" in the drafting of the program.

On the afternoon of June 24, Kennan and his colleague Chip Bohlen dropped by the British Embassy in Washington to talk to Archie Inverchapel and his colleague John Balfour. Kennan and Bohlen wanted to chat about the Russians. The Russians, Kennan thought, might not find it possible to think of the Marshall Plan from a fresh point of view. Rather, they would likely "relate the whole idea of European recovery" to their own need for reconstruction, as they always did with everything, and to be more interested in seeing what they might extract from the United States than in what they could actually contribute to the program.

The news that Kennan and Bohlen brought was sufficiently startling to bear repeating in several ways, to make certain that Inverchapel and Balfour got the message. What the Americans were saying was, they doubted the Soviet Union would want to join the Marshall Plan at all. But just in case they did want to join, they ought then be told that that would be fine - but that they would be expected to contribute to the plan, not receive from it.

Kennan restated the proposition from another angle to make sure the British got the point: "Responsible Americans," he said, "would welcome the participation of Eastern European countries, not excluding the Soviet Union, insofar as their Governments were ready to show their good faith by helping to restore the pre-war exchange of their primary productions with the industrial output of Western Europe," to see to it that "a reasonable share of the increased output of these countries was made available for Western European needs," to help, that is, in the reconstruction of the West to restore the prewar relationship in which the Eastern Europeans supplied raw materials to Western factories. The Russians would need "to permit their satellites to enter fully into economic relations with their Western neighbors" - and so the Russians would lose economic control of their sphere to the more powerful economic combination of the Americans and Europeans.

If the Russians were not willing to go along with this approach, said Kennan, the Americans wanted the Europeans to understand that America would like, then, to go with a plan for Western Europe alone - that is, to go the only course possible, or as Kennan phrased it, *pis aller*.

Kennan and Bohlen entrusted this information to Inverchapel and Balfour alone; they had no thought of conveying it to anyone else, not even to their ambassador in Paris.

That evening, Inverchapel cabled a secret report of the conversation to the Foreign Office in London, with copies to the British ambassadors in Moscow and Paris: The Americans were counting on the British to see that the Russians were knocked out of the Marshall Plan.

Meanwhile, Will Clayton landed in London for an informal conversation with Bevin. Clayton did not, as he stressed at the beginning of his conversation, have any intention of telling the British how to think about their response to Marshall's offer. It was entirely up to the British and the Europeans to frame their own program. It did seem to Clayton, however, that, if he *were* to think of how the British might frame their response, they might keep it in mind that what was wanted was a comprehensive coordinated plan from Europe as a whole, not a series of piecemeal demands from individual countries.

In drawing up a comprehensive plan, the British and Europeans might think of stating, first, their present rates of consumption of, say, coal, and their requirements for the next, say, four years. Second, they might consider the current rate of production. Third, they might set forth the ways that they planned to increase the rate of production. They might do similar analyses for foodstuffs, fertilizers, steel, fibers, transport, and machinery. These analyses would then make it possible to draw up comprehensive plans to show "(a) what Europe needs in order to get on her feet again; (b) how much of what is needed for the purpose can be found from within Europe itself and how much must be found from outside; (c) the economic objectives towards which Europe will agree to work, over the next four years."

All of this seemed eminently suitable to Bevin. Of course, said Bevin, Great Britain would be "on a different basis" from the rest of Europe.

Clayton wondered in what sense Britain ought to consider itself different from Europe.

In the first place, said Bevin (somewhat taken aback), he was "most anxious for some interim financial arrangement from the U.S. to stop the backbiting of [Bevin's plan for] foreign affairs moves by people at home who were pinched by the British financial position." That is to say, if Bevin were to do some special work for the Americans, which might give him trouble with his opponents in Parliament, then he would consider a quid pro quo only appropriate.

One of Bevin's colleagues chimed in that one way in which the British were different from the others was that Britain had contributed to the support of postwar Germany, using its own meager resources to help the American-led program of rehabilitating Germany.

The Soviet Union, said Bevin (with the barest suggestion of threat), was "flush with cereals," and maybe Britain would have to turn to the Russians to help with Britain's food shortage.

Unshaken, Clayton replied evenly: If America agreed to a special relationship with Britain, that would "violate the principle that no piecemeal approach to the European problem would be undertaken."

And incidentally, at this point, Clayton wanted to raise a couple of thoughts that - since they were "unpleasant" - he thought he might just as well get out of the way. He had a message to deliver from Secretary of State Marshall. Marshall was convinced, said Clayton, that the British had "failed in dealing with the Ruhr coal position" in the British zone of occupation in Germany.

The British were puzzled.

Marshall had not raised the subject before, said Clayton, because he had been uncertain of the facts, having heard only from the American occupation forces.

The British could not imagine what the problem was.

The Secretary, said Clayton, had had an independent investigation made, and he was now convinced that "an entirely new approach would have to be made to the coal production of the Ruhr." The British "set-up" was inefficient and British "methods" were bad. "Mr. Marshall, moreover, did not think that time permitted of experiments."

What did the Secretary of State have in mind?

As it turned out, what Marshall had in mind were British "schemes for socialization" of the Ruhr industries.

Bevin understood: Just as the Americans had advised the Italians and the French to eliminate Communists from their cabinets, so they meant to advise the British to slow down on socialism. As time went on, the advice hardly seemed to take in Britain, but Bevin did not hesitate at the moment to say whatever Clayton wanted to hear: American and British plans for Germany, he said at once, "were not far apart."

Then, returning to what he wanted, Bevin said he did not think that Britain could be considered "just as one European country among many." Its responsibilities in Germany, and in the Commonwealth, both of which gave it a special relationship with America at this particular time, were "not the obligations of an ordinary

European power." In truth, Bevin's feelings were somewhat hurt. He had thought that America and Britain could have some sort of "financial partnership." That Britain might be considered almost a special helper in leading Europe into the Marshall Plan. That Britain's guidance in shaping the plan might be appreciated by the United States, since Britain might have something very special, in the way of its ancient imperial diplomatic expertise, to contribute to the plan. Nor, frankly, did Britain relish the prospect of being thrown into a sort of "pool" with the Europeans, in which Britain would be dragged down to the lowest level of the Europeans. Actually, said Bevin, recalling Churchill's old ability to draw tears in a diplomatic negotiation, "we, as the British Empire," could assist the Marshall Plan materially. And in point of fact, he said with pride, the British simply would not want to go into the Marshall Plan "and not do anything." Such a prospect would, finally, sacrifice "the little bit of dignity we have left."

Sir John Henry Wood of the Board of Trade added a thought: He was "doubtful," he said, whether much advantage "would accrue" to Great Britain as an equal member of the Marshall Plan. It might be that Britain would find it more advantageous to stay outside the plan and make bilateral deals with the European nations.

Sir Percivale Liesching of the Ministry of Food said he thought that, on the whole, Britain ought to be a partner of the United States, but that the United Kingdom was "examining the Marshall Plan to consider how far it would help the British position."

Bevin concluded that perhaps the only effect on Britain, if the United Kingdom were thrown into the European pool, would be that "in time, a year or two, Europe would be in a somewhat better position to pay for British imports but . . . there would be little effect on the U.K. position except perhaps for an increase in dollar receipts from German exports."

Perhaps, said Bevin, Clayton ought to elucidate his notions of having Britain "lumped into the problem of Europe, because if that were the case, in forthcoming meetings" Bevin's approach "would have to be changed."

Sir Edward Bridges, Permanent Secretary of the British Treasury, had a thought. Had he quite understood the American proposal, he wondered. Was it not the case that the Americans wanted the British and the Europeans first to come up with an overall common plan, but that then the overall common plan would be implemented through "a series of bilateral agreements with individual European countries which would take into account the differences in economic needs of the various countries"?

Yes, said Clayton, with apparent relief, leaping at Sir Edward's nice formulation. The United States had no intention of throwing Britain into a European "pool." There would certainly be a common plan and then individual agreements with each country that could very well take into account their special situations.

Bevin was pleased. The British drafted a memo summarizing their understandings and showed it to Clayton for his approval. "It is understood that the United States Administration contemplates that, although the approach to the problem is essentially European, the arrangements for giving help for immediate needs would take the form of a series of agreements between the United States Government and each of the countries concerned. In this connection, it is understood that there might well be differences in the objects or purposes for which help was given to different countries according to the varying needs and situations of such countries."

In sum, America would recognize a special relationship with Britain, and Britain would make certain that the Russians were knocked out of the plan.

13
EXIT MOLOTOV

ON JUNE 27, at 11 a.m., the American ambassador in Paris cabled Washington that Bidault "told me last night that immediately upon his arrival Molotov asked him what he and Bevin had done behind his back."

At 4 p.m., Molotov, Bevin, and Bidault had their first meeting at the Quai d'Orsay. Molotov's first question was, suspiciously, "what additional information the French and British governments had received from the United States Government other than had been contained in the Secretary's speech."

Bidault and Bevin replied that they knew nothing more than Molotov did. Bevin said he had seen

Clayton in London, but that Clayton had had nothing to add to what Marshall had said in his speech.

Molotov then asked "what agreements the French and British had arrived at during the Bidault-Bevin talks last week."

Bevin and Bidault replied that their only decision had been to invite Molotov to meet with them.

Molotov wished "to make a proposal." Since none of the three governments knew anything more about the seriousness of the United States government's proposal than had been contained in the Secretary's speech, he proposed that they should ask the United States government: (1) the exact sum of money the United States was prepared to advance to aid European recovery; (2) whether the United States Congress would vote such a credit.

Bevin replied at once. "In the first place," he instructed Molotov, "in a democracy, the Executive Branch of the Government cannot engage the responsibility of the Legislative Branch." Second, said Bevin, Secretary Marshall had suggested that the European powers get together and formulate a common request for aid, and that was what Bevin thought they ought to sit down and do. And third, "Debtors do not lay down conditions when seeking credits from potential creditors."

Bidault agreed with Bevin. He softened the blow, however, by saying that since the United States had suggested that it might be willing to give "friendly aid" to the drafting of a plan, the three governments might ask Washington what was meant by "friendly aid."

Well, said Bevin, refusing to yield anything to Molotov (and refusing, too, to let the initiative slip out of his hands and back to the Americans), he interpreted that passage to mean that the United States would be willing, after the Europeans had done their job, to come in at the later stages and assist with a final draft of a plan so long as the original proposal seemed realistic to the United States. Meanwhile, Bevin said, he thought no "useful purpose would be served by Bidault's proposal."

With that, nothing more remained to be said, and the meeting was adjourned. Each side agreed to review the proposals of the others and convene again the following afternoon at four.

That evening, the men in the American Embassy cabled back to Washington that their sources in the British delegation said that they thought both Bevin and Bidault were determined "not to let the Soviets get away with any obstructionist or delaying tactics," but that "Bidault's position is more difficult because of the strength of the French Communist Party."

Molotov, meanwhile, back at his embassy, conferred with the small army of experts he had brought with him to Paris. That he had brought so many advisers suggested to some analysts that the Russians meant to take the Marshall proposal seriously. (To the more skeptical of the French, the platoons of "experts" showed nothing but that the Russians had decided to take advantage of their time in Paris by filling the city with spies and disrupters.) Whatever may have been the Russians' initial intention, by the next morning, Molotov had all but concluded that the Russians could not possibly join the plan. The dilemma of the Marshall offer was beginning to come clear to the Russians as they talked with the British and French: If the idea was to draw up a common economic plan, as Bevin and Bidault seemed to insist, then each country would need to take inventory of its economy, tell all the others what they had, declare what they needed, and allow some central body to set priorities and quotas. Each economy, including the Soviet economy, would in some sense become subject to American planning.

The Soviets, said Molotov at the meeting with Bevin and Bidault on the second day, "did not agree with certain of the proposals. . . . In particular, the Soviets felt that inquiry into the resources of European nations would violate the sovereignty of the individual countries." Each country, Molotov said, should make its own assessment of its needs and thus establish the amount of credit it would require from the United States. The individual credit demands could then be added up, and that total figure "transmitted to the U.S. Government."

Both Bevin and Bidault objected. Neither could see how this in any way constituted the sort of plan General Marshall had in mind.

At once, this, the essential matter before them, appeared clearly unresolvable. And so, with the practiced instincts of diplomats, the foreign ministers set the issue aside and moved to something easier - the question of which European countries should participate in the plan. Bidault suggested that all European countries join except Spain, which, as a former German ally still governed by Franco's dictatorship, ought to be "provisionally" excluded. Germany would be "provisionally" represented by delegations of the occupying powers. Italy, since it had a democratically elected government, could join.

Molotov replied that he thought only "allied countries which had suffered from the ravages of war should participate directly in the plan." In short, he meant to exclude Italy as a former German ally - a nice suggestion on his part, which would certainly go far toward breaking up Western Europe. Germany, he said, should be excluded until the Allies had agreed on reparations.

With that, the meeting drifted desultorily to a close.

Western diplomats were all somewhat puzzled by Molotov's behavior. He was not moving in one direction or another. One of the French delegates felt certain that the Russians wanted to break up the conference, but that Molotov was being mild because the Soviets "wished at all cost to avoid giving the French or the British a valid pretext to break with them." Bidault, however, thought Molotov might actually be "uncertain" about whether or not to join the plan. Molotov, said Bidault, "clearly does not wish this business to succeed, but on the other hand, his hungry satellites are smacking their lips in expectation of getting some [American] money. He is obviously embarrassed." To Bidault, it seemed that Molotov might be looking for some way to arrange the Marshall offer so that the Soviet Union could accept.

The next day, Bevin decided, matters ought to be "laid on the line," and Molotov's hand ought to be forced. Bevin drew up a one-page proposal that he thought the French would like. At eleven in the morning, he had the paper delivered to Bidault and Molotov as Britain's best suggestion. Bevin's paper called for a steering committee to draw up a program for four years. The program would state just what contribution European countries could make toward their own reconstruction and what external assistance would be required. The steering committee would be composed of Britain, France, the USSR, and four other countries. (Bevin and his aides had considered what might happen if Russia withdrew and France - stymied by Communist ministers - had to leave the drafting of the program up to Britain. In that case, Bevin realized, he would need some other countries to draw up the program so that it would not look like a mere Anglo-American scheme.) The steering committee would ask America's friendly aid in drawing up the final program. Subcommittees would be established at once on food and agriculture, coal and other forms of fuel and power, iron and steel, and transport.

That afternoon, the ministers met to consider Bevin's paper. Molotov spoke up at once. There could be "no infringement," he said, "on the sovereignty of European states." The Soviet position was that each state would have to make its own assessment of its needs and submit the dollar costs to America. Perhaps Molotov thought that Soviet insistence on this point would bring the others around; surely the Western European nations could not be eager to surrender any portion of their independence to America. Perhaps the others would be relieved to have the Soviet Union take the lead on this issue. In any case, negotiations had only just begun; there was time for haggling. In this instance, Bidault replied,

France disagreed with the Soviet position. France agreed with Britain that a common plan was called for, not a listing of individual needs. There would be no negotiating on this point.

Just then Molotov was handed what was, as Bevin later said, "an obviously partially decoded telegram." It came from Moscow, and it was, as Bevin thought at once, Stalin's response to the one-page proposal Bevin had put before the group. The telegram had no new angles to offer; it stamped as the final, position the one that Molotov had already taken: The Russians would not subject themselves to common planning.

Bevin then spoke. "I said with a smile," he recalled, savoring the moment, "in effect what you are asking the United States Government to do is give us a blank check. If I were to go to Moscow with a blank check and ask you to sign it, I wonder how far I would get at your end."

Bidault supported Bevin's remarks, then called for adjournment.

This conference, Bevin told one of the Americans in Paris, "will break up tomorrow. I am glad that the cards have been laid on the table and that the responsibility will be laid at Moscow's door. They have tried to sabotage it in the conference room from the very beginning as I knew they would."

Then Bevin added an uncharacteristically

pro-French note (no doubt he had been ingratiating himself privately with the French): "In the face of the breakdown of this conference, which I had anticipated and even wished for . . . I wish to raise another point: . . . the French are in a very dangerous position both politically and financially. I repeat that the French have supported me wholeheartedly and with great courage in view of the precarious French political situation. If the French . . . have no hopes for even interim credits which they can hold out to the French public . . . I fear greatly that they may waver. . . . If they stand with us, I hope you will not abandon them. Give them something to hope for."

Although, in fact, the conference was finished, each side had a little housekeeping to do before breaking up. In order to cover himself in terms of domestic politics, Bidault had to offer one last proposal as a presumed compromise between Britain and the Soviets. Europe (including Russia), Bidault proposed, would draw up a common plan and see what deficit it would have, and the United States would then supply the necessary "supplement"; this could be done without interfering in anyone's sovereignty. Bidault had said nothing; his proposal was a mere rephrasing of the British-French position. The Russians, as one of the French diplomats told the Americans, would be obliged to reject this last French offer and then the French would "be able to proceed with the British."

Indeed, the next day - the last of the conference - Molotov opened with a scathing attack on the French proposal. The question of American economic aid, he said, "has now served as a pretext for the British and French Governments to insist on the creation of a new organization, standing above the European countries and intervening in the internal affairs of the countries of Europe."

Moreover, said Molotov, Britain and France had simply assumed "a dominating position in this organization, or as is stated in the British draft, the so-called 'Steering Committee' for Europe." It was perfectly obvious, to Molotov, "that the European countries will find themselves under control and will lose their former economic and national independence to the advantage of certain strong Powers."

The Soviet government, said Molotov, "rejects this plan as totally unsatisfactory." Furthermore, he concluded, the plan "will lead to nothing good. It will lead to Britain, France and the group of countries that follow them separating from the rest of Europe, which will split Europe into two groups of States. . . . The Soviet Government considers it necessary to warn the Governments of Britain and France of the consequences of such actions."

Bidault replied, with some passion: "I have listened with great attention . . . to Mr. Molotov's statement. He concludes by warning my country. I, for my part, would like to warn the Soviet Delegation against any action which might lead to the separation of Europe into two groups."

The French government, said Bidault, rejected all suggestions that it had any ambitions toward dominating Europe. Furthermore, "the world is witness to the fact that France had done everything to prevent a rift. . . . Neither England, I am sure, nor France in any case, I say, seeks a dominant place in such a concert [of power]. But we have learned . . . that the role of the great Powers could not be underestimated."

The French, said Bidault, looked forward to cooperation in the Marshall Plan, not to any authoritarian fixing of directives. The plan that the French envisaged simply called for "knowing the production targets of these different countries and of harmonizing them in all freedom." Acceptance by the European countries would be freely offered, not enforced. "They will participate if they wish. . . . Their willing cooperation will be welcome; naturally, any cooperation other than willing would not be accepted."

The French proposal, Bidault concluded, "has not and will not have the effect of chaining the economy of the small countries, but, on the contrary, of liberating it."

Bevin then chimed in. "I said," Bevin reported in his own memo for General Marshall, "that Molotov's statement was based on a complete travesty of the facts. . . . M. Molotov presumably repeated misrepresentations like this in the hope that by constant repetition they would be believed. Our policy was to cooperate with all and dominate none."

With regard "to the division of Europe," said Bevin, "nobody has striven more than I for the unity of Europe, including the political and economic unity of Germany. I noted and regretted that M. Molotov had ended with a threat. Great Britain on other occasions had been threatened with grave consequences. Such threats had not and would not cause us to hesitate to pursue what we considered to be our duty."

The conference was at an end. Molotov said, with elaborate formality, that he "hoped the world at large would acquaint itself with the proposals of all three delegations." Bidault replied that the full texts of the various proposals would be published. Molotov said that he would consider it his duty to report in full, and exactly, just what had been said and done at this conference when he returned to Moscow.

"I am seeing M. Bidault early tomorrow," Bevin said, in conclusion, "when we hope to agree on a joint invitation to all European governments."

When Averell Harriman, who had recently been brought into the Truman cabinet as Secretary of Commerce, reflected on the Paris meeting, he thought "Bevin did a superb job of getting Molotov out of Paris - by careful maneuvering. Bidault claims to have had a part in it. But Bevin had the courage to invite Molotov and the bluntness to get rid of him. This confirmed my impression that Molotov is essentially a dull fellow. He could have killed the Marshall Plan by joining it."

Kennan, on the other hand, had never been worried that Molotov might join. One of the prices of Soviet participation, said Kennan, "would have been cooperation in overcoming real barriers in East-West trade." Such a move would have meant subjecting themselves to the influence of a more powerful, American economy: ". . . so, in a sense, we put Russia over the barrel. . . . When the full horror of [their] alternatives dawned on them, they left suddenly in the middle of the night."

From the American Embassy in London, an information officer wrote a colleague back in Washington: "I am enclosing an article in the *Spectator* . . . entitled "Why Molotov Said No" . . . which to my mind gives the clearest explanation yet I have seen of Molotov's action in Paris."

Some say, the article said, that Molotov left Paris "because the Soviet Government is reluctant to support in any way the United States' claim to world leadership. And it is clear that the Marshall speech is a claim to world leadership." But, *The Spectator* continued, more immediate practical considerations came into play as well. Russia, severely damaged by the war, needed help to rebuild. First the Russians had asked for a loan from the United States, which was not granted. Next, the Russians hoped to take reparations from Germany, which was also blocked by the United States. "So the third Russian alternative came into play - the industrial output of Eastern Europe. Czechoslovak and Polish output is being integrated with the Soviet economy."

Then, "by opening the doors of world trade to the countries of Eastern Europe, the Marshall offer threatened to destroy the whole of the East-European preference system upon which the speed of Soviet recovery now depends." At the moment, too, the Russians were taking reparations out of Finland, Hungary, and Rumania to buttress the Soviet Five-Year Plan. "So, without regard for any diplomatic niceties, without regard for even the normal courtesies of international relations, the Soviet Government slammed the door and slammed it quickly. There is nothing complicated about it."

Secretary of State Marshall cabled Paris asking the American ambassador there to deliver "the following personal and private message from me to Bidault and Bevin: 'I have followed with complete understanding the course of your patient efforts to find agreement with the Soviet Government. . . . We realize the gravity of the problem with which you have been confronted and the difficulty of the decisions which you have been forced to take . . . . We here are prepared to do all in our power to support any genuine and constructive efforts toward the restoration of economic health and prosperity in the countries of Europe."

The State Department's file copy of Marshall's cable bears the marginal notation "Approved by the President."

14
THE FRENCH THREAT

EVEN AS THE invitations went out from Paris inviting the various nations of Europe to send their representatives to a conference, where all would meet in an atmosphere of candor and equality, Bidault was arranging an intimate huddle with Undersecretary Clayton at the Quai d'Orsay.

Of course, Bidault told Clayton, one would have to act urgently to take advantage of General Marshall's generous offer. Particularly in France, where one faced "internal" as well as external "difficulties," alacrity and a certain smoothness were necessary in order that the Marshall Plan succeed. But he had to mention, incidentally, that "as concerns Germany" some people, the Communists in France for instance, were saying that the United States and Great Britain wished to see to the reconstruction of Germany even before the reconstruction of France. It was said that America and Britain even wanted the French to abandon their claim to certain reparations from Germany - to abandon, for example, French claims to the coal mines and the steel factories of the Ruhr and Saar valleys. Of course, Bidault did not believe that these rumors could be true.

It was obvious, said Bidault, "that Ruhr coal is essential for Europe, including Germany." But it had already been agreed (by the Americans, the British, and the French) that "henceforth the coal resources of the Saar and those of France form an entity." It had been recognized, too, that the French had a particular interest in the steel production of the Ruhr. To make a change in any arrangements at this point, said Bidault, would put the French government in a "difficult position." Indeed, it might be said that such an action could be thought to be "dangerous."

Clayton replied at once with an expression of gratitude for the "skillful and rapid manner" in which Bidault and Bevin had responded to the Marshall speech. As for the questions that Bidault raised concerning the Ruhr and the Saar, Clayton agreed with Bidault that it was necessary to get steel production going again in the Ruhr. It was "disastrous" that "two years after the end of hostilities Ruhr coal production only reached 45 percent of the prewar level." It was urgent that something be done to get the Ruhr factories going again (something in the way of management - though Clayton refrained from saying it - that might not exactly depend upon the French to carry out).

As for the Saar, Clayton said he could only speak "purely personally," although it was his understanding that the United States government had already expressed some "sympathy" for certain French objectives.

Perhaps Undersecretary Clayton had not quite understood Bidault's point. Bidault returned to the question of the Ruhr. The present situation, he said, was in fact "far from being satisfactory, and the adversaries of the French Government were using this very fact as an argument to attack it, saying: 'to assemble a conference at Paris to examine the Marshall proposals amounts to the same thing as abandonment of reparations and modification of the French position as regards the Ruhr.'" This situation, said Bidault, was "extremely serious." Perhaps it was not possible to settle the final question of the ultimate ownership of the mines of the Ruhr, but it certainly would be possible to change the management methods "with French participation."

Clayton replied that he could only speak "for himself." As a matter of fact, he could not agree more with Bidault about the question of ultimate ownership of the mines of the Ruhr; indeed, it seemed to Clayton that a "moratorium on nationalization or socialization plans for a period of five years should prove very beneficial in removing uncertainties now facing the mines management."

The conversation was becoming muddled as well as vexing to Bidault. The French wished to establish that they would not consent to having Germany restored before France was, that they would not consent to having Germany set up by the United States and Britain so that the Germans would dominate the Continent. Bidault wished to make it clear that the French would see to it, by taking the principal role in managing (if not owning) the great industrial valleys of the Ruhr and Saar, that - once again - France would dominate the Continent. But Clayton did not seem to understand the drift of Bidault's remarks, and instead, strangely, seemed to suggest that management of the resources of the Ruhr and the Saar might best be in some hands other than those of the French or even of the British, possibly even that the United States would have the dominant voice in the management of the Ruhr and Saar.

Bidault summarized his position: "The United States says that the Ruhr mines must not be nationalized; Great Britain, on the other hand, desires socialization; France demands internationalization. If it is impossible to settle this question now, it is at least necessary to improve immediately the management of the mines with participation by France."

As for steel, Bidault wished there to be "no misunderstanding." France was capable, "if it receives sufficient coke from the Ruhr, of increasing its steel production very substantially and of meeting . . . all the requirements of Western Europe, including German needs." For the moment, it was essential that absolutely no decision be made to raise the levels of German industrial production. Such a decision, said Bidault, "could lead to the belief that it is desired to restore the German economy before that of the countries Germany attacked."

Did Clayton fully grasp that he was talking to the former head of the French underground? Had Clayton heard Bidault? Bidault repeated himself: "To begin the attempt to settle European difficulties by abandoning reparations and by raising the level of German industry would have very serious consequences in Europe. No French government could consent to it."

France, said Bidault, "does not desire to reduce Germany to misery, it admits that the reconstruction of Germany is an element of

European reconstruction, but it must not take precedence. It is therefore necessary that the dismantling of [German] factories be pursued at an accelerated rate; that France receive a much more substantial share of reparations in equipment and in capital goods. Finally, the problem of the raising of the level of German industry must be reserved for the time being."

Clayton replied, hedging, that he agreed that first place in the reconstruction of Europe must not belong to Germany, but that it was nevertheless true that Ruhr coal production (again Clayton declined to say Ruhr coal production under the principal management of the French) constituted an essential element of European reconstruction.

If, said Bidault, the United States was determined to deprive France of reparations, and if the United States was determined in particular to raise the "German economic potential," then let Clayton understand at least that no public statement to this effect must be made. If such a statement were to be issued before the representatives of the European nations gathered together in Paris, then the Paris Conference would be doomed to failure, and let Clayton understand that, in such a case, then "there would be no Europe."

It may be that Clayton at last understood. Some historians had already argued that it had been the French, primarily, who were responsible for the continuing anarchy that followed World War I. The French, the argument goes, wanted to dominate the Continent after the war. When they found they could not, they also found that they could at least keep the Germans from doing so. And thus, frustrating the wishes of all others to establish a new order, the French kept the Continent in the chaos that led to World War II.

Clayton replied that he completely understood "the sentiments of M. Bidault, which are those of the French people." No one in the United States, he said, "was thinking of reconstructing Europe around a dominant Germany."

Nothing more remained to be said. The Undersecretary was "very glad," he said, to have had Bidault's reactions to the current situation in Europe, and he would "transmit them to the Secretary."

Bidault said that he wished once more "to express the gratitude of the French Government for the liberal and humane gesture made by the Secretary of State, the importance of which is appreciated by the entire French nation."

15
THE DIPLOMATS

D AIMLERS, MERCEDES-BENZES, Citroëns, Rolls-Royces rolled up over the gravel courtyard at the Quai d'Orsay on July 12 to deposit the elegant and the amiable, the curious and the expectant, the anxious and the opportunistic representatives of Austria, Denmark, Greece, Iceland, Ireland, Italy, Luxembourg, the Netherlands, Norway, Portugal, Sweden, Switzerland, Turkey; and, gossiping about who else was in Paris just then, they entered the gilt-trimmed Salon de l'Horloge - whose ladder-back gilt chairs, chandeliers, bare wooden floor, and immensely long table covered in green baize had provided the setting in 1919 for the daily meetings of the futile peace conference that followed the First World War.

Bevin was there, of course, for the opening of the conference, as was Bidault. Monnet was there. Sir Oliver Franks was there - tall, slender, slightly florid, a mere forty-two years old. The British had dispatched him to preside over the conference: Since the conference was to occur on French soil, it was only appropriate that an Englishman preside - and so, right off, the British had got the best of the deal.

Sir Oliver was a graduate of Queen's College, Oxford, where he read "Mods" and "Greats." He was a fellow and praelector in philosophy at Queen's College from 1927 to 1937, where he became known as an authority on Kant. At the beginning of the Second World War, he entered the civil service in the Ministry of Supply, and by the end of the war, he had become the Secretary.

A rigorously and dispassionately logical mind, a talent for lucid exposition, and what was noticed in the way of a "moral fervor" that often expressed itself as an unwillingness ever to give up, even in the face of the most vexing and complicated matters, a sense of discretion - all suited him perfectly to preside over what was destined to become a messy conference, and to muddle through to a conclusion compatible with his country's needs. "He has a strong sense of duty," *The Observer* once said of him, "but he also possesses a vigorous confidence that every problem, theoretical or practical, is soluble by the human intellect, given sufficient exercise of will to get the intellect working." Or, as one of the Americans would say of him, as Franks chaired a difficult meeting during an unusually warm day that summer in Paris and a bead of perspiration formed on his forehead, divided neatly, trickled down both his cheeks, and then met again under his chin: "I take my hat off to that guy. He even sweats symmetrically."

Duff Cooper, British Ambassador to France, was there too. The son of Sir Alfred Cooper and his wife, Lady Agnes Cecil Emmeline Duff, sister of the first Duke of Fife, Duff Cooper was there to help represent England, since Sir Oliver Franks was charged with being the impartial chairman of the conference. After an aimless adolescence and a tendency to drift that lasted even into his twenties, he joined the Foreign Office in 1913, having nothing else to do. Six years later he married Lady Diana Olivia Winifred Maud Manners, "a dazzling and valiant companion," and at their house they entertained many of the members of their own generation, as well as such older friends as Lord Beaverbrook and Sir Winston Churchill.

In 1922, Duff Cooper was elected as a Conservative member from Oldham and, after a single setback, managed to retain a seat in Parliament until 1945. "Although too reserved to win popularity," as Harold Nicolson once wrote of him, "and too proud to court it, he influenced his contemporaries by . . . the distinction of his mind, his manners, and his discourses. He was choleric in argument and pugnacious in debate; yet in his later manhood he was never, as some imagined, a fanatical conservative, since he regarded as 'barbarians' all extremists . . . he never lost his zest for literature, travel, conversation, shooting, wine, and the society of gifted and beautiful women."

Among the Frenchmen who began to take a noticeable part in negotiations was Maurice Couve de Murville, a tall man, lean and handsome, with the look of someone perpetually taken aback. His interests were homely: He smoked a pipe, played cards, rode horseback, and read the classics. But not many of his peers had quite as extensive a familiarity with economic matters as he did, nor as keen an array of instincts for finding his way through treacherous political situations. The son of a well-known judge, Couve de Murville was an adept politician; he was appointed inspector of finance in 1930, at age twenty-three. In 1937, he was promoted to assistant director in the Ministry of Finance. In 1938, he was made an associate director of foreign finance. As such, he became one of the principal architects of financial agreements between the French and the British in 1939. In 1940, he became director of external finance of the Ministry of Finance. Then, when the Germans conquered France, Couve de Murville was dismissed from the ministry for his "Republican sentiments" and deprived of his French citizenship.

By the summer of 1943, he was finance commissioner of the French Committee of National Liberation, and by the end of the war, with the resistance fighters established back in Paris, Couve de Murville had been appointed director-general of political affairs in the Ministry of Foreign Affairs.

The Americans had stayed in the background up until now, but once the conference got under way in Paris, a couple of Americans were seen around town avidly collecting gossip: Lewis Douglas and Jefferson Caffery.

Douglas, age fifty-three, often had a quizzical smile about his lips and a twinkle in his eye, as though he might be enjoying a situation and had nothing, personally, to lose. He was, in fact, the heir to a fortune; his family owned the richest copper mine in the world, the Copper Queen Lode, among others. After an aimless youth, Douglas had drifted into a career in politics in his late twenties, first in the Arizona state legislature and then in Congress, where he served four terms.

He was a conservative, and in 1933, when Roosevelt was looking around for conservative support, he appointed Douglas Director of the Budget. Douglas lasted only a little more than a year, resigning in August 1934 when Roosevelt began "pump priming" the economy with public works and unemployment relief programs.

But when World War II broke out, Douglas was ready to fight: he was among the first to advocate giving aid to Britain and cutting off diplomatic relations with Germany, and in 1941, Roosevelt appointed him a deputy of the new lend-lease program for Britain, where he worked with Averell Harriman.

In 1947, when Harriman retired as Ambassador to the Court of St. James's, Douglas succeeded him, and the English got along with Douglas at once. The new ambassador liked fly-fishing, reading, and horseback riding, and something in his well-to-do but unbusinesslike manner appealed to the English love of amateurs.

Caffery was a suave, almost prim man, meticulously groomed, who had learned, despite his Southern origins, to speak with the broad *a* so much in favor at the State Department. Clayton, another Southerner, who would soon join Caffery at the embassy in Paris, was disgusted by him. The ambassador had four butlers for six people at lunch, said Clayton, and for dinner he had a butler behind each chair. "If anything went on in Caffery's head," Clayton added, "you'd never know what it was, all he does is nod acquiescence, never has any ideas, never get anything constructive out of him."

Part of Caffery's problem was that he did enjoy a drink. At dinner once in Clayton's apartment in the Meurice Hotel, with Bidault and Monnet in attendance, Caffery said to Clayton that the minister (meaning Bidault) "likes a liqueur and you'd better order it."

Clayton ordered up some liqueur and then, on Caffery's further orders, some more liqueur. Bidault never touched it, and Caffery ended up, Clayton said, "tight as a knot on a log."

At the embassy, whenever Caffery wanted to pop down the hall and have a word with Clayton, a military guard would be sent on ahead to announce the Ambassador to the Undersecretary. And whenever Caffery went out for a meeting, his minions, as Clayton thought of them, would rush up and down the corridor - one to hand the ambassador his hat, one to hand him his cane, another to run ahead and open doors and hold the car door.

A native of Louisiana, Caffery started his career in 1911 as secretary of the legation at Caracas, Venezuela, and during the next couple of decades, he served in Stockholm, Paris, Madrid, Athens, Tokyo, Brussels, and Berlin. From 1926 to 1928, he was Envoy Extraordinary and Minister Plenipotentiary to El Salvador, and from 1928 to 1930 to Colombia.

In 1932, during hearings of the Senate Committee on Finance, it was said that Caffery had taken an active part in Colombia in promoting a grant of a large oil concession to the Mellon-owned Gulf Petroleum Company, which some members of the Senate committee considered evidence of "collusion of the State Department and bankers." Either in spite, or because of, these charges, Caffery was sent to Cuba the following December as Ambassador Extraordinary and Plenipotentiary, where he was soon accused of "meddling in Cuban internal affairs, especially in the interest of American capitalists," and of helping to install the dictatorship of Colonel Batista y Zaldívar.

With this background in Latin American affairs, Caffery was appointed Ambassador to Brazil in 1937, where he gained additional attention, largely praise, for bringing President Getúlio Vargas around to seeing matters from the Washington point of view, and of securing American support of Vargas's nondemocratic, military government. In 1943, in recognition of all of his work in South America, Caffery was given the Sign Las Americas Award for outstanding inter-American services by the Committee on Cultural Relations with the American Republics. Roosevelt appointed him Ambassador to France in 1944 - and Clayton, for one, was pleased when Monnet told him that "the French didn't appreciate, didn't approve of the style Caffery put on."

It could hardly escape the notice of the protocol-conscious diplomats in Paris that almost no one there had a rank as elevated as that of foreign minister. Evidently, Couve de Murville had talked with Bidault, and then phoned Duff Cooper, who cabled back to Bevin that the French "felt that invited nations should be politely discouraged from sending their foreign ministers." The French were fearful, he said, that if too many foreign ministers showed up they would all want to make speeches, and that would take "too long." Happily, too, though Bidault was not so vulgar as to mention it, if only Britain and France had their foreign ministers in Paris, then Britain and France would have the ranking diplomats, and the ranking diplomats would naturally take the leadership of the conference. Only two men managed to slip by this maneuver: Paul-Henri Spaak, Premier of Belgium, and Count Carlo Sforza, the Foreign Minister of Italy.

Spaak was a portly, round-faced, balding, resolute man. The son of Paul Spaak, a well-known Belgian poet and the director of the Brussels opera, and a mother who was an active Socialist and the first woman senator in the Belgian Parliament, the boy was fifteen years old when the Germans invaded Belgium in the First World War; he was a prisoner of war by the age of seventeen, when he was caught trying to cross the Dutch border to regroup with the Belgian Army.

After the war, Spaak took a degree in law and became a "firebrand" Socialist - a member, at age thirty-three, of the Chamber of Deputies, a co-editor of *L'Action critique,* a Socialist journal, Minister of Transportation and Posts, and, in 1936, at the age of thirty-seven, Minister of Foreign Affairs. By 1938, he was Premier - although his government lasted only eight months before the turmoil of prewar politics replaced his ministry with one led by a Catholic Conservative.

When the Germans overran Belgium in 1940, Spaak went with the other members of the Belgian cabinet to France. When France was attacked, Spaak tried twice to escape over the Spanish border, and succeeded the second time. Kept in Spain, in "enforced residence" under the order of the Nazis, Spaak escaped again, this time to London, where he served as Foreign Minister of the Belgian government in exile.

At the end of the war, governments rose and fell in Belgium with some frequency, and Spaak, by the time he arrived in Paris, was thoroughly accustomed to dealing with treacherous political situations. The sense of history he brought with him included the memory that Belgium had been invaded twice in his lifetime by the Germans and, not too long before that, by the French, led by Napoleon.

As for the Italians, the Italian government had not yet got around, by July 1947, to ratifying the treaty that had been drawn up for them to put an official close to the Second World War. When Italian ministers happened to mention to the British Ambassador to Rome that they were not certain the treaty would be ratified very soon, the ambassador said he thought that was unfortunate, since Italy "could not possibly have the same influence at the conference in Paris" if the Italians had not yet ratified the treaty.

On July 9, before the Paris meetings got under way, Count Sforza himself had come to call on the British ambassador. Did the ambassador think, Sforza wanted to know, and did Bevin think, that the Italian government (and Count Sforza himself) had been dealing honestly in trying to get the treaty accepted by the Italian Assembly? If the answer was yes, then Sforza would be prepared to go to Paris on either July 12 or July 15. But if Bevin thought the Italians were "up to their old tricks" (as Count Sforza had heard that the French were saying that the British were saying about the Italians), then Sforza would not feel that it was "worthwhile" for him to go to Paris.

Yet, on the other hand, if he were to go to Paris, would he be assured of a place on the Coordinating Committee? If so, he could get to Paris by the fifteenth. But, on second thought, it might be better for him to get to Paris on the twelfth in order to make certain of a good place on the Coordinating Committee. And he would not, he promised the British ambassador, make "any grandiloquent speeches" if he went to Paris.

But frankly, he did not care to go to Paris if he was not to be given his rightful place as the representative of "the biggest demographic and one of the biggest commercial countries in Europe." What did the British ambassador think? Actually, Sforza pouted, if he were not given his rightful place in Paris, well, then, "he would not make a scene but he would just return quietly to Italy."

Speaking for himself, Sforza thought that Italy had a contribution to make and that he personally could be useful. What did the British ambassador think?

Kindly, the ambassador put Sforza out of his misery. He was certain, he said, that Bevin was "genuinely looking forward" to seeing the count, and "the American, French, and British governments had all expressed their opinion that Italy should ratify the treaty as a condition of going to Paris."

Altogether, although the diplomats looked and behaved deceptively alike, as though they were all cut of the same pin-striped cloth, they were a remarkably diverse group, in background and temperament and idiosyncrasy - and, of course, in the diversity of conflicting national interests that they represented. Even though they had a fairly simple common denominator to their interest - cash on the barrelhead - bringing them around to a common understanding and a common interest in helping one another would be a feat not only difficult but entirely unprecedented.

The task had been simplified, however, as the diplomats were quick to take note, by the fact that, for the first time in several years, the Russians were nowhere to be seen.

Not only were the Russians absent, but the whole tier of Eastern Europe was conspicuously unrepresented in the Salon de l'Horloge. Bevin had tried - both frantically and without conviction - to ease the Eastern Europeans away from the Soviet Union: Telegrams had gone out from London to Warsaw, Prague, Belgrade, Budapest, and elsewhere to try to pry the Eastern Europeans out of their capitals into Paris. The responses came back with wonderful unanimity.

The Poles had hoped to accept the invitation to Paris. Frankly, one of the members of the Polish government said to a British diplomat in Geneva, "fifty percent of [Polish] planned exports for the current year are earmarked for the West." Passports were being prepared for a delegation to go to Paris. And then, abruptly, preparations were cancelled.

In Budapest, a British diplomat asked his Hungarian counterpart whether the Hungarians would send representatives to Paris. Most Hungarians, came the reply, wanted to attend the conference, but the Hungarian government had no choice in the matter; rather, "we will be directed what to do." The Russians had told the Hungarians, according to British sources, that if they sent anyone to Paris, the Soviet Union would be obliged to demand immediate delivery of maximum reparations from Hungary and would suspend the return of prisoners of war who were still in Russia.

As for the Czechoslovakians, they accepted at once and happily; 70 percent of their trade was with the West, and they regarded economic cooperation as nothing less than essential. Then, in Moscow, their representatives were called in for a meeting with Stalin.

Klement Gottwald, Premier of Czechoslovakia, and Jan Masaryk, Minister of Foreign Affairs, met with Stalin and Molotov at the Kremlin. At first, said Stalin sympathetically, the Soviet Union also had thought that it would be good to attend the Paris Conference, but then, after Molotov's visit to Paris, "another point of view prevailed." Evidently, said Stalin, through the "bondage" of Marshall Plan credits, the Western powers "were seeking to form a western bloc and to isolate the Soviet Union." By going to Paris, said Stalin, "you will participate in an action designed to isolate the Soviet Union."

Gottwald was silent for some moments. At last he spoke up: Even so, he said, Czechoslovakia depended on the West for 60 to 80 percent of her raw materials - for which "we had to pay in foreign exchange," of which "we had not enough."

Stalin burst out laughing. "We know that you have enough!"

Still laughing, he turned to Molotov: "They thought they could lay their hands on some dollars, and they didn't want to miss the chance."

After the meeting, back at the Czech Embassy, Masaryk, disgusted, told an English visitor that the word was definite: Czechoslovakia would stay out of the Marshall Plan. "And the real reason for this, if you must know, is that the Americans will be very happy to bribe both us and the Poles into loosening our bonds with the Russians."

"But," said the Englishman, "Marshall offered to give credits to Russia too."

"That," said Masaryk, "is the real crux of the matter. The offer of credits to us and to the Poles is quite genuine; I am less sure about the Rumanians and the Yugoslavs. But, as for credits for Russia, that is the biggest piece of eyewash in the whole scheme. Do you see Truman and Congress forking out billions of dollars to Enemy Number One, communist Russia, from whom we all have to be saved?"

Gottwald cabled home in what could only be called panic over the reprimand he had received: "Immediately call together all the members of the government within reach and inform them of the substance of our conference with Stalin and Molotov. We regard it as imperative that you agree to the withdrawal of our acceptance to joint conference at Paris and communicate it in such a way that it will reach here officially Thursday afternoon. In addition, telephone immediately your decision."

With the refusals from Czechoslovakia, Poland, and Hungary, refusals flowed into Paris from Rumania, Bulgaria, Albania, and Yugoslavia as well.

The American ambassador in Czechoslovakia was not cheered by what he thought would be the consequences of this brouhaha over the Marshall Plan. That Gottwald had first accepted Marshall's offer had been an embarrassment to the Soviet Union. Now, said the ambassador, there was a "feeling of intense discouragement over future prospects" for Czechoslovakia. Some Czechs thought that the Soviet Union would take "prompt steps to tighten control on Czechoslovakia and that Gottwald, whose position with Kremlin has been weakened by his error in acquiescing in acceptance of Paris invitation, will redouble Czech Communists effort in order to recover his prestige." The ambassador's sources felt, furthermore, "that while resolution and spirit of some moderates might be strengthened by outrageous fashion in which Czechoslovakia has been treated there is danger that many of rank and file will feel situation hopeless and cease to assert themselves." In short, it looked as though the whole unhappy business was simply going to cause increased repression in Eastern Europe - and a hardening of the Iron Curtain.

The startling casualness with which the United States and Western European nations abandoned Eastern Europe - with all its raw materials, its traditional role of supplying the grist for Western mills, the usefulness of its high volume of trade - illuminates, as perhaps nothing else so clearly does, how completely the leaders of the West had by this time acknowledged that Eastern Europe belonged to Russia. Stalin's armies were in place; agreements in private conversations, confirmed at Yalta and Potsdam, had, by this time, been taken for granted. None of the Western European leaders was prepared to go to war over Eastern Europe; all, accustomed as they were to balance-of-power politics, spheres of influence, and broken hearts, had written off the East. Although few of the leaders of the West spoke openly of this understanding of things, and many pretended that they had no intention of tolerating Russian domination of the East, not one, as the opening sessions of the Paris talks got under way, wasted a moment's effort on behalf of Eastern Europe.

In Paris, meanwhile, the opening meeting was coming off as planned. The British and French met beforehand to agree on arrangements: three seats would be provided for each delegation around the table; an additional five or six members of each delegation might be accommodated in seats just behind their principal representatives. They would be jammed in elbow to elbow around the table; fortunately, none of them would have to lift a fork.

Bevin and Bidault would sit side by side at the center of the table. Bidault, as Foreign Minister of the host country, would officiate. He would first ask whether the members of the conference wished to hold their meeting in public. If so, the members of the press (who would be kept waiting out in the courtyard) would be invited in. If not, the press would be allowed in for five minutes to take pictures, and then they would withdraw. Bidault would then make an opening speech, after which he would move that a chairman be elected for the conference. The chairman would be Bevin.

Bevin would then propose the nomination of a committee to draft rules, draft an organization plan, and address itself to the question of membership on the committees. The French would not be averse to having an Englishman named as Bevin's special delegate - as it transpired, Sir Oliver Franks - to serve as permanent chairman of the conference.

Sir Oliver suggested that some time limit might be set for the speeches, so that they would not drag on interminably, but the French thought that would be unwise, since it might give rise to the suspicion that there was some attempt "to impose Anglo-French will on the Conference."

The French suggested, too, that it would be wise for the central committee of the conference to be broad-based - to have all the participating countries have representatives on the Steering Committee - in order to allay the old Russian charges "of Anglo-French domination." This committee might be called the "Committee of Cooperation." Then, the "real work" could be done by an Executive Committee, with a membership of five - an Englishman, a Frenchman, Spaak representing the Benelux countries (Belgium, the Netherlands, and Luxembourg), Count Sforza of Italy, and someone from one of the Scandinavian countries. The Executive Committee would run the conference.

The Executive Committee (Bevin's Steering Committee) would be responsible for general setting of policy. Under it, a Working Committee would establish a series of ad hoc subcommittees to work with such areas as labor, agriculture, steel, and so forth. Since the French had given the chairmanship of the Executive Committee to Britain, Sir Oliver suggested that the French might like to provide the chairman of the Working Committee, and, indeed, the French provided Hervé Alphand, a diplomat so discreet as to be mostly unnoticeable - although Inverchapel was to say of him that he was "a man in whose proximity it was best to keep one's pockets sewn up."

At the appointed hour, eleven on the morning of July 12, the delegates were called to order in the Salon de l'Horloge, and the conference proceeded as planned. Bidault spoke. Bevin was elected chairman. Bevin suggested the formation of a Working Committee. The motion was carried. Cigarette smoke filled the air. Chair legs scraped the bare floor. Papers were rustled. Fingers were pricked on the little straight pins that the French (and some of the British) used to hold their documents together. The scents of a gorgeous variety of shaving lotions and hair tonics mingled in the air. The sunlight warmed and eventually overheated the room, glinting from time to time off eyeglasses of thin crystal lenses and thin gold frames with tracings of filigree. Close up, one heard the sound of a silk jacket lining rubbing against a crisp cotton shirt. And so began the detailed planning of the long-acknowledged division of Europe.

16
DIPLOMACY

ONCE THE DELEGATES had placed the pleasantries and formalities of their opening session behind them, they fell at once to bickering over agendas, schedules, committees - all the humdrum physical apparatus of an international conference that fixes, irrevocably, the relationships among the participants.

Hervé Alphand suggested an organizational chart for the conference: the showcase committee of the whole, the Committee of Cooperation, on which all nations were equal members; the Executive Committee - composed of Britain, France, Italy, the Netherlands, and Norway - which would really run the conference; the Working Committee, which would oversee the day-to-day work of the conference under the direction of the Executive Committee; and the Technical Committees, which would assemble the raw economic information on which the conference would base its planning. Britain and France were members of all the committees.

The other delegates rose up like so many honeybees whose hive had been jostled. The Turkish delegate requested recognition. He thought, he said, that the Executive Committee was admirable, as far as it went - although he did wish to point out that "it represented only Western Europe." The Turkish delegate wished to state that Turkey "had an economy complementary to that of Western Europe and, while agreeing with the need to keep the Executive Committee small, he suggested the inclusion in it of either Greece or Turkey in order to represent a region which is economically important and also comparatively unknown."

The Greek delegate "expressed his agreement with the views of the Turkish delegate."

Alphand swatted the Turks and Greeks at once, saying that he felt the concern of the Turkish and Greek delegates had been fully covered by their representation on the Committee of Cooperation, in which the ultimate authority of the conference reposed. In addition, either Greece or Turkey was represented on all of the Technical Committees, and they might well find themselves on some of the subcommittees that would be set up. Alphand thought, however, that an increase in the size of the Executive Committee "would be to the ultimate disadvantage of Greece and Turkey in that it would over-burden the machinery of the conference and make the accomplishment of its task difficult."

Sir Oliver Franks associated himself with the views of Alphand.

The Portuguese delegate requested the floor. He wished to state that Portugal was not represented on the Food Committee as proposed by the French, although Portugal - 90 percent of whose exports were comprised of agricultural and sea products - was particularly interested in food.

Sir Oliver Franks suggested that "at the present juncture, discussion of the sub-committees to be set up was anticipating the work of the Technical Committees themselves."

The Greek delegate spoke up to express the wish of Greece to participate in the work of any subcommittee which might be set up to deal with sea transport.

The Turkish delegate expressed the same wish in case an agricultural subcommittee should such be set up by the Food and Agricultural Committee.

Alphand stated that he considered the wishes expressed by the Greek and Turkish delegates to be quite normal.

The Italian delegate stated that Italy, as an industrial country, would like to participate in any subcommittee set up by the Iron and Steel Committee.

Franks soothed the delegates: The remarks made by various delegates, said Sir Oliver genially, "suggest a large measure of approval for the membership proposals submitted by the French delegation." The Working Committee, said Sir Oliver, was now anticipating future work rather than commenting on proposals before the meeting. He suggested that the Working Committee "might now express its agreement on the French proposals and terminate its work." Sir Oliver's suggestion was approved, and the Working Committee adjourned.

Caffery cabled home: "I submit following preliminary appraisal . . . based on day-by-day information contacts which we have maintained with number of delegates from participating countries: . . . Organizational plan. There is general agreement that organizational plan provides workable basis, consisting of: (a) conference proper which is now adjourned but will probably reconvene to receive and approve final plan. (b) The committee of European economic cooperation. This is in effect conference proper but committee device is used to permit closed sessions. . . . (c) Executive Committee. (UK, France, Netherlands, Norway, and Italy.) This is in effect steering committee. (d) Technical committees. Four of these (food and agriculture, energy, iron and steel, and transportation) have already been established and will begin work tomorrow."

In Washington, meanwhile, British Minister Sir John Balfour informed Secretary Marshall in a note: "I think that we can regard the limited size and actual membership of the Executive as extremely satisfactory. . . . The Turks, in particular, made an attempt to enlarge the membership of this Committee by the addition of themselves, but the other Delegations felt that this would have been quite inappropriate and their suggestion was therefore withdrawn. On the whole, I am glad to be able to tell you not only that the composition of these committees is satisfactory in itself, but also that it has been arrived at without any visible ill-will or dissatisfaction. Our final meeting today was conducted in a very genial atmosphere."

One of the English delegates, Sir Roger Stevens, wrote home to his wife: "Today has been relatively quiet. We started working at 9 a.m. and I stopped at 7:30 p.m. So far things have gone fairly well, the chief trouble *entre nous* being with the Dutch who have a one and a half year plan and obstinately say they cannot work to a four year plan which unfortunately happens to be what Mr. Marshall ordered. Their official representative is a fussy tiresome character with more than the usual quota of Dutch obstinacy. The national types are quite interesting. The Belgian is an insufferable and pedantic bore, the Turk - a former Foreign Minister - a pompous gas bag, the Swiss like a dormouse who wakes up at the end of the party and tries to go back to the beginning, the Scandinavians frightfully sensible, the only people - apart from the French and ourselves - who really understand what it's all about. But on the whole there is a general fund of goodwill."

As delegates from one country or another jostled to take advantage of the delicate balances of interests and power among the nations present, it fell to Alphand and Franks to discipline the negotiations. Sir Oliver said at once that he thought that the conference needed to reach clear conclusions on three broad areas: (1) measures to increase European production; (2) arrangements to stabilize the finances of the participants, both internally, within each nation's own economy, and externally, in the balance of trade and payments among nations; and (3) measures to facilitate European trade.

To solicit each nation's assessment of what it needed and what it could contribute, the Technical Committees sent out questionnaires to the home governments of all the participants. The detailed responses to these questionnaires would provide the conference with the grist for its negotiating mills. The individual governments were admonished to make honest appraisals of their needs - not merely to draw up shopping lists of all the things they would love to have if only they had the money.

The British set an example in this, as in so many other matters. Lecturing themselves mercilessly on the evils of shopping lists, a half-dozen members of the Board of Trade met with several members of the Foreign Office and the Treasury and bureaucrats from the Ministries of Transport, Agriculture, Fisheries, Fuel and Power, Supply, and other departments, and drew up a list of everything they wanted if they could get away with asking for it. On the matter of shipping, they naturally agreed that Britain, queen of the seas, would consider it proper to ask the United States, independently of the Marshall Plan, to postpone recovery of parts of its own shipping industry so as not to compete with Britain; as a part of Marshall Plan arrangements, the British thought they might get the gift or loan of American ships to make up for British deficiencies; and, as a general matter of policy, freight rates should *not* be reduced (although the French would undoubtedly urge reductions), since that would harm British balance of payments.

"Everybody cheated like hell in Paris. Everybody," said E. H. van der Beugel of the Netherlands about these early days of drawing up national estimates of needs.

In other areas of interest, the British decided to tell some small harmless lies. As for lorries, for instance, the British did not wish to end up having to import American vehicles, and so in the economic projections they would present to the United States they decided they would show that they did not project any shortage of lorries - whatever the facts might be. As for fertilizers for agriculture, the British decided they had two choices: They could estimate the amount of fertilizers they expected British farmers to use, or they could estimate the amount that it would be good to have British farmers use if an expanded agricultural program were to be devised. The negotiators had little trouble resolving how to handle that question: They would present the higher figures in Paris, and give in if they had to.

The question of fertilizers did, however, open up far more complex and momentous issues: The relationship of Britain to its empire raised scores of questions about nitrates, phosphates, potash, wheat, coal, wool, currencies, fuel, yarn, tractors, smelt. Committees proliferated with subcommittees charged to sort out the minutiae of trade on which the fates of whole peoples depended. The interrelationships of Britain with her colonies, those colonies with one another, and the colonies with other nations and with the colonies of other nations, the adjudication of the needs of one colony to balance its trade in phosphates with a dependency of another nation needing wool in trade for nitrates in trade for tractors: Such infinitely tortuous complexities had never been subject before to common, coordinated, detailed planning.

The nations of Western Europe, never having gathered before to take a complete common inventory - of themselves, and of their dependencies and colonies and possessions as well - were at once impressed by the sheer weight of facts - too enormous a burden, in fact, to deal with. Yet, the delegates were undaunted, for one thing was certain in the face of this vast complexity: The process of reasoning would be deductive, not inductive. These politicians were not economic determinists, after all. They would begin with their political wishes and deduce their needs from their wishes. They would not reason their way up from facts to abstract structures; they would begin with political structures and, to the extent they could, for as long as they could, invent the facts to fit the structures. Eventually, their planning might be tempered by some economic realities, but there was no reason to start with too much reality.

The essential task for each nation, as it sent its teams of negotiators in to grapple with the appalling complications of everyday planting and reaping, weaving and sewing, sawing and bricklaying, was to establish the guidelines along which each negotiating team would thrash out its particular batch of numbers.

The way things were thrashed out would depend, to be sure, on such factors as coal production, climate, agricultural machinery, skilled workers, and all the other constituents of economic power. But economic power was only one factor, among many others: more elusive considerations of sheer size, military power, colonial relationships, networks of longstanding agreements and simple compatibilities, national reputations, courage, and all the other elements that comprise political power, or weakness. As in poker, although the transaction would be in cash, the play was in nerve, bluff, pride, and luck. The diplomats would, of course, speak to one another in terms of money and production and trade, but the issue over which they tussled, and which they would resolve, was their relative political standing. Eventually - in the matter of foodstuffs in particular - questions would be raised about the differences in the standard of living in different countries. How much the British ate as compared to the Italians was not necessarily a given fact of nature or economics so much as a negotiable question of imports and exports and standards of production and consumption to be set by diplomatic negotiation. The various nations might agree to set a common standard for all countries - so many calories per person - which would mean trimming one nation's standard for the sake of raising another's. Or the various nations might agree to recognize a certain level of consumption as "normal" - say, the levels that had existed just before the war. Or they might hold other nations to "normal" standards while they raised their own.

The British were lucid on their aims. "Our interests," said one British policy paper, "are clearly against direct comparison of our consumption level with that of other participants" - to leave open the possibility of raising, say, agricultural levels in Britain but not elsewhere. If comparisons were to be made, however, the British would prefer taking prewar levels as a normal standard.

Some nations, as the British said to Caffery, might look on the Marshall Plan as an opportunity for nothing but a "spending spree." Not so the British: they wanted nothing but a boost back to their "normal" levels of production and consumption, and they wanted none of their rivals to get a boost beyond them. In fact, they insisted on writing in a paragraph in the working plan of the conference: "Standards of consumption during period under review, while they should be determined with regard to their effect on ability and incentive to produce, should not exceed those which each country expects subsequently to be able to maintain without special external assistance." No one, in short, should try to get the jump on Britain.

It seemed to the French, on the other hand, that the Marshall Plan was precisely an opportunity to get the jump on Britain - and Germany, and Belgium, and the Netherlands, and Luxembourg. In fact, the Benelux countries were irritated with the French from the beginning of the conference. "In order to get at the root of the problem," Caffery cabled home, "British first had Benelux group to dinner and found that Belgians took dim view of Monnet plan because in half dozen instances French were projecting large production increase for items which Belgians were either producing or expecting to produce and for which they regarded France normal market."

Furthermore, the French still - even at this late date - seemed determined, as Caffery reported home, to take a "pastoral" approach to Germany, an approach that included "pulling the heavy industrial teeth" of the Germans.

Léon Blum, writing in the Socialist journal *Populaire,* tried to put the French position nicely. While Germany would need to be reconstructed, said Blum, its reconstruction should not have "priority over Germany's victims or . . . lay a foundation for future German aggression." The problem, said Blum, was to determine, first, just how much the German people needed to get along (not much, in the view of some Frenchmen), and then set a level for its exports to the rest of Europe, while at the same time taking the "necessary measures to ensure security." Such measures ought to include a prolonged occupation of Germany, a decentralized German state (governed by the several occupational forces in their several zones), the prohibition of certain manufacturing activities (weapons, for instance), and the international operation of Germany's principal industrial regions, particularly the Ruhr.

The French wheedled the Americans relentlessly. Clayton and one of his aides were taken to lunch by the head of the Banque de France and the French Finance Minister, Robert Schumann. "They had us to lunch," said Clayton's aide, "to spell out in detail their financial plight. They took us to a cafe in Montparnasse (the one Hemingway used to frequent, I've forgotten the name), took us to a little room upstairs, and for lunch we had very little to eat: only a few vegetables, a salad, black bread, not any butter or any meat. They were trying to impress us with their poverty."

The French never lost an opportunity to plead their case - even if, as sometimes happened, they had to swallow their pride. One of the Italian delegates stopped by Clayton's office one day (the Italians were pleading their case, too) and reported that the waiting room was full of people. "Like a dentist's waiting room. An old chap sitting in a corner, looking as if he had a bad toothache. He'd been waiting fifty minutes. By Heaven, it was Ramadier, the French Prime Minister!"

France, said Monnet over dinner with Clayton, was "the key country in the implementation of the Marshall proposals." (Nearly all the diplomats in Paris agreed with him, although not in the way Monnet meant. Franks, for one, was going around discreetly complaining that France was the principal obstacle to progress in Paris. The French attitude toward Germany, he said, was "an emotional one.") Two things, said Monnet, must be done to bring about an understanding between France and the United States. "The German problem must be settled; France must put her financial and monetary house in order."

Clayton agreed. The German problem, he said, was composed of three elements: (1) security; (2) the political and economic power which the Ruhr gave Germany in her relations with her neighbors; and (3) competition between Germany and France. Clayton had sympathy for the French on the first two points, he said; but he had no sympathy for France if all the French wanted to do was forcibly curtail German production in the

Ruhr and allow corresponding French industries to be built up in France.

Some individuals in France, said Monnet, might harbor some wishes along the lines Clayton suggested, but certainly the French government and the French people as a whole did not want to hold German production down.

Still, for all their cheerful reassurances that they wished for an agreeable settlement with Germany, the French seemed impossibly stubborn to the Americans. At last, to try to whip Bidault into shape, the planners in Washington dispatched no less a figure than Averell Harriman to Paris to have a chat with the French Foreign Minister.

Harriman, Secretary of Commerce, former Ambassador to Great Britain, former Ambassador to Russia, was fifty-five years old. The son of a financier who had extensive railroad holdings, Harriman graduated from Groton and from Yale, where he was a member of Skull and Bones. He was an excellent polo player, with an eight-goal rating, and he had, even as a young man, as *Time* magazine would say of him, a "glossy" appearance, "an ingratiating if aristocratic charm."

His father died when he was seventeen, and he and his brother inherited a fortune estimated at between $70 and $100 million. By the age of twenty-nine, Harriman had parlayed his inheritance into a railroad and shipping fortune and a private bank, W. A. Harriman and Company, which he later merged with the investment firm of Brown Brothers. By 1932, at age forty, he was a partner in Brown Brothers, Harriman, the chairman of the board of the Union Pacific Railway, and a friend of President Roosevelt, who appointed him administrator of Division II of the National Recovery Act in 1934. As he moved from private to public business, acquiring a broader view of just how his personal interests sat in the context of national and international economic arrangements, Harriman became known as an instinctive diplomat - a man with a fine feeling for deft compromise. In business gatherings, he would oppose businessmen who opposed the New Deal, and in Washington, he would oppose New Dealers who wished to tax business heavily or favor the interests of labor.

Roosevelt promoted him swiftly up through the ranks: to chief of the raw materials branch of the Office of Production Management in 1941, to "defense expediter" in London in March of the same year, when the Lend-Lease Act went into effect to give wartime aid to Britain, as liaison officer between the British and American governments, as the American representative to Moscow to discuss extending lend-lease aid to Russia, and finally, in 1943, as Ambassador to Russia.

Harriman resigned as Ambassador to Russia in February 1946, before rhetorical fashions had thoroughly hardened against Russia. "Russia," said the retiring ambassador, "does not want war with the United States and is trying to cut off avenues of invasion by surrounding herself with friendly small nations." And again: "It is a fact that the Russian ideology is completely different from ours, but if we both adopt the attitude of live and let live, as to internal affairs, and if we both respect the right of all people to choose their own way of life, this barrier needn't be insurmountable. Most of the people of the world know that this is the attitude of the United States."

The next month, Harriman was appointed Ambassador to the Court of St. James's, a position in which his personal style seemed thoroughly at home. He had been in London, he said, "on and off since I was a boy," and the British press generally accounted him a "very close friend of Britain." Barely seven months later, however, when Truman scuttled Henry Wallace for making speeches against the policy of "getting tough" with Russia, Harriman was recalled to Washington to become Secretary of Commerce, and the new member of the cabinet had begun to change his tone about Russia. "A country," he said, "which attempts to gain security through unilateral action, through aggressive independent action, is only opening the gates of disaster." His appointment to Truman's cabinet was taken as a signal by Arthur Krock of *The New York Times* that Truman was consolidating his cabinet around a unanimous policy toward the Soviet Union.

Caffery sat in on the conversation between Harriman and Bidault in Paris. Harriman opened by congratulating Bidault for the work already accomplished by the conference, "which augured well for the future."

"We have, indeed, worked well," Bidault replied fretfully, "but elsewhere I am very alarmed." He had heard rumors "that an agreement has been reached between the United States and Great Britain relative to the Ruhr mines. That is serious. The management of the mines is to be put back in the hands of the Germans, and there are to be no reparations."

Bidault was on shaky ground. The French had been asked to join with the Americans and the British to fuse all three of their occupation zones into one. While the British had agreed at once (and so created the Bizone), the French had held back. It seemed somewhat unfriendly of them, suspiciously independent, as though it might be part of their game to remain independent between East and West; certainly it seemed as though the French did not want to be members of the team with the Americans and British.

Bidault could not satisfactorily explain this French reluctance to join with the others. "My answer," he said lamely, "is that it is impossible to do everything at once."

In any case, he said, "every decision made without consulting us renders fusion more difficult. There is becoming apparently a tendency to abandon federalism, and measures are taken which are definitely contrary to the interests I have to guard. I have done and am doing much, but I cannot do everything. And particularly not all at once.

"Although I regret greeting you with these words, I believe it is my duty to speak frankly: We have 180 Communists who say: 'The Marshall Plan means Germany first.' If something permits them to say this again, whether with ostensible or real reasons, I tell you the Government will not survive."

Bidault drove the point home: "I am not in a position to overcome the simultaneous opposition of General de Gaulle, the Communist Party, and a not negligible fraction of my own friends. Besides, I don't want to. All this has to do with Germany, of course. We know how things are going to come out. It is perfectly clear that we must accomplish the fusion of zones, that the Germans must be permitted to live and to produce, and that the categorical positions which we had defended at the beginning will have to be modified. But I repeat, if this additional burden is thrown on my shoulders in such conditions that I could not offer a valid answer, I would be in absolutely no position to confront the situation, after everything I have already done."

In a few days, said Bidault, he would be called before a Parliament that included 180 Communists and 120 Socialists and asked to explain the Truman Doctrine in Greece, the Paris Conference on the Marshall Plan, and the outright break with the Soviet Union. "If, in addition, I must explain the agreement contemplated among you with regard to the Ruhr and German production, I shall not succeed."

When Bidault subsided, Harriman took up the conversation calmly. He understood Bidault's preoccupation completely, he said. He was not, he said, "exactly up to date" on discussions about the Ruhr, or just what had been concluded, but he could assure Bidault that "they contained nothing contrary to the interests of France. The most important thing contemplated was the increasing coal production, which was, after all, in the interest of Europe as a whole."

Perhaps Mr. Harriman had not heard? "I am entirely in agreement to increase production of Ruhr coal," said Bidault, ". . . obviously, one can try to find a formula for agreement. But the wind is taken out of my sails when decisions are made in this fashion."

But no "definitive decision" had been made, said Harriman. As a matter of fact, there were still divergences between the British and American points of view. The United States did feel, however, "that if the Germans were made directly responsible for production, it would increase." But there was, in any case, "no question of giving the Germans management independence, but only of making them responsible for production."

Caffery spoke up to verify Harriman's remarks. The British had said they were in favor of nationalization, but Bevin had more recently agreed to put the nationalization question "on ice."

Bidault did not seem quite to believe it. "My associates have told me," he said, "from the little information they have available, that these agreements prejudge the final solution and at the very worst moment for my Government. I have, of course, my own ideas as to the final solution, but that this should intervene now carries the risk of wrecking everything."

Harriman repeated that no decision had been taken on the ultimate question of ownership, and nothing had been done contrary to French interests.

"My anxiety," Bidault said, "comes from the following: Ten days ago Mr. Bevin told me: 'We must discuss this.' I answered: 'Agreed.' Since then, nothing more has been heard."

As late as that very afternoon, said Caffery, nothing definite had been heard at the American Embassy in Paris about any Anglo-American agreement.

Still, Bidault insisted, he was "most alarmed." Of course, he said, "there is no question of leaving Germany in the depths. It is a very unfortunate nation today, but if a spectacular gesture is made, against which I should have to protest, I repeat that I can't imagine how I could stay in my present position. I apologize for using personal arguments, but that is how political problems are."

The attention of the Americans was suddenly seized. What, Harriman inquired, did Bidault mean by a "spectacular gesture?"

The British and Americans contemplated raising steel production in Germany, said Bidault. These steel figures were "very startling." "I am compelled to say that I absolutely do not see how I could explain the situation without saying things disagreeable for everybody . . . admitting that we are not in agreement. I should finally have to resign because I shall have been in the wrong."

The thought of the French Foreign Minister resigning - blaming the United States for fattening Germany at the expense of France - sobered Harriman considerably. He would, he said, pass Bidault's message on to Marshall.

"I know very well," said Bidault, "that Germans are Europeans, and I have never been a 'German-hater.' However, for political reasons there are people who are. I tell you again that I and the Government are in danger of being in a tragic situation. I don't need to repeat it, you have understood perfectly."

The conversation was ended.

And yet, if Bidault made the Americans uncomfortable, there were others who could make the French feel discomfort.

The tendency of the French, Belgian Premier Paul Henri Spaak said with nice understatement, was "to view the problem in too narrow scope."

The "smaller" nations of Europe had a few common interests, in Spaak's view: They had, many of them, long-standing trade relationships with Germany that were crucial to their economies, and a long-standing suspiciousness of the French. The smaller nations, if they could get together, could hobble France, bring Germany back into the European economy in such a way as to help the smaller countries, and so, by serving both themselves and the political needs of the Americans, hope to prosper.

Spaak had a sometime ally in H. M. Hirschfeld, who was in Paris to represent the Netherlands. Hirschfeld, like the British, took the position that Europe should be restored - not that more factories should be built here or there, but that the productive capacity of Europe, "including Germany," should be restored and put back into full use. Second, said Hirschfeld, trade had languished. If trade were restored, that too would help Europe's balance of payments. Third, European imports of food and raw materials from her colonies were insufficient. If these imports were brought back up to snuff, then Europe's economy would be enormously aided. As Hirschfeld saw it, the Marshall Plan did not need to finance grand new projects but simply assist Europe in getting its old productive capacities and economic arrangements working again.

Hirschfeld "emphasized the need to take short-term problems as a starting point. It was first necessary to make full use of existing productive capacity . . . . He did not wish to exclude discussion of national plans for increasing production, industrialization, etc., but pointed out that they might need reconsideration if a policy were adopted of making full use of existing European productive capacity."

Hirschfeld's remarks certainly seemed unexceptionable. But, nonetheless, Alphand took exception. "If the Netherlands delegate," said Alphand, "contemplated increasing German production beyond the level of security, the French Government would take an entirely negative position. . . . Security, for a country like France, which had been invaded, must be the overriding consideration. In the view of the French Government, the restoration of the German economy was not one of the tasks of the Committee."

Hirschfeld explained that he had "only intended to suggest that the German problem should be treated as a European problem." And then he pointed out, with only the faintest hint of impatience, that "Holland, as well as France, had been invaded."

Soon the Italian delegates, representatives of another of the "smaller" nations that was interested in the favor of the United States, would speak up to observe that Germany had been Italy's principal market for agricultural produce before the war, that exports to Germany had represented 20 percent of Italy's total exports, that Italy had received 27 percent of her total imports from Germany, that "the economies of Italy and Germany were largely complementary," and that Italy, therefore, "recognized the need for a renewal of trade between Germany and other European countries and agreed . . . on the need for the reconstruction of the German economy within the framework of European cooperation."

In Rome, meanwhile, Monsignor Giovanni Battista Montini, the Vatican Undersecretary of State (who later became Pope Paul VI), met late one evening with an American Foreign Service officer to see whether the Vatican could be of any use to the

Americans. At the request of the British, Montini had already been modestly helpful - planting a story in *Osservatore Romano* saying what a fine thing the Marshall Plan was, how important for America to help Europe and England. Montini wondered whether the Americans thought they would be able to bring Spain into the Marshall Plan. The American Foreign Service officer did not reply directly; he thought, he said, that American public opinion was not too favorable to the dictatorship of Generalissimo Franco. Indeed, he wondered whether Montini might not agree that the continuance of Franco's government might make it even more possible that the Communists would succeed in seizing power in Spain. Montini's reaction, the American officer reported back home, "was guarded." The monsignor said only that "he had not before heard this line of reasoning, which he characterized as very subtle." And the monsignor dropped the question of Spain at once.

Then Montini, "who is quiet, almost somber, spoke with rare enthusiasm" about the Paris Conference. The monsignor said - with what must seem, in the light of all the squabbling and backroom maneuvering going on in Paris, to have been either extraordinarily naïve or extraordinarily farsighted - that he thought the Paris Conference would lay the foundations for an eventual "United States of Europe."

17
MORE FRIENDLY AID

MARSHALL "PLAN" – KENNAN headed a memorandum summing up the current situation for Secretary Marshall on July 21: "We have no plan."

Actually, the State Department's plan had been exactly to have no plan, to force the Europeans to bring themselves together to come up with something. Yet the Europeans seemed a little slow in getting off the mark, in defining the basic assumptions on which their planning would rest - defining, for instance, just what level of "recovery" they were meant to achieve. And so, even though the Americans did not want to take over the task of designing the recovery program, it seemed that the State Department would have to offer a little help.

A committee met in the Old State Building to consider basic assumptions and definitions that might be passed along to the Europeans. Young Charles Kindleberger took notes. Members of Kennan's staff were there, along with other State Department men. The first subject was commodities.

"Question 1: What basis of requirements should be used by the European subcommittees; prewar, some planning standard, or a practical approach?" The committee concluded that no single standard could be applied to all European countries but that, in general, the plan ought to aim at attaining a self-sufficient European economy at a "practicable" standard of living in a period of four years, as the British had been saying. National economies would be restored to a level that they could then sustain on their own without additional outside help.

The plan would try, first, to break any bottlenecks in European trade, to get trade flowing, then to restore any factories and mines that were not productive, to get them working again - to concentrate, that is, on immediate, short-term goals.

As bland and sensible as the quick, short-term restoration strategy seemed, it did bring up just the sticking point that Hirschfeld and Alphand had been arguing about in Paris. If the Marshall Plan aimed at restoring Europe quickly to a level of self-sufficiency, then it would necessarily rebuild

Germany as a powerful member of a self-sufficient Europe. But the French had hoped to take a longer term view of things - the view that they had incorporated into their Monnet Plan - whereby Europe would be rebuilt with a less powerful Germany (and a relatively more powerful France) over a longer period of time. Whether one favored a short-term or a long-term plan, then, seemed to be a way of favoring a German-dominated or a French-dominated Continent. The committee declared itself for a short-term plan.

Next, the committee stepped calmly into another hornet's nest. The members of the committee wondered whether the United States might insist that the Europeans arrive at a better division of labor and allocation of resources than their current economic plans envisaged - whether, that is, spending on social programs should be curtailed. Having raised the question, however, the members of the committee quietly backed away from it. Although Clayton had not hesitated to reprimand the British for "socialization," the committee was more circumspect. It was enough that the Marshall Plan would buttress the incumbent governments of Europe; those governments would do the rest. More prompting would only hurt.

Then, finally, the committee stepped back into other treacherous territory. They suggested that the United States declare that it would look upon the formation of a European customs union "with favor." The question of such a union could not be ignored: It seemed to contain "the kernel of the problem of European recovery since it addresses the basic question of whether European recovery actually can be accomplished without the various European countries departing from their customary nationalistic approach to European problems and without a certain degree of infringement of their sovereignty." But the State Department did not want to make too strong a statement to this effect: America did not want to appear to be insisting upon such infringements on sovereignty. Also, the United States did not want to push Europe too quickly into a customs union, since "it is questionable whether Britain can [in a customs union] retain her present position as an important factor in European trade and at the same time the pivot of Empire trade." Any sudden move might sink Britain and give the Continent to France. But a slow, easy drift toward a customs union would be excellent.

Although in many such meetings the Americans refined these and other notions about what the Marshall Plan might be - and passed their gently worded thoughts along by cable to Caffery and Douglas and others in Paris - the Europeans seemed to continue to drift along drawing up their shopping lists and bickering, completely oblivious to the hints the Americans were slipping to them.

Toward the end of July, as a sense of anxiety spread from the American diplomats in Paris back to Washington, Paul Nitze was dispatched to France to meet with Clayton, Caffery, and Douglas.

Nitze was one of the State Department's bright young men, just forty years old at the time - an agreeable, modest, well-dressed, hard-working young man, skier, tennis player, product of Harvard and Wall Street, former chief of the metals and minerals branch of the Board of Economic Warfare, vice-chairman of the United States Strategic Bombing Survey, deputy director of the Office of International Trade Policy in the State Department - and capable, among other things, of tireless negotiations.

In conversations that took place over the next several days in Paris, Caffery spoke of the French situation and point of view, Douglas of the British, Clayton of the Italian, and Nitze listened. At the moment, Douglas said, the British were exhausting their dollar resources at the rate of $100 million a week. If they received no help, they would have to cut into their gold reserves by Thanksgiving. Soon enough, they would have to depreciate the pound, slash imports, withdraw from a number of foreign commitments, and radically alter their foreign policy.

France, said Caffery, faced a similar situation. In addition to the sort of dire possibilities Douglas raised for Britain, Caffery foresaw the results of a bad harvest in France: only five months more of bread.

Italy, said Clayton, might scrape through until January, but after the turn of the year, the Italians would not be able to contract for any more imports of food. Altogether, Clayton, Caffery, and Douglas thought that a special session of Congress ought to be called to get immediate aid to Europe.

It may be that Caffery and Douglas had succumbed to the usual disease of the Foreign Service officer: They had spent so much time in the countries to which they had been assigned that they had, as was sometimes said of Foreign Service officers, "gone native"; they had lost the American point of view and taken on the French and British points of view as their own.

Clayton, too, was moved by what he saw, and alarmed. If immediate steps were not taken to rescue Britain and France, "irreparable" damage would be done: "If the United Kingdom for example were forced to pull out of a number of areas for financial reasons . . . a vacuum would be created which would be filled then by another foreign power - maybe the Soviet Union."

Among the other aides and junior officers who were listening in on these conversations was Robert Murphy, who had flown in from Germany to represent the point of view of the U.S. Army occupation administration there - that is to say, of General Lucius Clay. Murphy was a great hulking fellow, fifty-three years old, six feet four inches tall, 223 pounds, red-headed and balding, a man who loved a game of high-stakes poker. The son of an Irish Catholic steamfitter from Milwaukee, Murphy had worked his way through college and law school and landed a job with the Foreign Service in Switzerland. He worked as a foreign officer in Germany, Spain, and France and established himself as something of a model of the career Foreign Service officer - dedicated to his country, plain-spoken in his dealings, shrewd but not devious, capable of playing a complicated hand well. At the beginning of World War II, he attended to American interests in Nazi-occupied France, juggling relationships with Nazi occupation forces, the collaborationist French government at Vichy, and French Resistance leaders. By the middle of the war, he had become chief civil affairs officer on the staff of General Dwight Eisenhower. He seemed to have a particular talent for mediating between the straightforward loyalty of military men to their country and the more complex attentiveness of politicians to political party, claque, class, and voters. At the end of the war, Murphy was appointed United States political adviser for Germany, with the rank of ambassador, where he spoke for the State Department while General Clay administered the zone in the name of the Army occupation forces.

As Murphy listened to the others, he began to worry that they were going to hog all American aid for their countries and neglect Germany. It had been "most interesting," Murphy finally said acerbically, "to listen to the exposition of the possible political effects of the deteriorating economic situation in France and the United Kingdom in view of the fact that the economic condition of Germany [is] so much worse than that in either the United Kingdom or France."

In case his colleagues might have missed his point, Murphy rubbed it in: The effect of "this adverse German economic situation remained to be seen," he said, but "the political direction in which 66 million Germans went might have a decisive effect on the European future."

As the American representatives to Europe threatened to dissolve into their own hostilities, Nitze stepped in to deliver the word from Washington. If American notions about European aid had been somewhat vague at first, clearer and firmer notions had been developing rapidly. The Planning Board of the State Department, said Nitze, had analyzed the European problem this way: America had already, in one form or another, given Europe about $10 billion worth of aid, and Europe was still a shambles. The only way to get Europe off the relief rolls and able to fend for itself was to see that the Europeans increased production. To achieve this goal, factories and transportation needed to be rebuilt wherever rebuilding could most easily and quickly be accomplished. Finally, conditions needed to be created whereby the Europeans could then trade their goods with one another, so that the revitalized production could be spread around for the benefit of all. Some multilateral trading system needed to be established. Politically - in terms, that is, of American domestic politics - Congress needed to be convinced that its appropriations would do the job. Congress could be most easily convinced if a program were designed for a specific, limited number of years, with the idea that appropriations would be made on a declining scale over that period so that, in the end, Europe would be self-sustaining. The goal, said Nitze, must be "a self-sustaining Europe at the end of three or four years."

As for Germany, said Nitze, the German economy needed to be rebuilt, and that was all there was to it. De-Nazification programs would need to be terminated so that the most qualified Germans could be employed in jobs and not be disqualified because of past political connections. (No political power, however, should be given to persons of "pronounced Nazi taint.") The American, British, and French zones of Germany needed to be brought into whatever multilateral trading system was set up for Europe. Management needed to be simplified and streamlined. More responsibility would have to be given to the German people. The Americans, British, and French would need to set up strict production controls, priorities, and allocations and ensure that the Germans directed scarce commodities to their proper ends. The French needed to be whipped into line.

Clayton, Caffery, and Douglas had long been eager to mix in with the Europeans and take a big hand in shaping the plan. Washington had told them not to interfere - that it was crucial for the Europeans to do their own planning, so that they could not complain later that the Americans had pushed them around, and so that the Americans would be free later on, if they did not like what had been drawn up, to reject it. Now the policy changed. In line with the directives laid down by Nitze, the Paris trio was instructed to offer the Europeans a little more "friendly" assistance.

18
THE WAR AGAINST THE ARMY

EVEN AS THE State Department was giving orders to its men in Europe, it was suddenly made the victim of a surprise attack by the U.S. Army. General Clay, in Berlin, was fed up with the dilatoriness of all the politicians and the continuing obstructionism of the French. Deciding that the Army ought to take matters into its own hands, Clay encouraged Secretary of the Army Kenneth Royall to speak up and tell the world what American foreign policy really was.

Royall found an opportunity to have in fact a full press conference and to tell the reporters - though he had cleared his statement with no one - that he knew "of no agreement by the War Department or the State Department to consult with France before the promulgation of the plan to raise the level of industry in Western Germany."

Bidault went mad. He demanded an explanation. A cable went out at once from the State Department in Washington to Caffery in France, instructing him to get hold of Bidault and tell him that Royall had spoken out of turn.

"You often reproach me for getting excited," Bidault said to Caffery when the American ambassador paid an afternoon call, "so I am going to keep calm."

Caffery did his best to reassure Bidault - although, by this time, the French Foreign Minister had all but given in to paranoia. Either the Americans were terribly disorganized, Bidault had concluded or they were just flimflamming the French. He listened, not too trustfully, as Caffery labored to reassure him; and then, at the end of the afternoon, as Caffery took his leave, Bidault, restraining himself from reaching any conclusions, told him, "I'll keep my shirt on."

Nonetheless, over the next several days, word trickled down from Bidault to his French colleagues - and the Americans began to notice something quite alarming: The French did not find it convenient to participate in any discussions in the Technical Committees until "satisfactory arrangements" had been made to discuss the

German level of industry. The whole conference was slowly grinding to a halt.

Who spoke for the American government? What was its policy? The conference in Paris awaited an answer before proceeding.

The questions were relayed to Washington and, since they involved matters of highest policy, were referred to the highest levels of the State Department, that is to say, to Secretary Marshall himself and to his new Undersecretary of State, Robert Abercrombie Lovett.

Lovett had replaced Acheson on July 1 - not because Acheson and Marshall had had any differences of opinion, but simply because Marshall, having been helped by Acheson to take over the State Department, now wanted his own man to come in as his principal deputy. Like Marshall, Lovett came from the South. His father was a Texas attorney; his mother was the daughter of a Confederate Army officer. In 1904, when Lovett was just nine years old, his father was named general counsel for all the Harriman interests in Texas, and when Averell Harriman's father died in 1909, Robert Lovett's father became president of both the Union Pacific and Southern Pacific railroads. The Lovetts moved to New York, and Robert was enrolled in the Hamilton Military Institute.

During World War I, the young Lovett took a leave from his student life at Yale and enlisted in the armed forces. He became one of the first of America's wartime pilots and flew repeated sorties over Germany during the war. At the end of the war, he returned to Yale, where he was a member of Skull and Bones, and graduated Phi Beta Kappa. After one year at Harvard Law School and another year at the Harvard Business School, he married Adele Quartly Brown and joined her father's investment banking firm, Brown Brothers. By 1926, at the age of thirty-one, he was a partner in the firm and a director and member of the executive committee of the Union Pacific Railroad. In 1931, by way of his father's connection with the Harriman family, he helped bring about the merger between Brown Brothers and Harriman.

Throughout the 1930s, Lovett kept his hand in at flying and made it his personal business to keep up with all the airplane factories in the United States. So it was that, when World War II broke out, Lovett knew all about planes and airplane factories in the United States - and, because of his business travels in Europe, all about potential industrial targets in Germany. He joined the War Department in 1940, and within four months he was named Assistant Secretary of War for Air. He pressed at once, and relentlessly, for the production of bombers as the number one priority of wartime industry.

By the end of the war, when Lovett returned to Brown Brothers, Harriman, he knew international relations and finance, and the politics of Washington; and he had established a close friendship with General Marshall. Like Marshall, he was not afraid of the Army.

Like Marshall, too, Lovett was a self-effacing, private, and strictly self-disciplined man. Bald, five feet ten inches tall, fine-boned, with a certain delicacy to his hands, he was given to the silk ties, French cuffs, and dark suits of the banker. He engaged in no sports; he liked to read westerns; and, as members of the State and War departments soon discovered, he did know, in the great American game of human relations, how to play hardball.

When word of Secretary of War Royall's press conference reached him, Lovett fired off a memo to Marshall. Royall's statements, said Lovett, represented a "disavowal" of Marshall's promise to consult Bidault on the German level of industry, which had been approved by Bevin on behalf of the British government, and which thus constituted a position taken jointly by the governments of the United States and the United Kingdom. Marshall's policy statement had been "personally cleared" with Secretary Royall by Charles Bohlen and by Marshall's personal assistant, General Marshall Carter, a memorandum of understanding having been drawn up and initialed by Secretary Royall.

Royall could not now undercut the State Department or declare that the State Department was in any way bound by some sort of right of veto by the War Department. "The Secretary of State with the responsibility for the conduct of American foreign policy by direction of the President, cannot be limited in foreign matters by any agreement with another Department of this Government without divesting him of the authority to carry out his responsibilities."

In order to gather the French back up again, Lovett continued, the State Department would need to have a tripartite meeting with the British and French in London and give the French a feeling of real participation in planning for Germany - and, in the meantime, stomp on the Army.

Within just a few days, Marshall found an opportunity after a cabinet meeting at the White House to take Secretary Royall aside for a moment. Marshall told Royall gently that the State Department intended to hold tripartite talks in London with the British and the French and that the American occupation forces in Germany would be invited to send General Clay as an "adviser." In short, Royall was made to understand that the War Department could advise, but the State Department would set policy.

Royall, Marshall said, in a memo back to Lovett, "accepted my views."

General Clay, on the other hand, flew into a rage. Murphy (at that time with Clay in Germany) cabled Washington that Clay declared the "decision is not acceptable to him and that it destroys any vestige of prestige he may still have, placing him in an impossible position. He spoke with bitterness over what he considers absence of conviction and principle on part [of the State] Department in this matter. He indicated he could not agree to go to London ... and he would also telegraph ... regarding his immediate retirement. He further said that all of this would make some form of public statement by him inevitable." In the past, Murphy said, he had been able to persuade Clay to stay on the job. "This time he really seemed to have lost interest and does not react to suggestions."

General Clay, great-grandnephew of the famous Henry Clay, grew up with an apparent assumption that he was born to command. He attended West Point, where, as historian Daniel Yergin has written, he "ranked first in English and history, but at the bottom in conduct and discipline." He was assigned to engineering school at Camp Humphrey, Virginia, and rose to become an instructor in engineering at West Point, company commander of the 11th Engineers in the Panama Canal Zone, assistant district engineer on the Allegheny River, adviser to the Philippine government on engineering projects, district engineer in charge of the Red River Dam construction in Texas. If

Clay knew anything, he knew construction, and reconstruction. At the end of the war, he was appointed deputy military governor, and later military governor, of the American occupation zone in Germany.

He loved being in charge. "Military governor," said another American administrator in Germany, "was a pretty heady job. It was the nearest thing to a Roman proconsulship the modern world afforded. You could turn to your secretary and say, 'Take a law.'" Or, as one of Clay's economic advisers said, all of Clay's opinions "are either black or white because he knows that when decisions are put into operation down the line the chiaroscuro will develop in sufficient quantities anyhow."

"I find talking to Clay very difficult," Charles Kindleberger wrote home during a visit to Germany. "He is personally very cordial, and frequently after a sweeping denunciation of the Department says with a smile that he doesn't mean me."

When he did not manage to get his way, he resigned. During his term as military governor, he threatened to resign at least eleven times. "The guy is really jealous on lines of authority," said Kindleberger. And usually, when he threatened, he got his way.

This time, however, he was threatening General Marshall. Marshall did not even deign to reply.

Then when Lew Douglas, in a panic, began firing off cables from London, Marshall replied to Douglas.

The "situation," said Marshall - that is, Clay's threat of resignation - "has arisen on frequent occasions in the past." Marshall was not impressed. "I feel that this is entirely a matter for War Dept. decision and that this Dept. should not inject itself in the matter." Clay then flailed and floundered, and in the end withdrew his resignation.

Marshall, having set his policy, put Lovett back in charge of carrying it out; and Lovett, having been quick to sense, and squash, a threat to his control of foreign policy, established himself in his new job with a sense of command that was communicated at once to the diplomats in Paris. And so, having disciplined the U.S. Army and secured his place at home, Lovett proceeded to discipline the French.

"From your cables," Lovett wired Caffery and Clayton, ". . . we gain the impression that too little attention is being paid by the participants to the elements of self-help and mutual aid. . . . We are concerned over this. . . . An itemized bill summing up prospective deficits against a background of present policies and arrangements will definitely not be sufficient. In approaching this problem, the Europeans might make more progress if they were to assume there was no one to help them, to imagine that they had no choice but to try to work out an acceptable economic future without any outside support, to elaborate the best program they could, and only then to undertake to define the gaps which absolutely could not be filled out of their own resources even by the most strenuous individual and collective effort." Unless the Europeans were ready to dispense with shopping lists and draw up realistic plans, the State Department might simply lose interest in presenting any plan to Congress.

"Furthermore, we consider that the problem of the leading Western European countries is not only to make up deficiencies caused by the vicissitudes of war, but *to adjust themselves* [the emphasis is added here] *to certain basic changes which have occurred and are continuing to occur in their international positions.*" Such adjustments might require "courageous and incisive action" on the part of the Europeans, "both individually and collectively," but the adjustment had to be made. "We are," said the Undersecretary of State, "entirely serious about this."

19
SKIRMISH IN THE
FOREIGN SERVICE

IN PARIS, CLAYTON, Caffery, and Douglas huddled with Sir Oliver Franks. The reports of the Technical Committees had begun to trickle in to the Executive Committee. It had already been learned, Franks had to admit to the Americans, that it would be necessary "on a global basis" to scale down some of the countries' minimum requirements for commodities "because they exceeded any possible availability."

The report of the financial experts was not heartening, either. Sir Oliver Franks' colleague Sir David Waley figured that "the deficit of the participating countries with the American continent for the four years was likely to be over $28 billion." Moreover, at the end of the four years, the Europeans would not yet have a viable economy; they would still be running a deficit for 1951 of more than $5 billion. The British and the Europeans, Franks said to Clayton, Caffery, and Douglas, were doing their best to keep the overall dollar amount low and to attain a viable economy in a period of four years; but early reports of the Technical Committees were not encouraging.

Next, said Franks, as far as a customs union was concerned, the French and the Italians were in favor of the idea. The British were not enthusiastic. The Benelux countries were not enthusiastic about a union that did not include the British. The Irish detested the idea, and the Turkish delegate had made a speech about the idea that nobody had understood. The other delegates were waiting for instructions from their home governments.

Clayton, Caffery, and Douglas replied that the United States did not insist on a customs union; the State Department wished only to point to the need for a constructive, long-term program, not just "an itemized bill summing up prospective deficits against a background of present policies and arrangements." The United States would favor "the eventual elimination" of trade and other barriers among the European group.

The three Americans then tried out some of Lovett's phrasing on Sir Oliver. The Europeans "might make more progress if they were to imagine that they had no choice but to try to work out their problems without any outside support."

Sir Oliver did not doubt for a moment the implications of such a suggestion: "If such a planning approach were used," he said, "it would result in a program based on self-sufficiency (as contrasted with a viable economy) and . . . the pattern would be entirely different from one based on fitting Europe into a world economy and on the assumption of some kind of outside assistance during the transitional period."

Clayton, Caffery, and Douglas thought about Sir Oliver's rejoinder and cabled Lovett: "We are inclined to agree with this point of view."

Then Clayton, Caffery, and Douglas began to slip away even more from their boss in Washington. They had decided simply not to pass on some of Lovett's remarks to Sir Oliver. The State Department's directions calling for "the full productive effort of European countries to solve their production problems in concert" seemed to suggest to the three Americans that the old "cartel practices" of Europe would be revived, and all the monopolistic practices of price-fixing and nationalistic economic competition would retard reconstruction and lead to "economic chaos."

"We hope," said the three Americans in their cable home - as they joined bureaucratic undertow to the active subversiveness of the Army and the French in trying to undo Lovett's orders - "the Department will . . . approve our action in not passing . . . on to Sir Oliver" some of Lovett's suggestions.

Lovett cabled back a reprimand within hours: "Department deeply concerned by indications that Paris Conference is not facing necessity of subjecting stated requirements of participating countries to critical analysis with a view to producing a final program whose statements of needed aid would be justifiable as realistic and based on maximum self-help and mutual aid."

The State Department felt that European statements of requirements were simply "being accepted" by Clayton, Caffery, and Douglas "without discussion." The American trio seemed remarkably passive; they seemed not to be forcefully representing American interests. If all the Europeans did was to add up separate estimates of their needs, with American acquiescence, it would "obviously result in unacceptable program."

Lovett's cable was gently, but firmly, worded. Was it clear? "Will Clayton, Douglas, and Caffery please comment re Depts apprehensions?"

Douglas, chastened, cabled home at once. "I share your apprehensions," he told Lovett. ". . . there is danger that final program may be both unrealistic as to product and inordinately large as to our assistance. . . . Agree important all countries at Paris adjust their production programs to realities."

Nonetheless, the Paris trio continued to try to wriggle out from under the directives that were coming to them from Lovett.

In Washington, Kennan met with Bohlen, Kindleberger, and a few others. "It was concluded that the time has come to firm up the overall departmental position. . . . It was the consensus that Mr. Clayton, while generally aware of departmental thinking with regard to the 'Plan,' holds fundamental divergent views on some aspects." In short, the men in Washington wondered what the hell was going on in Paris.

Lovett cabled Secretary Marshall, who was off attending the Inter-American Conference for the Maintenance of Continental Peace and Security in Brazil. "Progress," said Lovett of the conference in Paris, "so far is disappointing . . . all that has come out so far is sixteen shopping lists."

Lovett was impatient with the foolishness. "The present grand total of the shopping list approach is unreasonable." And not only was the grand total huge; even so, "these huge sums will not accomplish the rehabilitation over a four-year period, still leaving a deficit at the end of that time."

Lovett was convinced that "the time has now arrived for us to give some indications that the present plan is not acceptable." He suggested that a message be dispatched at once to the trio abroad saying that the State Department was determined to have from the Europeans a plan that would enable Europe to become self-supporting "at whatever minimum scale is tolerable" according to principles of "self-help and mutual help," rather than encourage them in the belief they can "lean on us to rebuild, on a long-term basis, their entire production machine."

To be sure, said Lovett, it would be desirable for the Europeans to rebuild their economies entirely. But such a thing could not be accomplished for years, "and we cannot support the drain of rebuilding Europe on a grand scale."

Clayton and Caffery, Lovett told Marshall, "have been out of touch with headquarters for some months and may not be wholly familiar with the work that has been done here." They needed to be put in the picture. It might be necessary to send out a couple of fellows from Washington to put them straight.

Finally, said Lovett, he thought it was common in all conferences that "no real progress will be made in obtaining real concessions involving the abandonment of national prestige or transitory competitive advantages until the deadline for adjournment approaches." So he thought it would be good to keep the pressure on the

Europeans - let them think that the Paris Conference needed to be brought to a close quickly - but let Sir Oliver Franks know confidentially that the United States would be prepared to have the conference extended for an extra two weeks for a final bumping together of heads.

What Lovett wanted from Marshall was the authority to go ahead with his plan. "Will you please authorize or amend the action outlined above at your earliest convenience."

Marshall cabled back from Brazil: "I concur completely in your views and action proposed."

In fact, even before he had heard from Marshall, Lovett had gone ahead and cabled Clayton, Caffery, and Douglas and told them how to go about shaping up Sir Oliver - that is to say, to "express to Franks . . . our grave concern."

Caffery seemed a trifle slow at grasping the idea that Lovett had stopped asking advice and started issuing instructions. Caffery, still tending to see things from the European point of view, cabled back to Washington to try to explain the tangle the Europeans were in.

The trouble was, said Caffery, that Western Europe before the war had been consuming $2 billion worth of goods and services more than it had been producing. With the war, the resources for financing such a deficit had disappeared. "The commercial isolation of Eastern Europe under Soviet controls has greatly reduced an important source for foodstuffs . . . and other materials which Western Europe previously financed by the sale of its manufactured products to the same area."

The job that the conference had done so far was simply to assemble the various countries' estimates, which, as one delegate said, "were aimed at prewar standard of living." These estimates, said Caffery, "presuppose a continuation of the basic economic pattern of the European economy with all the implications regarding low labor productivity and maldistributions of effort which derive from segregating 270 million people into 17 uneconomic principalities."

Grappling with all these problems, said Caffery, was not easy. The Europeans resisted really trying to solve the problems: The conference's "terms of reference" made the diplomats feel that they could not try to force any one country to change its position for the sake of all. "Home governments tend to act as a brake on the enthusiasms of some individual delegates who would be disposed to push through a bold constructive program." The United Kingdom, for instance, had been reluctant even to let the question of "living standards" be raised at the conference.

Clayton seemed a little quicker than Caffery. He wasted no more time explaining the European point of view. The European point of view had become tiresome, perhaps even to some of the Europeans. Clayton fell into line behind Lovett at once. On Saturday afternoon, August 25, Clayton sat down with Sir Oliver to chat for a couple of hours.

The numbers that the Americans were hearing come out of Paris, said Clayton, were "very disturbing." The total balance-of-payments deficit for 1948 through 1951 was said to be estimated at $19.9 billion for the United States and $28.2 billion for the American continent as a whole, starting with an $8.1 billion deficit for 1948, and gradually scaling down to $5.8 billion in 1951. Of course, said Clayton in his report to Lovett, "I told Sir Oliver in my opinion the $28.2 billion figure was out of the question."

Any notion the Europeans had about running a deficit actually higher than the deficit of 1946, said Clayton - and he thought that deficit had been somewhere between $5 and $6 billion in 1946 - would "create a very bad impression at home."

Franks replied rather coolly that what Clayton was suggesting would mean "a standard of living below prewar and would raise grave political problems for most of the countries."

The destruction to the European economy by two world wars, said Clayton, "was so enormous" that he doubted whether Europe could achieve "in the next decade" the sort of living standard it had had before the war, "even with all the help which had been provided by the United States." For at least several prewar years, he said, Europe had been living off its foreign investments - that is, its colonial possessions and other concessions - to the extent of $2 billion a year; all that was gone now, and would never be recovered.

Without a moment's hesitation, with barely a wave of the hand, Franks cut $5 billion from the $28 billion figure. A "quick examination of the supporting documents," he said casually, showed that the total could be "trimmed" by $5 billion. Some of the early estimates had included provisions for capital equipment that could be financed through the International Bank; some provisions called for commodities of such magnitude as to exceed total world supplies. Cutting $5 billion was no trick at all.

But, said Franks, if the total had to be reduced even further, "say to $15 billion," then he was certain that could only be done if the Americans "told" the Europeans that it had to be done.

Franks' hint was broad enough: He seemed almost to be asking for the Americans to dictate some terms. The Europeans on their own could not discipline themselves; their political problems at home were such that they could not be caught trimming their own requests. No diplomat could demand less than he was demanding. No one could be willing - or appear willing - to agree to a lower standard of living for his country. But if the Europeans were told what to do, Franks suggested, they might become very cooperative very quickly.

The time had finally come, Clayton concluded - and both Lovett and the Europeans had reached the same conclusion - "to impose certain necessary conditions."

20
AMERICANS IN PARIS

Gᴇᴏʀɢᴇ KENNAN STEPPED off the plane in Paris, accompanied by Colonel Charles Hatwell Bonesteel III, a regular Army officer who had been detailed to Kennan's planning committee. "Tick" Bonesteel was a tall, slender, gray-haired man with ice-blue eyes whose father and grandfather had gone, as he had, to West Point. The suave Kennan and the trim Bonesteel, the diplomat and the warrior - looking as though they had split Secretary Marshall between them - made a fine, up-to-date picture of two Americans in Paris.

The Europeans were, by this time, getting accustomed to seeing Americans in Paris. During the summer, as one of Clayton's aides put it, "almost every Congressional group that could think up an excuse to come over to Europe came over. Within six weeks, we had about 15 groups come over."

The groups were getting a lot of encouragement to visit Paris. The State Department - and the President - worked feverishly to round up congressmen and send them abroad, in the expectation that if the Marshall Plan were made sufficiently entertaining, votes would be easier to line up for its eventual approval by Congress. A young man named Philip Watts in the State Department served as tour director for the hastily formed Herter committee. Congressman Christian Herter, said Watts, "felt that by studying European conditions firsthand, members would convince themselves as to the desirability of Marshall's program." Wives and dinner jackets were left at home, and the congressmen did manage, despite the press of business, to have a good time in Paris.

Among many others who took the tour was Congressman Richard M. Nixon, then thirty-four years old, the newly elected Representative from the 12th District of California, where he had won by associating his opponent with Communists, who had established himself quickly in Congress as a member of the House Un-American Activities Committee, a strong internationalist, and a man of perfervid ambition and flexibility.

Even Vice-President Alben W. Barkley turned up in Paris along with Douglas MacArthur II (the General's nephew). Ivan White, the first secretary at the American Embassy, and his wife threw a dinner party and invited Barkley (who was Mrs. MacArthur's father), the MacArthurs, and the Claytons. The social whirl was maintained.

But of all the Americans in Paris, the Europeans had no trouble sensing at once that George Kennan was the significant one in the crowd. They knew of his background, of his current position as the chief of the Policy Planning Staff, and they had heard of a paper that had just been published in *Foreign Affairs* magazine, by a "Mr. X."

The "X" article was nothing other than Kennan's memo for Secretary of the Navy Forrestal on "The Sources of Soviet Conduct." Published in July, in the establishment magazine on foreign policy, under the mysterious byline of "X," it received even more attention, perhaps, than it would have if Kennan had merely put his name to it. The "X" gave it the caché of a piece of insider's gossip, and journalists and diplomats parsed every paragraph and word of it. Arthur Krock, writing in *The New York Times,* identified Kennan at once as the author of the document, and excerpts were picked up immediately and run in *Reader's Digest* and *Life.* The article's talk of "containment" was taken at once to be America's newest, official doctrine of foreign policy.

"Feeling like one who has inadvertently loosened a large boulder from the top of a cliff," Kennan recalled, "and now helplessly witnesses its path of destruction in the valley below, shuddering and wincing at each successive glimpse of disaster," Kennan began at once to take some criticism from the press. Walter Lippmann, for one, leapt on the "X" article as dangerously bellicose. It was filled with some of Kennan's most regrettable phrases about Russian paranoia and barbarism. (Even Kennan, in later years, was apologetic about such passages and protested he hadn't quite meant them as they were taken.) Moreover, said Lippmann, the notion of containing the Soviet Union within its borders was strategic nonsense. To announce it as a policy would require (as Wallace had pointed out months earlier over the Truman Doctrine) that the United States police every inch of the Soviet borders. The Russians would be automatically given the upper hand: they would be free to choose the time and place of any advance they might wish to make; America would be obligated to counter whenever the Soviets made a move, even if the time and place were the worst for America and the most advantageous for the Soviet Union.

Kennan was somewhat shocked at the response his article got. So, too, was Marshall. "It was a firm principle for him," Kennan said of Marshall, "that 'planners don't talk.' The last thing he had expected was to see the name of the head of his new Planning Staff bandied about in the press as the author of a programmatical article - or an article hailed as programmatical - on the greatest of our problems of foreign policy. He called me in, drew my attention to this anomaly, peered at me over his glasses with raised eyebrows (eyebrows before whose raising, I may say, better men than I had quailed), and waited for an answer."

Kennan explained the origins of the article, and that, before he had submitted it to *Foreign Affairs* magazine, he had sent it through appropriate channels for clearance. "This satisfied him. He was . . . an orderly man, accustomed to require and to respect a plain delineation of responsibility." If the article had been cleared, Marshall had no further questions.

And so Kennan, however bruised, was not knocked out of center place as an articulator of American foreign policy. With all its flaws, his article still commanded interest and respect, among the diplomats. Indeed, although Lippmann did point out the policy's essential flaw, and although Kennan continued to insist that he had not meant it as a "doctrine," and had not meant to be so harsh about the Russians, or so aggressive about his recommendations for American conduct - and although Marshall never formally endorsed the paper, and Kennan disowned it, and Lippmann disproved it - it nonetheless did become the basis of American foreign policy, accepted as a doctrine by many in Washington as well as in the rest of the world. For, however fatally flawed the policy might have been, it did express just what the Americans and their Europeans friends hoped to do.

Kennan and Bonesteel went at once into a two-day meeting with Clayton, Caffery, and Douglas, and from there into a session with Sir Oliver Franks, Hervé Alphand, and the other members of the Executive Committee of the Paris Conference.

Each time the basic assumptions of the Marshall Plan were talked through - however tedious the repetition had become - the thinking behind it became clearer. And, with Kennan leading the discussion, the ideas and aims of the plan were laid out very clearly indeed. The objective of the plan, the Europeans were told, was "the speediest possible reactivation of the European economic machine and for its restoration to a self-supporting basis." The conference's preliminary estimate of its dollar needs (in this discussion the ever-changing figure was quoted at $29.2 billion, another billion above previous estimates) was "much too large." The fact that the Europeans supposed they would still have a big deficit at the end of the four-year program "reflects the unsatisfactory nature of the methods by which it was calculated and the assumptions on which it was based."

The Europeans must understand a few essentials, said the emissaries from Washington. First, the plan must provide for a workable European economy for four years, able to sustain itself thereafter without outside aid. Second, the dollar amounts that America would provide should diminish over the period of four years, until aid was phased out entirely. Third, during the time of the plan, the Europeans would be expected to show "convincing evidence" that they were making progress. Fourth, long-term projects - such as the Monnet Plan for France - must not take precedence over immediate rehabilitation of existing productive facilities. Germany would be rebuilt at once. Fifth, the European countries would need to stabilize their currencies and generally get their financial houses in order. Sixth, the European countries would need to take steps toward eliminating trade barriers (a step toward a customs union). And, seventh, the Europeans must set up an organization that would oversee all these matters on a continuing basis.

At least the Americans were straightforward; there was no shilly-shallying. And Kennan always spoke graciously, without ruffling feelings. Nonetheless, Alphand and Franks were reduced to weak mutterings in response to this American laying down of the law.

Franks did venture the opinion that he was "doubtful" that the European economy could be self-sustaining at the end of four years, or that it could have brought its deficit down to zero. "We can get to a low figure," he said. But if the Americans insisted on planning toward zero, "we will have gone from the area of reasonable assumptions to paper construction."

One of the Scandinavians present said that "it must be assumed that after 1951, Europe would be a capital importing country in the broad sense."

Bonesteel agreed. The Europeans might still need to bring in outside capital, but such capital would need to come from private sources, or from the International Bank, not, after 1951, from the United States government.

Sir Oliver, said the Americans, might think that the Europeans could not reach a zero deficit in four years, but his expectations that deficits would persist might be "based on a higher standard of living than Europe's productivity will support."

The vision that sprang to some American minds was that of a bombed-out street: Walls were destroyed, roofs caved in, basements flooded, plumbing and wiring a ruined tangle - and the Europeans, rather than tightening their belts and doing without for a time, were gathering in the parlor for tea as usual, hoping the Americans would finance it all, and that the Europeans, meanwhile, would not have to cut down on their cakes and ale.

The European projections of steel production, for instance, seemed absurd to the Americans. The reports of the Technical Committees, said the Americans, "do not reflect a concerted effort to direct European production, trade, and manpower, in the most efficient and economic manner . . ." For example, "in determining the requirements of coal for steel production, account should be taken of the relative efficiencies of available plants" - that is, again, the French should let German mines and plants be rehabilitated. The problem of French intransigence on this matter had simply not been faced by the Europeans. "The report on steel avoided this problem by assuming that all existing steel capacity in the 16 participating countries would be operated at its maximum . . . and that there would be sufficient coal and transportation for this purpose." Everyone knew this was not the case. Some "selective utilization of productive capacity" would need to be made; that is, the French would need to agree to let German factories revive.

The French government, said Alphand, "had definite views on the question of utilization of productive steel capacity." He said no more.

Franks added some sympathetic murmurings in aid of his French colleague. It was true, he said, that the conference had not set standards of consumption for the sixteen nations, or engaged in critical analysis of one another's programs, or tried to force one or another nation to back down from its demands. The reason for this, he said, was that "the terms of reference for the Conference made it clear that there would be no diminution of sovereignty."

Neither Kennan nor Bonesteel replied to Sir Oliver's remark; their silence confirmed the worst suspicions - that some diminution of sovereignty, some lowering of expectations, some understanding of "basic changes in European conditions" and of America's new relative strength would need to be taken into account.

Sir Oliver found it hard, even in talking with the more realistic members of his own delegation, to face entirely what Kennan had to say. Sir Oliver persisted, even after his conversation with Kennan, in telling his colleagues that what the Americans wanted was a "good report" rather than an "indifferent report" - even if it took a little longer to produce a good report.

Kennan, meanwhile, did not depend on the members of the Executive Committee to convey his remarks in all their clarity to the rest of the delegates in Paris; he made his own diplomatic rounds, repeating himself at cocktail and dinner parties. And, once he had made his main points and moved along to more idle topics of conversation,

Kennan slipped in a characterization of his own government - and a suggestion for how the wily Continental diplomats ought to think about dealing with the Americans. There was "a new set of men in Washington," Kennan said, "with simple, honest minds." Subtlety on the part of the Europeans "must at all costs be avoided," and the Europeans ought to send "simple, honest men" to represent them in Washington.

Having accomplished his mission, having finished his whirlwind tour of Paris dinner parties, Kennan got back on the plane to Washington. Soon after he landed, he submitted, to the "simple, honest men" in Washington, his report.

The diplomats in Paris, said Kennan, were generally a hapless lot. None of the diplomats was a strong political figure in his own country. "There is none who could take any extensive liberties with the anxious reservations of the home governments." In the absence of the Russians as a focus for irritation and hostility, "the gathering has reverted, with a certain sense of emotional release, to the pattern of old-world courtesy and cordiality in which many of the participants were reared and for which they have instinctively longed throughout the rigors of a postwar diplomacy dominated by the Russian presence."

This political insignificance and this sense of luxuriating in the day-to-day comforts of diplomacy had given the conference a certain easygoing, pleasurable pointlessness. The general atmosphere of politeness had "practically ruled out any critical examination of the other fellow's figures - particularly as most of the delegates must have lively doubts as to the entire validity of some of their own, and cannot be eager to enter a name-calling contest between pot and kettle."

Nonetheless, the tendency to fiddle at the Paris Conference was no laughing matter. Many of the governments were operating under "formidable strains, internal and external." Some had economic problems with which they were politically too weak to cope. Some, perhaps all, were overcome by a sense of the terrible differences they harbored over Germany, and the difficulty of resolving those differences. The conference reflected, in sum, "all the weakness, the escapism, the paralysis of a region caught by war in the midst of serious problems of long-term adjustment, and sadly torn by hardship, confusion and outside pressure."

Under the circumstances, said Kennan, the Americans must not look to the Europeans to accomplish the impossible. The Europeans had scaled down their requests a little; they would scale down the requests even more. In the end, Kennan thought, the Europeans might even make a largely honest estimate of their financial situation.

"But glaring deficiencies will remain. No bold or original approach to Europe's problems will be forthcoming. No startling design will emerge here for the removal of the pitiful dependence of much of this great peninsular area on overseas supplies for which it cannot pay." Historically, the Europeans had always had a genius for living off the fat of other people's lands; they could not change all at once.

Britain in particular was a ruin. "Britain's position today is tragic to a point that challenges description. Her problems . . . are deep-seated and grave . . . as a body politic Britain is seriously sick. She is incapable of viewing her own situation realistically and dealing with it effectively." The tragedy of the Labour Party in England, said Kennan, was that it had waited decades to have a chance to put certain principles of social welfare into effect: "It has finally come into power at precisely the moment when those principles became essentially inapplicable" because Britain no longer had wealth to redistribute. "It is too much to expect the leaders of that movement to recognize that, as an intellectual proposition, and to take the consequences out of their own logical deduction." No, rather, the British leaders would have to be pushed into dropping many of their aspirations for social justice.

No one should hope, however, that the British could be pushed too quickly into seeing things from Kennan's point of view. The British would try to cling to their social programs. A gap between reality and vain hope would remain for some time - "a gap in which British governmental behavior will be unrealistic, erratic, slap-happy."

In the largest perspective, in any case, there was no hope for Britain at all. "With many of England's traditional sources of income lost" - that is to say, with the end of its empire - "I think there is for her no satisfactory economic future." America would simply need, in one way or another, to continue to keep a flow of money going to England; and, as a result, England would need increasingly to relinquish certain powers to the United States. The only real long-term solution for England's problems would be "some closer form of association between England, Canada, and our own country; something which would involve a sharing of certain of the powers of sovereignty among the three countries" - however upsetting such a prospect might be to the British. Kennan continued calmly: "There is no necessity that a move in this direction should take a form of any sudden or abrupt act. It can well be planned as a gradual process, to be completed through a five- or ten-year program."

As for Europe as a whole, most of the governments were "afflicted just at this time with abnormal weaknesses, fears, and prejudices. The illness of which the British government suffers is endemic among all governments in one degree or another. Britain's is an extreme case. But it is not the only severe case. . . . And the work of the Conference cannot logically be stronger than the political and psychological fabric of the war-torn, fear-wracked, confused and maladjusted area which is the object of its labors."

Kennan did not say that the United States ought to absorb all of Europe in quite the same way that it would need to absorb Britain. Still, only one major conclusion was possible. Whether or not such an approach might develop into a permanent habit, as far as present planning was concerned, said Kennan, the Americans would need to listen "to all that the Europeans had to say, but in the end we would not ask them, we would just tell them what they would get."

21
HARDBALL

A STONISHINGLY, EVEN THOUGH the Europeans sensed their economies collapsing about them and feared for their political future, after all the advice and the pressure they had taken, after all the nagging and threats, after Kennan himself had been dispatched to Paris, they still tried to wriggle away from reaching any unpleasant conclusions.

The central issue remained, as it had been from the very beginning, whether the Europeans would come up with a set of shopping lists or with an integrated plan. Molotov had left Paris saying that an integrated plan - which would require someone, some nation or some multinational body, to set priorities, to decide which factories in which countries would be given aid first, to allocate raw materials, to insist on lowering certain trade barriers, to designate markets - would necessarily require recipient nations to give up some of their sovereignty. The Europeans, who had resisted that conclusion for some weeks, were discovering they could not avoid it. And so, as they finally faced the prospect of giving up power, they discovered they had new resources of resistance.

The members of the Executive Committee, led by Sir Oliver Franks, accepted the need for an integrated plan and agreed to pare down the total amount in American help that the Europeans would request. But the Technical Committees kept turning in their reports, day after day, without any paring down. The Technical Committees behaved as though they had not heard of the understanding reached by the Executive Committee. More and more shopping lists were turned in - and then, to make certain the United States would be embarrassed if it tried to cut the lists down, the Technical Committees, in an extraordinary breach of diplomatic etiquette, held press conferences to announce the completion of each of their reports.

Caffery cabled home in a swivet. Not only were the Technical Committee reports entirely unrelated to the agreement to reduce the total amount of aid, but the Europeans continued simply to list their wishes, to avoid bargaining with one another to bring their wishes into line, to avoid any plans for giving one another mutual aid to help support the American assistance, to avoid any discussions of the need to adjust their standards of living, to avoid distinguishing between capital requirements for reactivating basic industries and capital requirements for long-term investment, even expansion. And furthermore, said Caffery, he had heard that one way the Europeans planned to reduce the total aid they requested was by naming a commodity they would accept from the United States - say food, or coal, or timber - and then simply knocking down the prices; in this way, they planned to get the same amount of commodities, but reduce their dollar deficit.

From Washington, Lovett fired off a cable to "certain American diplomatic officers" in the capitals of the sixteen nations represented in Paris. The American diplomats were instructed to call on the foreign minister or prime minister in each of the countries and inform him that the report that the Paris Conference was about to produce contained "numerous deficiencies" that would make it "unacceptable to State Dept."

The program being worked out in Paris "shows little more than lip service to principles of European self help and mutual help." The United States recognized how difficult it was for the Europeans to come together on such a plan, to recognize their common interests, even to subordinate their national aims; however, such efforts were "essential."

The diplomats in Paris might think they could get away with releasing their reports to the press, but Lovett knew how to undercut them. The home governments, said Lovett, were to instruct their delegates in Paris that they must clearly state that the report they would issue "is not final," that it would be "useful as basis for further discussion," and that the "initial technical reports require further work."

In London, Bevin complained to Douglas (who was by this time in constant motion, traveling back and forth between London and Paris). The seven points that Kennan had talked about in Paris were not new to the British, Bevin said. The British were trying to incorporate the points into the final report of the conference. But, frankly, any attempt the British might make now to force the other nations to screen their requests and pare them down "would only tend to slow up the report." Sir Oliver, said Bevin, had brought the participating countries "as far toward a cooperative effort as is possible." Any effort to press further would, Bevin feared, "so impair national sovereignty that many countries would rebel."

Two days later, in Paris, Clayton, Caffery, and Douglas met with the members of the Executive Committee. Perhaps the Americans had not been specific enough in their objections to the work of the conference. The three Americans had some examples of "weaknesses" in the proposed conference report. The balance-of-payments report, they said, would include a large provision for capital equipment. By looking at the technical report, the three Americans had found that provisions were included for steel plants, power installations, oil refineries, and railroad equipment - $2 billion worth - which were outside the range of short-term needs, which were just attempts to build new, expanded industrial capacity. Second, the Americans said, they had discovered that the petroleum estimates had been prepared on the assumption that there would be no gasoline rationing in Europe. Back home, said the Americans, opponents of the Marshall Plan would object to American taxpayers paying for European "joy riding." Third, the food and agriculture report had failed to state import requirements by source of supply - leaving entirely outside its considerations the question whether and how much European nations would contribute to one another, and shifting too great a burden onto the United States.

Sir Edmund Hall-Patch was in the room for this meeting of the Americans and the Executive Committee. "It was apparent," he said, "that neither Mr. Clayton nor Mr. Caffery . . . had read the report." In point of fact, said Hall-Patch, gasoline rationing "was specifically mentioned in the proposed report." The Americans also contended, Hall-Patch later said to his fellow Britons, "that the figures which had been supplied in the replies were either incorrect or they had not been compiled honestly." To this, none of Hall-Patch's colleagues could summon a reply.

The Americans suggested that the conference be prolonged to work out some of these difficulties and that the presentation of the report be postponed.

Sir Oliver Franks replied that that was "not possible."

The Americans then suggested that the conference report would need to be issued as an "interim report," not a final report.

Franks replied that it would not be possible to call their conclusions an "interim report." (America had made a generous offer; the Europeans had accepted. Did the Americans now want to appear to the world to be taking back their offer?)

Going around the table, the members of the Executive Committee then spoke individually to Clayton, Caffery, and Douglas. It was apparent, Caffery said, "that they had previously reached agreement on a joint position."

Essentially, said the Europeans, "it is not possible to label the report as tentative or preliminary." Such a label would indicate that the conference had been a failure, and the political repercussions of that in Europe would be "serious."

The Executive Committee was prepared, however, to indicate in the body of the report that it was " 'provisional' in some respects." The Americans should keep in mind, in this connection, "the importance of public reaction in Europe as well as in the United States."

The notion that the conference should be prolonged so that the Europeans could work out a more integrated plan was pointless. "A short period of delay would not permit a fundamental change." While the Europeans recognized that their report fell short of some of the desires of the Americans, the Americans needed to understand that the "difficulties in part arise from the terms of reference of the Conference and in part from national decisions at a Cabinet level" - that is, from the reluctance of the European nations to surrender any part of their sovereign rights to do their own planning for their own countries in deference to the United States, or to one another, or to some new multinational planning body. To meet the wishes of the United States entirely "would require a change in the terms of reference, and this would mean a new conference, which might not" - because some of the nations might withdraw - "include all of the countries participating in the present work."

During the next several days, the conference might make some "adjustments" to accommodate American wishes, "but there is no possibility of the present Conference agreeing on an integrated plan."

Apparently, said Sir Oliver disdainfully, the Americans had in mind some sort of directorate, a *"dirigisme* under which an overall control agency would plan and regulate the basic economic activity of the individual countries." Merely to mention the idea was to dismiss it with contempt.

The conference was prepared to put together its report and send its representatives to Washington to "mutually review" the program with the Americans, and then to reconvene the conference in light of the Washington conversations - and, in that manner, to suggest that its report was not "final." But the conference could not agree actually to label its report as an interim one.

Finally, said Sir Oliver, it was "impossible to obtain agreement on a specific undertaking for the formation of a multilateral organization." He had, he said, been able to bring the delegates to the point of agreeing that, should the "necessary means for carrying out the program" be made available - that is, should the United States come up with the money - then it would be desirable for the European countries "mutually to consult together" during the period that Europe received aid.

So, at last, with the Europeans in Paris still eluding and resisting the Americans in Paris, Washington resorted to pulling in its heaviest artillery: Cables started coming out of the State Department from General Marshall himself.

To Douglas, the Secretary of State cabled a wonderful, intricate set of compromises on the issues of "interim" and "final" reports and "shopping lists" and "integrated plans," in such a way as both to ensure and compromise the sovereignty of the European nations.

First, said Marshall, the Executive Committee ought to gather and revise its general report "so far as is possible" to meet Kennan's seven essentials.

Second, the phraseology of the report should be changed to make it clear that the report was "preliminary."

Third, if possible, "although admitted unlikely," the technical reports might be further improved along the lines of the general principles accepted by the Executive Committee.

Fourth, the revised report would then be published about the third week in September and submitted to the participating countries and the United States simultaneously.

Then, the Executive Committee would adjourn, but leave the Technical Committees still working, "with US technical reps offering technical aid" and to "apply to technical reports the principles agreed in revised general report." This friendly aid would include screening the technical reports, paring some down, trading off priorities and allocations, and, in short, doing the work of the conference that the Executive Committee refused to do.

Incidentally, Marshall informed Douglas, Bevin's prediction that the European nations would fear giving away their sovereignty did not seem to be materializing. Lovett's cable instructing American diplomats to visit the home governments had been effective; the home governments thought the American requests were reasonable and were going to so instruct their representatives in Paris.

In fact, some of the smaller nations were delighted to imagine a multilateral system that would help to inhibit the larger nations. Hirschfeld was quick to make it clear that neither Holland, Belgium, nor Luxembourg would sign a report that would prove unacceptable to the United States.

At the same time, word was trickling back to Paris from Washington that Marshall had finally become convinced that the Europeans needed immediate interim aid - before the larger plan would take effect - to tide them over their present difficulties. Such assistance had been requested repeatedly by the Europeans; Clayton, Caffery, and Douglas had all begged their Washington colleagues to agree to some interim aid program. Now Marshall added the carrot to the stick.

At his weekly press conference in Washington, Marshall declared that Europe had two requirements, one for a large aid plan, one for immediate assistance. And, while the nature of the plan was being worked out, droughts and crop shortages had made the immediate problem even more critical. By the end of October, said Marshall, he expected to have in hand some "working papers" from the Paris Conference. Congress could look them over. The papers would show "that every effort has been made locally to meet the critical needs" of Europe. Soon, Marshall would expect Congress to get down to taking appropriate legislative action. Meanwhile, the Europeans needed immediate aid, and that could not wait. Immediate needs, therefore, would be given urgent consideration.

In less than forty-eight hours, Hervé Alphand, in Paris, informed the Executive Committee that the French government had changed its position and was prepared to "proceed along the lines suggested by the U.S."

Hirschfeld suggested that the conference get down to work at once to make as many improvements in their report as possible, that the report then be issued as a "first report," that European experts continue to work on details of the program while the Americans were reviewing it, and that then a conference group meet with an American group to consider revisions. The Italians agreed immediately.

In London, Bevin called in Ambassador Douglas. The British would go along with the Americans, Bevin said, but he asked Douglas to pass along a message to Marshall. Bevin was "much disturbed," he said, by the impression that had been created in Paris "that the work of the conference has been unsatisfactory and is now having to be done again under American pressure." That impression, said Bevin, would give critics an opportunity to snipe at the conference. Although Bevin did not say so, the American action also seemed to be an implicit criticism of Sir Oliver Franks, and of the British, who had been entrusted with running the conference and who appeared to have failed to do their job. Bevin thought that the bad impression could only be corrected from Washington, by Secretary Marshall, who ought to find an opportunity to make some reassuring statement.

Lovett replied coolly: "There seems little use," he said, "in a statement from Washington at this time."

In Paris, as the momentum of the conference switched to the Americans' favor, Douglas, Clayton, and Caffery pressed the Europeans even more energetically. On September 17, Caffery cabled Lovett and Bonesteel that the Europeans had given in on most points; the new provisions the

Americans had demanded were "satisfactory," and "in some cases exceed[ed]" American demands.

The Europeans had agreed to obligate themselves to the group to attain certain production targets for key commodities. They agreed to commit themselves to reducing and eventually eliminating trade barriers. They agreed to segregate capital equipment items meant for investment or expansion that ought to be financed by the International Bank or other lending agencies rather than the Marshall Plan. They agreed, too, that they would "recess" the conference, not "adjourn" it, so that they could meet again to revise their planning after Washington responded to their initial report. Still, Caffery said, the Europeans were resisting some of the aspects of integrated planning, particularly the notion of a multilateral organization.

The opinion "held by a few," said Caffer - meaning, especially, Lovett - "that the European participating countries should designate without regard to national frontiers the productive facilities that should first be brought into production . . . sounds plausible at first, but its implications, we think, are far-reaching. First it inevitably requires for its execution an international organization to select the plants that will be given priority; second, it inevitably requires an international organization to allocate the necessary raw materials for the operation of plants enjoying priority; third, it inevitably requires an international organization to allocate among several or all of the participating countries the products of plants and facilities to which priority has been given. The evidence is clear, we think, that the 16 participating countries would not accept this sort of system and organization."

Douglas, back in London once again, cabled Marshall and Lovett. Certain people in Washington might think the British were being "sticky," but, in fact, the British had a point. The idea that a multilateral organization would be empowered to indicate, "without regard to national frontiers, the plant facilities which would first be brought into production necessarily entailed, in their view, the allocation of a relatively large list of raw materials and of the finished products among at least several participating countries. This sort of an undertaking, the British felt, would necessarily mean an impairment of sovereignty."

The conundrum over the multilateral organization was solved, finally, one evening when Sir Oliver Franks sat down for a chat with the delegate from Sweden, Dag Hammarskjöld, who would soon become Secretary-General of the United Nations. With Hammarskjöld's expert help, Franks was able to conceive of an international organization that would sound good on paper, offer some vague hope of international cooperation, but be, in fact, politically impotent. And so, with their sense of national sovereignty intact, the Europeans were able to agree, at last, to a multilateral organization.

Clayton, Caffery, and Douglas were overjoyed. First they met with Franks to express their appreciation for his work, and then they were escorted once more to the Quai d'Orsay, into the gilt-trimmed Salon de l'Horlage for a meeting of the full sixteen nations.

Clayton addressed the delegates. He could not speak for Washington, he said. Washington might still have some additional suggestions to make about the conference report - and, indeed, they would all have an opportunity to hear Washington's reaction when they took the report there, and went themselves to brief the State Department and work with the department's economists in further refining the report. But, for his own part, and on behalf of Caffery and Douglas, Clayton was ready for a celebration. He thought the conference had done a splendid job. In his personal judgment, said Clayton, "the representatives of the 16 European nations have blazed a new path in the history of Europe, if not in the history of the world." The "magnitude of the task," the "tight time schedule," and so forth. He looked forward, he said, to seeing members of the committee in Washington soon.

Cabling home, Clayton, Caffery, and Douglas were bubbling with pride: They sent home the conference report to Lovett with a sense of great personal accomplishment. Lovett, however, was a tough man to please. When he received the report, he was not overly impressed. He saw more work to be done, a few more turns to put the Europeans through. "For your info," he cabled the Americans in Paris on September 22, "we believe it will become clear from discussions in Washington that further substantial work by committees in Paris will be necessary."

22

THE MOLOTOV PLAN

O N SEPTMEBER 22, in Polish Silesia, in the middle of a large park, in a country house that had been converted to a sanatorium by the Polish State Security Service, representatives of the principal Communist parties in Europe gathered to meet with Andrei Zhdanov and Georgi Malenkov.

The Russians had called the meeting to set up the Communist Information Bureau - an association that would aid, the Russians said, in the exchange of information among Communists in Europe. The meeting had been called on Polish soil to emphasize the notion that the Soviet Union did not mean to exercise undue influence on the Cominform, that all Communist parties were equal, and that the Soviet Union was merely *primus inter pares*. Representatives were there from Yugoslavia, Poland, Hungary, Rumania, Bulgaria, Czechoslovakia, Italy, and France as well as Russia.

The delegates to the conference must have been sensible of the fact that, only a few years before, many of them had been unknown workers in sometimes clandestine movements across Europe. By the autumn of 1947, many of them, with the help of the Russians, had become influential and well-known politicians or even taken over the governments of their countries. And yet, not all of them felt entirely appreciative of the Russians.

Far from being docile, willing functionaries, they were national leaders, the heads of parties, embodying the hopes of millions of followers for national independence and even, in many cases, for Western-style parliamentary democracy. They represented nations that had, in some instances - indisputably in Italy and France and Czechoslovakia - freely voted them into office with fervent hopes for freedom and social justice, or merely, on the part of the truly oppressed or impoverished peasants and farmers, for some simple form of fairness.

Some of the Communist leaders who gathered for the Cominform conference - still feeling the pain of having been forced to stay out of the Marshall Plan - were resentful. Some - the Yugoslav, French, and Italian parties - had pointedly not sent their top leaders. All - in a conference lasting a brisk seven days - were about to be disciplined.

The disciplining had begun, in fact, even before the conference got under way. During the summer, while the Western Europeans were meeting in Paris, Stalin had sent a message to Wladyslaw Gomulka, the first secretary of the Polish Communist Party, suggesting that Gomulka invite the other European Communists to a conference in Poland. The Poles, Gomulka replied at once, actually considered communism a foreign import, and one of his hardest jobs was to convince them otherwise; now, to have a Communist conference on Polish territory would make the work in Poland that much harder. Stalin disagreed. Gomulka called the conference.

In 1919, Lenin had founded the Comintern to direct the Communist parties throughout Europe - and, indeed, the world - in their efforts to gain control of their own governments. The Comintern had been abolished by Stalin during World War II, in accord with his policy of cooperation with the Allies and his declaration that, henceforth, all Communist parties were to become national parties, not directed by the Soviet Union.

The idea that the Russians needed to resurrect the Comintern, or something similar, had been discussed as early as 1945, but Stalin had dismissed the idea each time it was raised. By 1947, however, the Soviet Union had come to feel increasingly threatened by the United States, at the same time that it needed to ensure control of its own followers. And so Stalin gave the word to create a sort of pocket Comintern, no longer global in scope, limited only to Europe: the Cominform.

With the Truman Doctrine and the Marshall Plan, Zhdanov told the delegates to the conference, the world had now been divided into two camps - the "imperialist and antidemocratic forces" and the "democratic and anti-imperialist forces." The doctrine and the plan, he said, were "an embodiment of the American design to enslave Europe." The United States had finally launched "an attack on the principle of national sovereignty."

Although Soviet policy continued to be based on the hope of peaceful coexistence, said Zhdanov, the United States had set about constructing a bloc against the Soviet Union, using American economic strength to expand into the world, to create a base for its expansion by creating a sphere of influence over Western Europe and Britain and its empire, and to secure its position by planting military outposts around the world.

As he surveyed the postwar world, said Zhdanov, he saw that, of the six "so-called great" imperialist powers, three - Germany, Japan, and Italy - had "dropped out." France had been desperately weakened. Britain was entirely dependent on the United States for its survival. Only America had emerged from the war strengthened. America had abandoned its traditional isolationism. It had become expansionist. It meant not only to hold the position it had won, but to build on it - to replace Germany, Italy, and Japan in the world markets, to transform Britain into its vassal, to sweep former British colonies into its own sphere of influence. The most extreme of American politicians were even advocating a preventive war against the Soviet Union.

For its allies, the United States counted on Britain and France, which had now become American satellites; on Belgium and Holland, with their little colonial empires; on Greece and Turkey, with their extremely reactionary governments; on Middle Eastern countries that were heavily dependent, economically and militarily, on America; and on the antidemocratic and pro-Fascist regimes of South America. American military bases were established all over the world - in Japan, Italy, South Korea, China, Egypt, Iran, Turkey, Greece, Austria, Western Germany, even the Arctic.

As for its economic aid, said Zhdanov, all it achieved was to allow the powerful American economy to move in and dominate the weakened European economies, to use assistance to help friendly (non-Communist, non-Socialist) parties and politicians gain and hold control of their governments in Europe, and to arouse hostility toward the Soviet Union, claiming America is "protecting" its friends against an aggressive Russia.

The Soviet Union, by contrast, said Zhdanov - in words that required a considerable suspension of disbelief from the Eastern Europeans - "indefatigably upholds the principle of real equality and protection of the sovereign rights of all nations, large and small." The Soviet Union remained a "reliable bulwark against encroachments on the equality and self-determination of nations."

After Zhdanov sat down, Malenkov rose to add a couple of flourishes to Zhdanov's speech. "The ruling clique of American imperialists," he declared, ". . . has taken the path of outright expansion, of enthralling the weakened capitalist states of Europe and the colonial and dependent countries . . . . The clearest and most specific expression of the policy . . . is provided by the Truman-Marshall plans." Then, leaving analysis behind, Malenkov finished off with a little extra flair of rhetoric: As for Yugoslavia and Poland, he said, "the United States and Great Britain are pursuing a terrorist policy. . . . Plans of fresh aggression, plans for a new war against the Soviet Union and the new democracies, are being hatched. . . . Imitating the

Hitlerites, the new aggressors are using blackmail and extortion."

When Zhdanov and Malenkov had finished speaking, they opened the floor to the other delegates - and to considerable, though muted, complaining. If Lovett had trouble cajoling the Western Europeans, it was nothing compared with the trouble Zhdanov and Malenkov had whipping the Eastern Europeans into line. While most of the delegates at the conference dutifully rose and thanked Stalin and the Red Army for liberating their countries from the Nazis, Gomulka got up - still smarting from having to call the conference in the first place - and spoke of the great work the Polish party had been doing to eradicate anti-Soviet sentiment: And so ensured that the Russians knew how much anti-Soviet sentiment there was in Poland.

Yugoslavia's foreign minister, Edvard Kardelj, managed not to mention at all that his country owed its liberation to the Red Army. Actually, said Kardelj, it was a "slander" against the Yugoslav party to suggest that the national liberation movement did not begin in Yugoslavia until after Germany had attacked the Soviet Union.

And yet, if all the Eastern Europeans had not quite learned how to toe the party line, some, at least, were happy to join Zhdanov in his attacks on the West. The Yugoslavs in particular - who had the distinction of being listed just after the Soviet Union in the roster of Cominform members - took some pride in making their own credentials look even better by attacking those of the French and Italians. Even Milovan Djilas, who would eventually become thoroughly disillusioned with the Soviet Union, and who would spend some years in jail for his independent ways, joined his Yugoslav colleague Kardelj in roasting the French and Italians.

The French Communists, Kardelj and Djilas said, could have seized power in 1944 but had behaved, instead, like a bourgeois political party - even helping the reactionary government by holding back on strikes and supporting the government's economic "reforms." In 1946 and 1947, although the French Communists were the largest political party in France - had gotten the largest vote of any party in national elections - they could not even manage to stay in the government. In short, said the Yugoslavs, the French Communists were contemptible; they were mere "opportunists" and "parliamentary deviationists" - and, as it turned out, they were not even good at it.

Jacques Duclos, the leader of the French delegation, replied heatedly to the charges. France was in dreadful straits - in terrible need of food, coal, dollars. The French working class had a living standard 50 percent below the prewar standard.

Inflation was out of control. And the Americans were doing their best to cash in on the situation. The propaganda was enormous - touting the idea that "America alone could help" - and the French Communist Party had a hard job counteracting it. In 1946, even though the Communists had won a great election victory, the Socialists combined against them to keep them from power. Then came the short-lived Socialist coalition led by Léon Blum, who took the French into the Anglo-American camp. Blum was rewarded at once with American aid that gave an immediate boost to the French economy. Then Blum took France into war in Indochina. Thus, when the Communists were able to join Ramadier's coalition government in January 1947, they were brought into the position of having to support a wage and price freeze and a Southeast Asian war, which helped to discredit them. Then, in May 1947, they were finally eliminated from the government.

In all this, the French Communist Party had in fact been trying to follow the Russians' advice. And now they were being asked to persuade the French people that the Marshall Plan was a bad thing. It would not be easy. The Communist Party in France had been driven into a "political ghetto" from which they found it increasingly difficult to get anyone's favorable attention. Now, on top of all his other troubles, Duclos had to listen to the Yugoslavs criticize him and brag about their own accomplishments - of their party of 400,000 members, of the fact that half of retail trade had been taken out of private hands, big landowners had been eliminated, three-quarters of their farms had been made into cooperatives, and overall, they had become the very model of a Communist state outside Russia. Indeed, it was true, as Kardelj had so smugly said, that "reactionary forces were often willing to cooperate in the government with the communists - but only so long as they themselves felt weak; once these forces felt they were strong, they were only too ready to throw the democratic principles and parliamentary conventions overboard, so as to get rid of the . . . communist members." So Duclos had learned, painfully, at first hand. Duclos accepted some criticism. He even had some self-criticism to add: There might be "some doubts" whether the French Communists had done well in that most crucial piece of maneuvering when they were knocked out of the Ramadier government. They might, then, have lost their greatest opportunity. But they had not failed to try. They had been defeated by American imperialism, by the power of the dollar, against which they were helpless. The Marshall Plan had, in fact, knocked out the Communist Party in France as a viable parliamentary power. The party would need to turn - and it would turn - to strikes and sabotage, to the strategies of the outsider, to fight against the American "colonization" of France.

Duclos, having had to admit that all his hopes for having a parliamentary party had been destroyed by the Americans, left the little building after his speech and wandered out into the park, where his friends found him sitting alone, swinging his legs, and crying.

When Luigi Longo of Italy was attacked by Zhdanov and the Yugoslavs for the same sort of "parliamentary deviationism," Longo talked back. It was quite true, he said, that Communists had been eliminated from the Italian government - because of a split in the Socialist Party in January of that year, and because of maneuvering by the Americans and the Vatican. In fact, said Longo, it was "a real *coup d'état*," carried out on the instructions of the Americans (and eased along with a $600 million American credit to the hard-pressed Italian government). And now Alcide de Gasperi, Italy's Premier, had begun a police terror against the Communists.

But Longo was undaunted. He regarded the de Gasperi government as "an antinational government threatening the very existence of Italy as an independent state." The Italian Communists, said Longo, would continue to rely on democratic parliamentary means to return them and their political allies to power. "We are struggling for the constitution of a government in which all the popular and republican forces of the country would be represented."

Zhdanov could not contain his contempt for Longo. The Italian Communists, he said, were "more parliamentary than de Gasperi." Longo's hopes were absurdly sentimental. "You are the biggest political party, and yet they throw you out of the Government."

Zhdanov was powerless to change the behavior of Duclos or Longo, but he turned fiercely on the Eastern Europeans. Gomulka had been talking about the "Polish road to socialism," which could accommodate small entrepreneurs and private farms along with collectivization. On the contrary, said Zhdanov, there needed to be an end to "national communisms" that went their separate ways. Indeed, before Zhdanov was finished he would have the conference endorse collectivization as the only appropriate way toward socialism, and so he would arrange a victory, and a defeat, at the same time. While he had his way with the Eastern Europeans, Zhdanov's conference, by making the delegates look so subservient to Moscow, actually helped discredit the Euro-Communist movement for decades among Western Europeans.

In the declaration that the members of the Cominform drew up as their formal conclusions, they declared that "the Truman-Marshall plan is only a constituent part, the European subsection of the general plan for the policy of global expansion pursued by the United States in all parts of the world. The plan . . . is being supplemented by plans for the economic and political enslavement of China, Indonesia, the South American countries . . . . Under these circumstances it is necessary that the anti-imperialist democratic camp should close its ranks . . . and work out its own tactics against the main forces of the imperialist camp, against American imperialism and its British and French allies."

Indeed, whereas Stalin had until recently continued to speak of the possibility of "peaceful coexistence," henceforth the phrase was dropped from his language. Whereas certain national diversities had been tolerated in Eastern Europe, henceforth such idiosyncrasies were ended. Regimes in Rumania and Hungary were stiffened. And it became clear that the Western-style parliamentary government in Czechoslovakia - where Foreign Minister Masaryk and President Eduard Beneš had tried, like the French, to look both east and west - would have to be sacrificed as a luxury.

Czechoslovakia's last chance to stay in touch with the West occurred that autumn. As it happened, the summer harvest in Czechoslovakia had been a disaster. Only 63 percent of the expected grain harvest came in, only 48 percent of the potato harvest. The government appealed at once to the United States. The United States declined to extend aid unless the Czechs were prepared to alter the orientation of their government. The Russians promised at once, and with a flourish of publicity, to provide 600,000 tons of grain for Czechoslovakia.

"Those goddamn Americans," said the Czech Minister of Foreign Trade as he went to Moscow to close the grain deal. "It's because of them that I've had to come here to sign on the dotted line. We told the Americans, and asked for 200,000 or 300,000 tons of wheat. And these idiots started the usual blackmail. . . . And now these idiots in Washington have driven us straight into the Stalinist camp."

Later that autumn, General Marshall informed his cabinet colleagues in a secret briefing that according to the State Department's best estimates, a general "halt in the Communist advance" had occurred in Europe. Western Europe was holding firm. One result of this phenomenon, however, was that it was "forcing Moscow to consolidate its hold on Eastern Europe. It will probably have to clamp down completely on Czechoslovakia." As long as the Communists had been doing well in Western Europe, said Marshall, they liked for Czechoslovakia to have the "outer appearances of freedom," such as free elections, to make communism look enticing to the West. But once possibilities to the West were closed off, Czech freedoms became a dangerous example to the other countries of Eastern Europe. So Russia would have to clamp down on the Czechs. To clamp down would force opposition underground, and so the Russians would "proceed to this step reluctantly." Nonetheless, they would have to proceed as "a purely defensive move." Not so incidentally, Czechoslovakia was Russia's principal source of uranium.

Thus, Washington was not surprised by the events of the following spring. In the most recent elections, the Communists had won 37 percent of the vote in Czechoslovakia and so named a number of cabinet ministers, including the Minister of the Interior. The Interior Ministry, which controlled the police force, had taken to stocking the force with Communists. In protest, twelve non-Communist cabinet members resigned. Apparently, the twelve had an understanding with President Beneš that he would not accept their resignations; a cabinet reorganization would be forced, or else new elections would be held. Instead, five days of utter confusion followed. The Minister of the Interior ordered the police to arrest non-Communist opposition leaders. Panic spread. Rumors of a Russian invasion circulated. It was said that the Russians were massing troops on the Czech border. And President Beneš - old and ill, having had a stroke during the summer of 1947, fearful of war - turned to the Communist leader Klement Gottwald to form a Communist cabinet.

"The Communists took power," as Daniel Yergin has written, "by pushing hard against a door that was already half open." There were no Soviet troops on the border. The Beneš government simply collapsed. And when the government fell, the Communists seemed more surprised than the Americans.

To be sure, once they had taken over, the Communists went on to arrest opposition politicians, stage trials, and execute erstwhile enemies.

And then, several weeks after the fall of the government, unexpected and truly shocking news came from Prague. Jan Masaryk - a man with a wry, ironical sense of humor, the American-educated son of a former president of Czechoslovakia, who had agreed to stay on as Foreign Minister in the new Communist government to help in the transition and to assist those who wanted to leave the country - had committed suicide by jumping from a window. Or else he was murdered - suffocated by a pillow and then thrown from the window to make it look like a suicide.

What could be said? Nothing but that it had been foreseen back in the spring of 1947, this final setting of the division of Europe into Eastern and Western spheres - though not in all its tragic implications.

PART THREE

23
WASHINGTON

THE EUROPEAN DIPLOMATS who gathered up their papers in Paris, searched through their wardrobes for their most brightly colored neckties, and set out in the early weeks of autumn for Washington to argue their case for help before members of the State Department and Congress were astonished to find, among other things, that hardly anyone in America had heard of the Marshall Plan.

The plan might be a topic of urgent conversation on Capitol Hill and in Georgetown, but outside Washington, according to opinion polls, barely half the population had heard of it, and of those who had, many were opposed. How America could have remained a nation of isolationists, even late into 1947, must seem phenomenal - and the isolationism was not confined to pockets of rural indifference in Kansas and Nebraska. The historic roots of isolationism ran deep. If America was a nation of immigrants, it was, necessarily, a nation of those who had fled foreign lands, turned their backs on those lands, and hoped never to have to do with the ceaseless wars, tyrannies, persecutions, power politics, spheres of influence, and other deplorable complications of Old World life. If the men in the Defense Department, and the President, sometimes forgot this deep suspicion Americans had about war fought for the sake of national pride, or commercial markets, or imperial conquest, or merely ancient, tangled disputes - and sent a bill up to Congress calling for universal military training, so as to have a trained "citizens' army" ready at all times should the need for mobilization arise - congressmen never forgot. Each time the bill for universal military training was sent up to the Hill, the representatives - their nerve endings quivering with messages from home - would vote it down.

Nearly every schoolchild, no matter how poor the rest of his education might have been, was taught that George Washington had warned future generations to avoid foreign entanglements, and - lest Washington's warning be dismissed as the simple-minded thoughts of an earlier, naive age - men like Senator Taft were reminding Americans after the war of what foreign involvements might lead to: of the inevitable tendency, in a nation constantly preoccupied with foreign affairs, for political power to flow to the office of the President, and for the President to pursue foreign adventures unchecked by the Congress, until the Republic had been compromised, or entirely undone, by unending foreign wars.

History, culture, political theory all combined with lesser instincts - self-satisfaction, laziness, parochialism - to instill a profound sense of isolationism in America. A wish for international adventure did not come even from those sources that common sense (and Karl Marx) would suggest: Most American businessmen, Republicans and supporters of Senator Taft, were firmly isolationist. Who could trust a foreigner to pay his bills, after all? Who could trust a Socialist or Communist government not to seize an American plant? A few American businessmen, men like Clayton and others who had had some experience of international business, were eager to get into the big European and other foreign markets - but they were a precious few.

When the President called a few congressmen into his office that September to talk to them about the interim aid package that the Europeans had been promised in order to sweeten up the bargaining in Paris, Truman discovered that the congressmen were still not happy about all this talk of international plans.

The President did not try this time to overwhelm his former colleagues with big set-piece orations. His manner was offhand. Nonetheless, he did manage to threaten the possibility of the immediate fall of the French and Italian governments if they did not get aid at once. If France and Italy fell now, of course, there would be no point to the Marshall Plan later - and, under those circumstances, the President was not even sure whether the United States "could stand up in such a situation."

"This is serious," Truman said. "I can't overemphasize how serious." He thought he would call a special emergency session of Congress to put through an interim aid bill, to hold Europe while Congress debated the Marshall Plan.

The congressmen were sullen.

"I had hoped very much, Mr. President," Sam Rayburn said at last, "there would be no special session of Congress."

"It doesn't seem," said Truman, "we can get the money any other way, Sam."

"Then the plan had better be well worked out, right down to the details."

Charles Halleck, the Republican House Majority Leader, spoke up: "Mr. President, you must realize there is a growing resistance to these programs. I have been out on the hustings, and I know. The people don't like it."

In truth, Truman had anticipated the response of Congress, and of the country. He had not gone to the trouble of switching gears from the Truman Doctrine to the Marshall Plan with the thought, then, of just hoping for the best. Already, back in the spring, Truman had gotten hold of Averell Harriman and asked him to gather up those precious few businessmen who might be in favor of some international financial dealings and form them into a committee to study whether the Marshall Plan might have a good or bad effect on American business. Harriman brought together Hiland Batcheller, president of the Allegheny-Ludlum Steel Corporation, W. Randolph Burgess, vice-chairman of National City Bank of New York, Paul G. Hoffman, president of Studebaker Corporation, and other businessmen and international-minded academics. They spent the summer conferring with one another, dining together, contributing their thoughts on the subject at hand. In the autumn, one of their number drafted a report on their conclusions: They thought the Marshall Plan would be good for American business. The report was timed to appear at just the time Truman was calling Congress together to consider his special request for interim aid - and henceforth, in these hearings and later ones, whenever a Republican congressman or businessman came up to Vandenberg to question the plan, Vandenberg would refer to the Harriman report and say, "It's all right . . . these are good people."

Nothing was left to chance. Acheson, too, was brought into service, and the former Undersecretary of State got together a privately organized, "grass roots" Citizens' Committee for the Marshall Plan. Former Secretary of War Robert Patterson joined Acheson as co-chairman of the committee, and both took to the road to make speeches. Acheson's speeches, he said modestly, were not important in and of themselves but only as a contribution to the "efforts of hundreds, perhaps thousands, of other speakers and workers who . . . reached the minds, or at least the attention, of innumerable others."

Secretary of the Treasury Clinton Anderson hit the trail too, speaking of America's abundant agricultural production and the need for "export outlets for some of our most important commodities." Edwin G. Nourse of the Council of Economic Advisers formed another committee whose members met and conferred and dined and issued another favorable report. And Secretary of the Interior Julius Krug formed still another committee to determine whether the United States had sufficient natural resources to preserve national security and the American standard of living at the same time that it supported a large program of foreign aid. The conclusion: It did.

Attorney General Tom Clark, meanwhile, commenced to take the lead in a great campaign to reawaken America's sense of patriotism. Americans, said the Attorney General, seemed to have lost their enthusiasm for "the American way of life." What the country needed was a massive program of public "education" at all levels, in all areas of the country. The Commissioner of Education considered the Attorney General's remarks and somberly agreed. The most urgent educational task of the United States, the commissioner said, was "to bring up young citizens who really understand and cherish American democracy." A presidential commission was formed. The commission met, deliberated, and issued a report: What the country needed was a comprehensive program that would instill "a fuller realization of democracy in every phase of living."

The champions of universal military training, meanwhile, were feeling somewhat neglected. A bill had gone up to Congress not long before and been voted down. Over at the White House, and even in the Defense Department, everyone's attention was focused on the campaign for the Marshall Plan. And so, a presidential commission that had been appointed some time before to issue a report on the need for universal military training temporarily realigned its sights and wrote up a report instead on education. The "single most important educational frontier of all," said the Commission on Universal Military Training, was "to strengthen national security through education."

Finally, the Office of Education got together its comprehensive program. The program was called "Zeal for American Democracy," and it was designed, said the Office of Education, to "vitalize and improve education in the ideals and benefits of democracy and to reveal the character and tactics of totalitarianism." Budgets were drawn up, appropriations earmarked, and the Office of Education set out to provide schools across America with pamphlets and study guides that would assist teachers in giving a "patriotic emphasis" to education. (To help get the teachers on the bandwagon, the American Federation of Teachers - traditionally a Democratic organization, and eager to help the President - decided to give its annual convention the overall theme of "Strengthening Education for National and World Security.")

Certainly the Office of Education did its job: A whole generation of Americans was raised to believe fervently in the values of the Republic, in its Constitution, its inherent goodness, even its nobility. This was the generation that would be disillusioned in the ensuing decades, and that would object with such intensity to American involvement in the Vietnam War and presidential intrusions against the Constitution. In 1947 and 1948, the Office of Education did its job better than subsequent presidents would appreciate.

Nor was the Office of Education left alone in its efforts to promote patriotism. The Attorney General had other ideas, too. Along with FBI Director J. Edgar Hoover, Clark conceived the notion of promoting a vast, nationwide campaign for patriotism that would feature a coast-to-coast whistle-stop journey of a Freedom Train - a special train that would be fitted up into a traveling museum of Americana, containing such truly sacred documents as the Declaration of Independence, the Constitution, and the Emancipation Proclamation, copies of the Magna Carta and of Christopher Columbus's letter describing his first voyage to the New World, Tom Paine's pamphlet *The American Crisis* ("These are the times that try men's souls. The summer soldier and the sunshine patriot will in this crisis, shrink from the service of his country"), a letter from George Washington describing the dreadful winter of 1780 in Valley Forge ("It would be well for the troops if like Chameleons they could live upon Air - or like the Bear suck their paws for sustenance during the rigour of the approaching season"), the Virginia aristocrat George Mason's original draft of the Declaration of Rights that was the basis of the Bill of Rights, Benjamin Franklin's editorial defense of free speech ("Freedom of speech is a principal pillar of a free government; when this support is taken away, the constitution of a free society is dissolved, and tyranny is erected on its ruins"), a letter from Louis Kossuth, a leader of the Hungarian revolution of 1848, to President Fillmore, the head of state of "this great Republic . . . this great and generous country . . . this glorious home of liberty," the copy of the Gettysburg Address from which President Lincoln spoke, General Mark W. Clark's proclamation of Allied victory in Italy in 1945, the logbook of the USS *Missouri,* in which the surrender of the Japanese was recorded in 1945, General Dwight Eisenhower's personal flag, the flag that was raised by United States Marines on Iwo Jima, a United States 6 percent loan certificate of 1779, a 6 percent loan certificate of 1862 that was used to help finance the war that saved the Union, a 2 percent Panama Canal Zone certificate, a 4¾ percent Victory Liberty Loan Convertible Gold Note of 1918, a Defense and War Savings Bond, Series E of 1945.

The Freedom Train traveled all across the land, stopping at more than 200 towns and cities, returning at last to Washington to culminate a "week of rededication" (the same week that the Senate opened hearings on foreign aid) that featured mass demonstrations in which thousands of government employees turned out to take a "freedom pledge" and sing "God Bless

America" - all topped off at the end of the week by the National Guard staging a mock bombing raid on the nation's capital.

If much of the campaign to reawaken patriotism seems wonderfully jolly and rambunctious in retrospect - and to arouse deep nostalgia for a time of real love of country - other aspects of it managed to mix in some more disturbing strains. Secretary of Defense Forrestal, for instance, decided to pitch in and do his part for the campaign, and Forrestal's mind tended to turn to rather serious matters. It seemed to Forrestal that there were a number of newspaper reporters writing about military affairs whose loyalty to the country was not entirely certain, and that some of these reporters ought not to be allowed into places where they might uncover material that could prove embarrassing or even damaging to the country's defenses if it were published. Was not the country, in some sense, locked in deadly combat with the Communists? Should not the rules that applied to journalists during the war still apply? Forrestal thought the system needed tightening up and that any journalist who wanted to be accredited to cover military affairs should pass a loyalty test.

The Security Advisory Board of the State-War-Navy Coordinating Committee took Forrestal's notions to a more systematic conclusion. The board issued a set of guidelines for handling sensitive material within the government. Traditionally, the military had marked documents with the legends "unclassified," "restricted," "confidential," "secret," and "top secret." Henceforth, the Security Advisory Board recommended, all documents, throughout the entire government, ought to be so marked, and any employee who disclosed "confidential" information should be subject to dismissal on the ground of disloyalty.

This confidential report of the board was - who would not have bet on it? - leaked to a newspaper reporter, who took it to his editor, who raised such a horrible, clamorous fuss that President Truman himself had to disown the board's report at a press conference. The guidelines were ostentatiously buried - and then put into effect several years later.

Much of what the executive branch did that summer, whether by design or coincidence, seemed to feed the general atmosphere of fear and a renewed sense of discipline. The Central Intelligence Agency was formed during the summer of 1947, too. At the end of the war, President Truman had disbanded the Office of Strategic Services, which had functioned as America's wartime espionage organization, and distributed its agents between Army intelligence and the State Department. Later, when he came to consider setting up a permanent peacetime intelligence operation, he approved an awkward idea that called for a National Intelligence Authority to set policy and a Central Intelligence Group to carry out policy, the latter having a vaguely conceived set of duties that would include collecting and evaluating intelligence and performing "such other functions and duties related to intelligence affecting the national security as the President and National Intelligence Authority may from time to time direct."

The CIG was the creature of three departments - State, War, and Navy - and before long, the three departments were suggesting that the CIG could not function efficiently unless it were spun off on its own as an entirely independent agency. Marshall was one of the few who objected. It seemed to him dangerous to detach such an organization from the restraining influence of the State Department. "The powers of the proposed agency," he said, "seem almost unlimited and need clarification."

But Truman went ahead and proposed legislation to Congress to establish the Central Intelligence Agency. During the summer of 1947, Congress debated whether this new agency might bring police state activities to America. Clarence Brown of Ohio asked whether the CIA "might possibly affect the rights and privileges of the people of the United States." Another congressman worried whether it might "become a Gestapo or anything of that sort." Still, with their misgivings unresolved, Congress passed the CIA enabling legislation on July 25. By autumn, the CIA was already planning its very first covert activities, which seem, in retrospect, almost sweet: Among other things, a secret printing plant was to be established in Germany and a flotilla of hot - air balloons was to be organized to drop propaganda leaflets into Eastern Europe.

In the autumn, too, the Department of State contributed more to the general aura of choosing up sides to fight. In October, the department announced that it had adopted a set of standard practices whereby any employee would be dismissed who was a member of a subversive organization on the Attorney General's list or who was "associated," as the historian Richard Freeland has phrased it, "with any individual so associated." Soon enough, across the country, people seeking jobs in private corporations would be asked to sign loyalty oaths as a condition of employment.

At the same time, the Attorney General was setting a few precedents with the House Committee on Un-American Activities. Whereas it had been the custom during the Roosevelt Administration for the executive branch not to cooperate with HUAC - and even, when the occasion presented itself, to make jokes in public about HUAC - the Truman Administration set a new course, treating the committee with respect and giving top priority to securing indictments on people who had been charged by the committee with contempt of

Congress. In part, it was said, the President and his men were forced to this by the temper of the times; in part, the President found the atmosphere well suited to his own needs. HUAC was geared up for the showiest set of hearings in its history in the autumn of 1947. The committee had summoned before it some of the stars of Hollywood to testify whether Communists had infiltrated the movie business and were using it for Communist propaganda and whether, as a result, the actors and directors and screenwriters thought Congress should break all precedent and outlaw a political party in America. At last, Communists and anti-Communists were brought together for a full-scale knock-down, drag-out investigation in front of microphones, floodlights, movie cameras, and even one of the new television cameras. Niceties of dialogue and plot were not the crucial elements in these hearings: the hoopla was all.

Gary Cooper, one of the good guys, star of *Unconquered, Pride of the Yankees, Mr. Deeds Goes to Town,* and (then in production) *Good Sam,* wearing a well-tailored double-breasted suit and a powder-blue silk tie, ambled in to the accompaniment of flashbulbs and sighs, smiled his disarming, self-deprecating smile and testified that he hadn't read Karl Marx and didn't know much about communism, but "from what I hear, I don't like it because it isn't on the level."

Had he ever noticed any Communist propaganda in films?

"Well, I have turned down quite a few scripts because I thought they were tinged with communistic ideas."

Cooper was followed to the stand by Robert Taylor, who declared right off: "I shall never work with anyone who is a Communist."

"You would refuse to act in a picture in which a person whom you considered to be a Communist was also cast, is that correct?"

"I most assuredly would, and I would not even have to know that he was a Communist. This may sound biased. However, if I were even suspicious of a person being a Communist with whom I was scheduled to work, I am afraid it would have to be him or me, because life is a little too short to be around people who annoy me as much as these fellow travelers and Communists do."

Cooper and Taylor were tame compared to Adolphe Menjou, however, who said stoutly: "I am a witch-hunter if the witches are Communists. I am a Red-baiter. I make no bones about it. I would like to see them all back in Russia. . . . I would move to the State of Texas if [communism] ever came here because I think the Texans would kill them on sight. . . . I believe America should arm to the teeth."

All of which made Congressman Richard Nixon, one of the younger members of the committee, look like a calm, philosophical defender of the Constitution, as he chided Menjou for concluding that a person was a Communist because "he acted like a Communist." And Ronald Reagan, president of the Screen Actors Guild, not only seemed to be, but was a defender of the Constitution, gently, mellifluously reminding the committee: "After all, we must recognize them at present as a political party. . . . In opposing these people, the best thing to do is make democracy work. In the Screen Actors Guild, we make it work by ensuring everyone a vote and by keeping everyone informed."

But the bad guys provided the best show: a group of screenwriters on whom the committee had the goods, including the numbers on their Communist Party cards, the so-called Hollywood Ten. And the Ten did their part to make it good theater - refusing to testify, challenging the right of the committee to exist, heaping scorn on the chairman, shouting, ranting. Proofs were not important to either side: Both sides merely wanted to hold the other up to derision, to let the enemy expose himself.

"I am not on trial here," said John Howard Lawson, the first of the Ten to appear. "This Committee is on trial before the American people. Let us get that straight."

Thus provoked, Chairman J. Parnell Thomas came down gaveling on Lawson.

CHAIRMAN: Please be responsive to the question.

LAWSON: I wish to frame my own answers to your questions, Mr. Chairman, and I intend to do so. . . .

CHAIRMAN: And you will be responsive to the questions or you will be excused from the witness stand. . . .

LAWSON: I stated that it is outside the purview of the rights of this committee to inquire into any form of association . . .

CHAIRMAN: The chair will consider what is in the purview of this Committee.

LAWSON: My rights as an American citizen. . . .

In this atmosphere, then - of spies and counterspies, censorship and the Freedom Train, Hollywood stars and mock bombing raids - the Europeans, who must, in this context, have seemed innocent by Washington standards, arrived in the capital to argue their case for aid, and the President summoned Congress to an emergency session.

24
SELLING CONGRESS

THE PRESIDENT COULD, of course - and would - twist arms, swap favors, logroll, pork-barrel, and engage in all the other legislative tactics of persuasion that a President customarily applies to Congress; and those tactics would give senators and representatives an incentive to vote for the Marshall Plan. But members of Congress like a reason, too, for their votes, something they can take home to their constituents when it comes time for reelection - particularly when they have to return to an isolationist country with a proposal for foreign adventures. Lovett and his colleagues in the State Department were not yet happy themselves with what the Europeans were presenting to them. Under the circumstances, the administration could hardly feel confident that it had come up with something that Congress could believe, and sell to its constituents.

Early in September, Inverchapel had cabled home to London, "I saw Lovett yesterday and he expressed to me his despondency at the probable outcome of the Paris Conference. He referred repeatedly to what he called the 'shopping lists' . . . and said that the report . . . could not in its present form meet with a favorable reception here or be supported by the representatives of the United States Government."

Inverchapel had been upset. "I was unable to elucidate from Mr. Lovett exactly what were his specific criticisms of the report. I asked him whether the visit of Mr. Kennan, together with representations made by Mr. Clayton, had done anything to meet United States criticisms. . . . He replied that small improvements had resulted but the report was still unsatisfactory."

Inverchapel had then dined with George Kennan and found him no more cheerful. Kennan "expressed the concern of high officials that the Committee's report would not be positive enough in commitments and specific plans for the degree of integration of the European economies which was thought to be necessary in Washington."

Specifically, as an anonymous State Department official told Inverchapel's staff, the sixteen nations had not looked carefully at what they were requesting. In some cases, their total requests for a given commodity were actually more than the entire world's supply of that commodity. In other cases, the sixteen had used utterly arbitrary methods to cut their dollar requirements down from $29 billion to make the plan appear less expensive. Some of the Marshall Plan funds seemed to be earmarked for the purchase of supplies from Canada and Latin America, which would "in effect provide those countries as well as Europe with dollar assistance." That was not at all what the United States had in mind. It seemed to some of the Americans who considered this riddle that the Europeans could only avoid the problem by expressing their needs in commodities, not dollars. America would send goods, from its own farms and factories - not spending money.

Even late in September, after the European delegates had arrived in Washington to explain their requests, the anxieties at the State Department persisted. Inverchapel cabled again: "The lack of what they consider to be adequate co-ordination and integration . . . is entirely responsible for their feeling that they will not be able to justify the Paris report to Congress and the country."

In truth, the American objections had rattled even Inverchapel, whose faith in his European colleagues was becoming shaky. A new "glaring inconsistency" had just been pointed out to him. "I am told that the grand total of the mining equipment which participating countries expect to export to each other amounts to something like four times the grand total of the same equipment which participating countries expect to import from one another." How did his colleagues rationalize that?

"The hopes of American officials during the last few months," said Inverchapel, "have depended on the ability of the European countries to prove, not only to the United States Government but to the United States as a whole that they were able to work hard and work together." Frankly, Inverchapel was disappointed by his colleagues' work.

By this time, the British who had worked on the report in Paris were sick of Inverchapel's cables. The British negotiators cabled back: "Washington telegram . . . shows the Americans in Washington to be in as confused a state of mind as their representatives in Europe." The negotiators replied point by point. "We cannot understand the reference to mining machinery." Perhaps the Americans were confused by the fact that the French occupation zone in Germany needed four times more mining machinery than could come from the British-American zone. That anomaly naturally raised a question about where the mining machinery might come from. Perhaps it would be necessary to reactivate certain German factories. The negotiators had not felt they could solve this question, but by no means had they overlooked it. Inverchapel's quibbles about fats, oil, steel, and other commodities were answered by the negotiators with fiercely phrased specifics. Then, as for the idea that America would provide only commodities or would provide dollars only to purchase commodities from America, that suggestion was "extremely disturbing. Until the last few days it has never been suggested that European requirements should be expressed in terms of commodities rather than of dollars." What did Inverchapel think he was doing?

Sir Oliver Franks stepped into the midst of these anxieties and mutual recriminations with perfect aplomb. Of course, the British were right. But the Americans were not to be unduly criticized. Lovett, after all, was a relative newcomer to the State Department. "I gather," said Franks, a young man who had been born an old hand, "that Lovett started fairly soon after his arrival to create . . . an organization to decide the policy to be followed." But the State Department, he thought, was "short of experienced personnel," and they got off "to a slow start." To be sure, a number of policy questions should have been decided long before this time. "In theory it should have been possible to decide the form which aid should take (commodities or dollars), whether the United States was to assist in purchases of goods outside the United States and if so by what means . . . etc. In fact, however, no discussions were taken on these points by the time the technical committee representatives from Paris arrived." Nothing was to be gained by apportioning blame for these shortcomings.

And the question of dollars and commodities was a complex one. Europe needed imports from Canada and South America. This created a political problem for the Americans. A Kansas farmer, said Franks, might be willing to work extra hours (that is, to be taxed) to send aid to Europe, but he would not be so willing to work so that Europeans could buy wheat in Argentina for a higher price than the farmer gets in Kansas. The Americans knew, he said, that at least some American aid would have to be in dollars - to make normal European trade possible - "but what form this assistance might take was still obscure and would probably remain obscure for some time."

Sir Oliver's reasonableness and clarity of mind were enormously reassuring to the Americans once they were given a big dose of it, and he managed, for the whole of his Washington stay, to keep his equanimity. On October 6, at the first plenary meeting of the European delegates with Lovett and a few other Americans, Lovett made a welcoming speech in which he (insincerely) praised the Europeans for the "amount of thought" that had gone into making their report. He wondered, he said, "whether a similar agreement could have been written by sixteen States in the Union." Inverchapel replied that, of course, "a report full of detail, composed in so short a time and which dealt with so many issues, must give rise to many questions." During the next several weeks, the representatives all agreed, they would work with American experts to clarify the reports, to settle any questions of policy that might arise, and to revise any estimates that did not hold up to scrutiny.

Franks, meanwhile, had a quiet conversation one evening with Lovett. The program they were all talking about, Sir Oliver reminded the American, "was a *recovery* program and not a program of temporary relief. It has therefore to be a long-term program and the amounts available under it have to be sufficient to do the job. Otherwise it loses its character, becomes a further installment of relief, and at its end the people of Western Europe will be on your doorstep again." By that time, though, Europe would be in terrible shambles and could probably not be repaired, and America would be thoroughly disillusioned about foreign aid programs anyway. Thus, "the forging of the recovery of Western Europe can only be done once, and it has to be done now."

Therefore, although the program Lovett had had presented to him indisputably had its faults (and some of those faults could be corrected), still "I should be misleading you," said Sir Oliver, "if I were not to say at this stage that I am a little disturbed at the way discussions . . . have been going [with the Americans]. There seems to be a tendency . . . to 'chip away' [at the European proposal] and the risk is that the cumulative effect of this process . . . would have the result that the amount the Administration might support before Congress might in aggregate be sufficient only to support a relief program and not a full program of recovery."

What was really essential for the Americans to do, said Sir Oliver, was to decide whether the assumptions the diplomats made in Paris were "broadly reasonable." The Europeans had cut and pared their estimates of their needs. If estimates of needs still exceeded current world supply - as, for instance, in cereals - perhaps, in fact, some "physical sacrifice" was being asked from the United States. "This may well create problems of real difficulty." But if Europeans could not get sufficient food, they could not work. Lack of cereals could destroy the whole program. "Even as it is the people of Europe must live to some extent on deferred hope."

Under Sir Oliver Franks' patient tutelage, Lovett commenced to come around. The Europeans had, after all, not been sloppy or carefree; they had thought particularly hard, for instance, about the conundrum of aid in dollars or commodities. American questions evoked answers - perhaps not the ones that Americans wanted to hear, but answers, nonetheless, that showed the Europeans had tried to think through the problems they faced. The Europeans had tried to keep in mind the demands of American politics and business. As he listened to Franks, Lovett began to appreciate, too, how well the potentially impossible politics within and among the sixteen nations had been worked through. As Sir Oliver said, the report had "involved four years of crystal gazing; it had to be completed in eight weeks; it had to be agreed to by 16 nations." When the full realization of the accomplishment finally struck Lovett, said Sir Oliver, it had "an almost startling effect." Lovett was overcome with admiration for Franks.

Then, too, the Americans had had to realize, however reluctantly, that although they might have the strongest nation on earth, although they might have the wealthiest nation on earth, although they might be the only ones to possess the atomic bomb, although they might have an extremely clear policy and exceptionally clear-minded men who could carry it out with the clearest and strongest of managerial competence, although they might enjoy the goodwill of the world to a greater extent than ever before, although Europeans might be begging for them to cross the ocean, although America might never again have such overwhelming strength in the world - nonetheless, even then, even at the very height of their powers, the Americans were still only one among many sovereign nations in the world, and America's powers were limited. That Lovett was able, at last, to absorb that fact was some measure of his wit and maturity.

"After a difficult first three weeks," Franks reported back to the home office, the atmosphere in Washington had "changed completely." The men at State had been reassured, and they turned now more enthusiastically to the job of putting the program through Congress. First, they concentrated on the bill for interim aid; next, after that was successfully shepherded through Congress, they would turn their attention to the bill for the full Marshall Plan.

Those who went up to the Hill to lobby Congress used every argument in favor of aid that had been kicking around the Capitol for the past year: Whatever worked seemed good, and the State Department lobbyists did not pick and choose among the arguments so much as toss them all at the Congress to see what gathered votes. Soon enough, however, they discovered that the argument about European cooperation was awfully abstract and, to most congressmen, boring. The argument about building an integrated European market for American goods seemed also to lack fire. The words that were really electrifying up on the Hill were "Communist threat," and that was the theme that the salesmen tended to return to again and again as they worked the halls of Congress.

Meanwhile, reports trickled back to Washington about conversations that Georges Bidault had had with some senators who had visited him in Paris. The situation in France, said Bidault, was desperate. "At the present time, we are being literally strangled." But he had been encouraged by a visit of his own to Washington, he said. So many Americans had been so friendly. "I am very specially grateful in this emergency to all the Americans of both political parties . . . who were kind enough not to make me feel the humiliation of my position as beggar for my country."

The fundamental situation in Europe, Bidault told the senators, was "a huge wager between the Communist and anti-Communist forces. . . . I am sure we will win, but, of course, we can't do so alone."

Some Americans questioned France's hard attitude toward Germany. Bidault understood completely, he said, the need to rebuild the German economy, which was "an essential part of Europe's." Nonetheless, he could not quite go along with the "hand-in-hand" theory. France came first, not Germany.

Could France ensure that its government would not be dominated by Communists?

"I don't know what will happen. I have no idea as to the form which coming events shall take. I don't know whether I will long be at this desk. As a matter of fact, I don't think it will be for very long, but, of one thing I am certain, and that is that France shall not be governed by the Communist Party. With reasonable assistance from the United States . . . the French anti-Communist forces shall triumph."

Would France be satisfied to get commodities instead of dollars?

France only wanted dollars, said Bidault, to spend in the United States. These dollars would "not stick to France's fingers."

At the end, Bidault thanked the senators, and hoped that his "frankness should not be misunderstood: I am convinced that ours is a just course, and it is whole-heartedly that I entrust it to you."

Douglas and Caffery, meanwhile, peppered Washington from London and Paris with cables meant to be transmitted to Congress. "I am sending you this secret message," Douglas cabled Lovett, "which you may show Eaton, Chris Herter, Joe Martin. . . . There is in France a very real struggle for power. [Maurice] Thorez, the French Communist leader, has just returned from Moscow, probably with a promise of wheat, which he may make public in the near future at the proper time, in an effort to throw the balance of weight against U.S. If we are not to run the serious risk of losing France, we should act promptly. . . . Time is of the essence. Hardly a day can be lost. This is not, I promise you, a cry of 'wolf, wolf.' This we firmly believe is a brute reality.

Actually, Caffery cabled from France, the Communists had come to realize that the strikes they had been fomenting throughout the country were not only a failure, but that, as a result of them, "French public opinion is daily crystallizing against the French Communist Party." Lest the men in Washington take heart from this, however, Caffery had other news: The Communists were resorting to even more intransigent tactics; "flying squads of hardened Communist shock troops are being shuttled about to combat the police"; some Communists were deliberately provoking the police to fire on them; in some areas, non-Communist political leaders, "including deputies," were joining Communist protests and riots. "Moscow is convinced that the Marshall Plan to aid European recovery would serve to promote the formation of a Western European bloc which would permit the U.S. under cover of economic aid to expand and organize its zone of influence in Western Europe to the point where this zone would prevent extension of Communist influence and would serve as a dangerous jumping-off place for attacking Soviet Russia." Faced with such "menacing activity," Soviet policy seemed to encompass the possibility even of stepped-up "revolutionary activity," although, for the time being, Caffery understood, Thorez had told Communist "shock troops" not to "resort to the use of firearms."

The French Interior Ministry even went so far as to suggest - either out of conviction or because it seemed another good selling point - the possibility of war. The ministry had previously held the position that the United States had no reason to launch a preventive war against the Soviet Union, and that the Soviet Union needed five to ten years to get ready for a war. At the moment, however, the ministry had "a very severe case of the jitters." No one could figure out what Moscow wanted. The Russians seemed to be encouraging the European Communists to behave so extravagantly as to force European governments to outlaw them and drive them underground. Why? To aid the Soviet Army, "say within the next year or two . . . in an international conflict."

From Italy, at the same time, came news that the Italians were running out of dollars and "there would be nothing at all left for November imports." Should Italy not receive emergency American aid, Ambassador Alberto Tarchiani told Lovett in Washington, "a complete breakdown of the Italian economic system would occur." The American ambassador in Rome cabled home: "There was a time not long ago when I believed Italy would pull through, at least until the first of the year. Such is no longer the probability."

Tarchiani had another conversation with some of Lovett's aides. Communist-instigated strikes were becoming more widespread; the Communist leader Palmiro Togliatti had threatened violence, if necessary, to overthrow the government. Tarchiani thought (or at least he panicked the Americans by saying that he thought) that Togliatti might set up a Communist government in northern Italy, where the greatest Communist strength lay. That government would probably receive recognition from Tito. There would be civil war. A situation would exist similar to the one in Greece. Only one thing could prevent this: aid from America, to prove that only Tarchiani's government could rebuild Italy.

Kennan's Policy Planning Staff prepared a memo on the situation in Italy: "The Communists were excluded from the Italian Government in June, 1947. Since then, their rapid increase in strength and power appears to have been checked, and their influence seems to have declined, although they remain the strongest single force in Italian politics.

"Resenting their exclusion from the Government . . . the Communists have exerted increasing pressure . . . to bring about the downfall of the . . . cabinet and the formation of a new government with Communist participation. . . .

"For the first time, the Communists have threatened the use of force to overthrow the Government."

A memorandum was prepared for the President. France and Italy, the memo said, "have now reached the bottom of the barrel." France required $100 million worth of imports a month, to be paid for in dollars. The French would be out of dollars by mid-October. Italy's needs were almost as great ($85 to $95 million worth of goods), and the Italians were out of dollars too. In Italy, a summer drought had severely cut the most recent harvest. In France, the wheat crop was down from 6.7 million tons in 1946 to less than 4 million tons in 1947. Communists had been successfully excluded from both governments, but hunger and unemployment "will enable the communists to gain a dominant if not controlling position in the government before the winter is over."

Perhaps it would have taken uncommonly cool, or cynical, temperaments to withstand the sense of high anxiety that swept through Washington in the fall of 1947. Some of the unease about Communists exercising influence over (if not, in fact, "taking over") European governments was well founded. The Communist parties had, after all, won large votes in recent elections. Having been excluded from cabinets, they were prepared to strike, disrupt, spread disorder - whatever might bring down the incumbent governments and give the Communists another chance: any tactic was permissible, so long as it did not make more domestic enemies than supporters. Yet, in the private memoranda that circulated at the State Department, the coolest heads understood that the Communists had lost, that these were the last, desperate maneuvers of defeated factions, and that much of the furor over the Communists was now being trumped up, not least of all by the established Italian and French leaders, who saw in hysteria a chance for dollars. Or, as Pierre Mendès France, then the French executive director of the International Bank, said, "The Communists are rendering us a great service. Because we have a 'Communist danger,' the Americans are making a tremendous effort to help us. We must keep up this indispensable Communist scare."

And the Communist scare, whatever the more skeptical men at State might have thought of it, did help on Capitol Hill. Soon enough, the gossip networks began to carry good news from Congress. An Englishman in New York wrote a friend at the British Embassy in Washington about a dinner with Allen Dulles, "brother of John Foster Dulles . . . who used to be in the State Department . . . [and] has been working in an advisory capacity to the Herter Committee . . . he really felt very hopeful . . . . One of his chief reasons . . . is directly connected with the frame of mind which the members of the Herter Committee, and indeed virtually all the 215 members of Congress who have visited Europe this summer, have exhibited on their return to the U.S. ... Despite a certain amount of political opposition in Washington, Dulles said that he cannot recall such serious attention being given to any measure ever submitted to Congress as that which is currently being given to the Marshall Plan."

Confidentially, Lovett told Inverchapel, when the legislation came before Congress for debate, they must not be upset by what would happen. Interim aid would pass. But the British and Europeans should expect "very considerable delay and frustrations ... at every step," he said, and there would be "plenty of occasions for us to keep cotton wool in our ears." The Europeans could be quite certain, said Lovett, that Congress "will certainly demand every time a quid for their quo." And Sir Oliver wrote home, "During this stage almost everything possible that could be said about Europe would be said."

As the interim aid legislation moved through Congress, the President made a speech about the "totalitarian pressures" that might bring down the governments of France and Italy - and the rest of Europe. Marshall and Lovett and Harriman all testified about the crisis in Europe. Clayton published an article in the *Saturday Evening Post* about how failure to support foreign aid would lead to Communist domination of all Europe. "Never before," Congressman Busby of Illinois said with some wonder, "has the Congress been so bombarded with propaganda."

By the end of November, the mix of domestic and international politics - of real and trumped-up fear, of self-sacrifice and greed, of honesty and reasonableness, calm and hysteria, humanitarianism and political ambition in both America and in Europe, of real hunger and potential violence - had become so potent that the interim aid bill sailed through Congress. "I shall be greatly surprised," Vandenberg confided to his diary, "if more than a dozen senators dare vote against the Bill." In fact, in the end, only six voted against it. Even Senator Taft cast his vote in favor of aid.

The momentum had begun at last to shift in the administration's favor. Congress and the country had begun to move. In a moment - no more - the momentum would assume the proportions of an avalanche, for the President, with the most certain of political instincts, sent his men up to Capitol Hill at once, on the very day that the interim aid bill was passed, to submit the legislation for the full Marshall Plan. And then, as Averell Harriman told the British when he dropped by their embassy for a chat, if they thought they had seen unusual behavior on behalf of the interim aid bill, they should just wait: They had seen nothing compared to the "flood of organized propaganda which the Administration is about to unloose."

25

PASSAGE

I HAVE NEVER seen better work," Senator Vandenberg wrote in his diary as he surveyed the preparations the administration had made for its final campaign for the Marshall Plan. "The preparations that the State Department have made for this next showdown are amazing." Indeed, so thoroughgoing, so complete, so assiduous were the preparations that one of the men working Congress on the administration's behalf found it appalling. "Everything," he said, was "one dimension too big. The stuff was so elaborate that [the congressmen] couldn't leaf through it." The final report of the Harriman committee, for example, was three inches thick - and hard to lift.

Charles Bohlen, Kennan's colleague at the State Department, was detailed to take charge of public relations. Ambassador Lewis Douglas was recalled from London to take over liaison between the department and Congress. Marshall, Clayton, Forrestal, and Attorney General Clark all went out on speaking tours. Acheson's Citizens' Committee went into the business of ghost-writing testimony for such groups as the Farmers' Union, who sent representatives to testify before Congress. In the first five weeks of 1948, Vandenberg's Senate Foreign Relations Committee heard more than ninety witnesses and received written testimony from scores of others. Congress was buried in lobbyists and testimony. The National Cotton Council (Clayton's old friends) had a delegation in every state who knew the principal financial backers of every senator and representative - and the council's board voted to go all out on the Marshall Plan. The Citizens' Committee financed women's groups, and the women's groups held meetings and sponsored speeches.

"Cabinet members, ambassadors, and other government officials were heard," Vandenberg recalled, "so were leaders in industry, agriculture, and labor. College professors, editors, and trade association representatives appeared; so did the women's clubs, church groups, and organizations interested in various means of keeping the peace. Veterans' groups, civic groups, and such leading citizens as Bernard M. Baruch were heard; plain citizens, One-Worlders, isolationists, socialists, and those who, quite frankly, were not certain where they stood took their turn on the witness stand." What was said mattered less than the overall impression this all made: that here was something very big and important.

Even Acheson put in a cameo appearance before Congress and displayed the character that many congressmen had already come to love to hate. "When you go up to Congress," as Dean Rusk (one of Acheson's later assistants) once remarked, "you should have a little hay behind your ears. Acheson wouldn't do that." Quite the opposite: At one point in his testimony, Acheson - mustache bristling, eyebrow arched, head cocked to one side - fixed his withering gaze on a congressman and snapped, "If you didn't talk so much and listened more, I think you would understand better what this is all about."

Clayton, too, irrepressible, bouncing back from every rebuff or reprimand, looking perpetually newly showered and freshly combed and ready to advance once more into the fray, popped up whenever he could to argue the need for a strong European market to buy American exports - although, by this time, the people in Washington were generally confused about the economic issues involved in the Marshall Plan.

Calvin Hoover, a member of the Harriman committee, told the Senate Foreign Relations Committee that "we do not need to give foreign countries money to buy our surplus goods. There need never be any net surplus of goods which cannot be easily disposed of to our own citizens, either by lowering taxes or by raising real wages or by other means of increasing purchasing power whenever such action is appropriate. . . . We could easily consume much more in the form of goods and services than we are currently able to produce." Any competent economist, said Hoover, could show that surpluses would disappear if domestic purchasing power were raised. "There can be no question, therefore, but that the goods which we furnish Europe must come out of our own potential standard of living and not out of some mythical surplus."

But Clayton would have none of this. As he thought, "If Western Europe is overrun by communism, I think the situation which we would face in this country would be a very grave one. . . . The economic consequences of such a disaster would be very, very great to us. We would have to reorder and readjust our whole economy in this country if we lost the European market." Whatever Calvin Hoover might say, Clayton knew for a fact that the cotton business and other such multinational enterprises needed strong international trade to survive and prosper; and in any case, as always,

Clayton was not just interested in a few years' surplus; he was eager for a few decades' expansion. And so he kept it up, proselytizing whenever and wherever he could – "Doctrinaire Willy," Hugh Dalton, the British Chancellor of the Exchequer, had taken to calling him.

Forrestal, who was hurtling himself mercilessly from meeting to business lunch to conference to dinner speech - struggling with his own department to finish the job of unifying the three branches of the armed forces, and badgering others to support universal military training - took time to do his part on behalf of the Marshall Plan, even finding it possible to take the position (if only briefly) that the Marshall Plan must take precedence over the needs of the Defense Department. "I believe," he wrote to Chan Gurney, the chairman of the Senate Armed Services Committee, "that economic stability, political stability, and military stability must develop in about that order." Although the Soviet Union had the greatest army in Europe, the United States, said Forrestal, had the greater sea power, the atomic bomb, and the greatest industrial capacity in the world. "As long as we can outproduce the world, control the sea, and can strike inland with the atomic bomb, we can assume certain risks otherwise unacceptable in an effort to restore world trade. . . . The years before any possible power can achieve the capability effectively to attack us with weapons of mass destruction are our years of opportunity."

Of all who testified, however, none made a greater impression than General Marshall. He was, as President James Conant of Harvard said of him, the only American in history who could be compared with George Washington. He was, indeed, first in war, first in peace. For all his aloofness, for all the difficulty that even his closest friends had in penetrating his character, he remained a warmly revered man, a national monument. His word was still the best in Washington. And he had, during the last several months, come a long way in talking to congressmen.

"So long as hunger, poverty, desperation, and resulting chaos threaten the great concentration of people in Western Europe," Marshall told the Congress, ". . . there will steadily develop social unease and political confusion on every side. Left to their own resources there will be, I believe, no escape from economic distress so intense, political confusion so widespread, and hopes of the future so shattered that the historic base of western civilization . . . will take on a new form in the image of the tyranny that we fought to destroy in Germany. . . . We shall live, in effect, in an armed camp, regulated and controlled. . . . There is no doubt in my mind that the whole world hangs in balance." Congress, said Marshall, was about to make "the greatest decision in our history." If it turned down the European Recovery Program, he said solemnly, he would not be held responsible for the consequences.

Having outlined a basic array of arguments, the administration played them like a piccolo through the following weeks. If a congressman wanted protection from Russia, the Marshall Plan would stop the Communists; if a congressman resented scare tactics, administration spokesmen shifted ground and talked economic benefits. If it was said that the Marshall Plan was too expensive, then the Defense Department had an analysis to show that the budget for the armed services would need to be increased immediately by 25 percent if the Marshall Plan were defeated. When a congressman complained, with the reasoning of Calvin Hoover, that there was no necessary surplus of goods in America and that Marshall aid would strain the American economy and cause inflation, Truman's men would refer to the Harriman report.

The Marshall Plan was, Congress was told, a means to fight communism, a way to prevent postwar American depression, a way to reduce the need for more military spending, a humanitarian act, a way to rebuild the important German economy (but only after the rest of Europe, and in a way to keep Germany from rearming), a way to establish

European economic and political union, a way to restore France and Italy - to keep Communists out of their governments.

Nothing was excluded from the administration's pitch if it looked as though it might attract a few votes. If economic arguments failed, references were made to charity; if charity failed to arouse interest, the plight of Western civilization itself was worked into the conversation. At one meeting of Vandenberg's committee, someone objected that a reference in the ERP bill to "impact on our domestic economy" was too vague and should be deleted. "That's perfectly all right," said Vandenberg, "just leave those words in. I can tell nineteen different senators from the floor of the Senate who are worried about something - your problem is taken care of by that clause in the bill." Finally, what the Marshall Plan had above all was something for everyone. And everybody won. Nobody lost.

Of course, Senator Taft was not happy. "We have seen in the past three months," he had complained over the interim aid campaign, "the development of a carefully planned propaganda for the Marshall plan, stimulated by the State Department by widespread publicity and secret meetings of influential people in Washington."

Taft and his Republican colleague Kenneth Wherry commenced to gather a group of twenty senators to oppose the administration. They joined forces with Christian Herter of the House - who could be considered an expert, having taken a committee to Europe that summer - and they suggested, since they concluded they could not stop the momentum altogether, that the Marshall Plan be slashed to an appropriation of $4 billion for a year, and then be reviewed to see how it was doing. Toward the end of January, former Republican President Herbert Hoover - another foreign aid expert for having run a European relief program after the First World War - announced that he agreed with the idea of a $4 billion program. If the Republicans could not halt the Marshall Plan, they could at least trivialize it.

At that moment, Vandenberg proved his mettle. Where the administration had been talking about $17 billion or $18 billion for a four-year program, Vandenberg had a suggestion for Marshall: Let the Secretary of State ask for a general authorization, without a stated price tag, for the plan as a whole, but for a specific dollar appropriation only for the first year. Such a thing was common, Vandenberg told Marshall, in programs extending over several years, and in any case, it was all Congress could really do. One Congress cannot bind the next one on spending; specific appropriations would have to be made annually anyway. Under the circumstances, there was no reason even to mention such a large number as $17 billion.

Furthermore, said Vandenberg, the administration was asking for an authorization of $6.8 billion for the first fifteen months of operation. Let it rather request $5.3 billion for the first twelve months. The difference between 4 and 5, then, was almost unnoticeable, and men like Taft, after all the fuss that had been made on Capitol Hill, would seem like Scrooge for quibbling over such a little difference. With the approval of the State Department, Vandenberg added his amendment - and the opposition was scattered. At the same time, a Gallup poll was taken to sample public opinion across the country. After all the tumult in Washington, how much impression had the politicians made on the American people? How many had come to the conclusion that the Communists had to be stopped, and were sold on the idea of throwing the Marshall Plan at them? How many saw the economic benefits for American capitalism? How many had even heard of the Marshall Plan?

Encouragingly enough, more Americans had heard of the plan than not. As for what it was worth, 56 percent of Americans thought the Marshall Plan was best considered an act of charity; 8 percent thought it would "curb communism"; and 35 percent offered back the grab bag of explanations the administration had given them, or had no opinion, or had, still, never heard of it. Perhaps it could be said that the poll showed that the American people were naive - that they had little idea what their government was really up to, or why. Certainly it can be said that the American people did not constitute a vast constituency eager for a large international role for themselves, or that their political leaders were merely the weak pawns in the grip of a people determined on exercising great power in the world. But of all the tentative conclusions one might draw, there can be no doubt that the most poignant and touching is that, in the autumn of 1947, the Americans were by and large still an astonishingly generous people: They were, in fact, prepared to support the Marshall Plan, and to support it for largely humanitarian reasons.

Yet nothing was left to chance. *Time* magazine pronounced support for the Marshall Plan to be "shallow," and so, in the midst of the congressional debate, the State Department leaked a file of documents that would not, under ordinary procedures of editing and processing, have been released for another several years: the report of a conversation between Molotov and the German Ambassador to Moscow, reports of conversations between Hitler and Molotov, and several other papers which confirmed that Stalin and Hitler had signed a mutual nonaggression pact in 1939. The documents confirmed, too, as it had been rumored, that Stalin and Hitler had come to another secret agreement to establish clear spheres of influence and, what seemed even more offensive, that the Russians had greeted the German invasions of

Norway, Belgium, and Holland with enthusiasm and delight, and that Stalin might even have preferred to be allied during the war with Germany, instead of Britain, France, and the United States. It came as no surprise to Americans that Stalin was an evil character, but this fresh reminder, this linkage with Hitler, called up all the passions of the recent war and sent a new wave of revulsion against the Russians across the country. Several weeks later, on February 13, when the Marshall Plan came before Vandenberg's committee, the bill went through in a breeze, passed by a vote of 13 to 0.

Then, toward the end of February, the Communists in Europe gave the Truman Administration another gift when they brought on the downfall of the Czechoslovakian government. Newspaper reports described grown men weeping in the streets of Prague - recalling Hitler's blitzkrieg invasion to the east at the outbreak of World War II. In an entirely unrelated incident, General Lucius Clay sent a cable from Germany. Clay had been asked by Army intelligence if he could furnish a little something that would help when the Army went up to Capitol Hill to ask for a larger military budget. Without much thought, he dashed off a cable: "For many months, based on logical analysis, I have felt and held that war was unlikely for at least ten years. Within the last few weeks, I have felt a subtle change in Soviet attitude which I cannot define but which now gives me a feeling that it may come with dramatic suddenness. I cannot support this change in my own thinking with any data . . . other than to describe it as a feeling of a new tenseness in every Soviet individual with whom we have official relations. I am unable to submit any official report in the absence of supporting data but my feeling is real. You may advise the Chief of Staff of this for whatever it may be worth if you feel it advisable." Forrestal took Clay's telegram and broadcast it around Washington.

Kennan, of course, was quick to remind his colleagues that the Czech crisis was merely the anticipated consolidation of the Russian sphere of influence (as Marshall had informed the cabinet the previous November), but now, once again, Kennan's voice no longer carried. His brief time of influence in American foreign policy was already waning. Once again his advice sounded overly balanced, cool, not useful. He was on his way, once again, to becoming an outsider. The atmosphere had become best suited to hard men.

Within hours of the fall of the Czechoslovakian government, Forrestal got together for dinner with former Secretary of State James Byrnes and stoked Byrnes's imagination with fears of the Communist menace - and with opportunities to get Congress to agree to that same old pet project that would beef up the Defense Department: universal military training and a reinstatement of selective service (the draft). Forrestal provided Byrnes with grist for a speech and with some publicity. "There is nothing to justify the hope," said Byrnes in his speech, "that with the complete absorption of Czechoslovakia and Finland the Soviets will be satisfied." Just as Hitler had taken advantage of the appeasers who would not stop him, so Stalin would keep moving until he was stopped. Italy might well be next. What could America do? Get Congress to pass UMT, selective service, and the Marshall Plan.

The main thing, as Forrestal sensed at once, was to put a couple of things through Congress while the atmosphere was right, "to capitalize," as he noted in this diary on March 2 after having lunch with Marshall and Lovett, "on the present concern of the country over the events of the last week in Europe."

Truman may, in fact, have believed war was possible. "We are faced," he wrote his daughter Margaret, after conferring with Marshall and Forrestal, "with exactly the same situation with which Britain and France were faced in 1938-39 with Hitler." Or else the President was just in love again with crisis and action and decisiveness and bragging to his daughter. "Things look black. A decision will have to be made. I am going to make it."

Newspaper reporters, kept in a turmoil by releases and leaks from the Pentagon and the

State Department, filed story after story about "how war might come," "whispers of war," "that awful three-letter word, war."

At last, when the news of Jan Masaryk's death reached the West, even those who had been rather routinely using the tragedy of Czechoslovakia for their own political purposes found their words suddenly informed by genuine feeling. All at once, the Americans were unable to distinguish - perhaps not for the first time, certainly not for the last - between what they said and what they deeply believed and feared.

The Joint Chiefs of Staff gave Forrestal an emergency war plan to counter a Soviet invasion of Europe. The Council of Economic Advisers prepared a query for the President, asking whether the economy should be put on wartime wage and price controls. And Truman's new CIA informed the President that, although it did not anticipate war within sixty days, it would not predict further than that.

As it happened, the spring primaries for the 1948 presidential election were fast coming up, too, and Clark Clifford, Truman's principal adviser on the campaign, had just returned from Florida with some thoughts on strategy. As one of Clifford's aides put it, "Pres. *must* for his prestige, come up with a strong foreign speech - to demonstrate his leadership - which country needs and wants. . . .

The strongest possible speech for the President would be one on Russian relations. . . . The President could deliver a Russian speech better than a speech on any subject. His best delivery has been on occasions when he has been 'mad' . . . His poorest deliveries have been when he is merely *for* a 'good thing.'" An address to Congress was called for.

As Clifford had written in an earlier memo on campaign strategy, "There is considerable advantage to the Administration in its battle with the Kremlin . . . the nation is already united behind the President on this issue. The worse matters get, up to a fairly certain point - real danger of imminent war - the more there is a sense of crisis. In times of crisis, the American citizen tends to back up his President."

The President's speechwriters went to work at once - with such enthusiasm that General Marshall began to feel anxious and sent Charles Bohlen in with instructions to say that the Secretary "wants a weak message, drop intemperate language . . . simple, businesslike, no 'ringing phrases' - nothing warlike or belligerent. Don't denounce, just state the facts."

Clifford was disgusted: "It has to be blunt, to justify the message! He asks for legislation - how does he explain it?"

Marshall had been worrying lately about all the positions America seemed to be taking in the world - and all without armies and navies and an air force to back them up. The trouble was, as he had confessed to Forrestal just a couple of weeks before, "we are playing with fire while we have nothing with which to put it out."

Marshall, Truman told his staff at their daily meeting on March 16, was afraid that he, Truman, might "pull the trigger" with a speech that was too forceful. But Truman dismissed the notion without a second thought: "Better to do that than be caught, as we were in the last war, without having warned the Congress and the people."

And so, once again, Truman walked down the aisle - preceded by members of the cabinet, senators, congressmen, watched from the galleries by friends, the press, Mrs. Truman - and to the applause of the chamber took his place at the podium to address a joint session of Congress.

This time the groundwork had been done. Congress had been prepared. The President's proposals would not be sprung as a surprise: They were the culmination of many months' work.

"The situation in the world today," said the President, "is not primarily the result of natural difficulties which follow a great war. It is chiefly due to the fact that one nation has not only refused to cooperate in the establishment of a just and honorable peace, but - even wors - has actively sought to prevent it . . . . Since the close of hostilities, the Soviet Union and its agents have destroyed the independence and democratic character of a whole series of nations in Eastern and Central Europe. It is this ruthless course of action, and the clear design to extend it to the remaining free nations of Europe, that have brought about the critical situation in Europe today. The tragic death of the Republic of Czechoslovakia has sent a shock-wave through the civilized world."

The Prime Minister of Canada, Mackenzie King, was listening to the President on the radio and made a note afterward in his diary: "This was a day that had its place in history. It really is the line of demarcation between the past and efforts to adjudicate difficulties with the USSR by conciliation and beginning of settlement by force."

"There are times in world history," said Truman, "when it is far wiser to act than to hesitate. There is some risk involved in action - there always is. But there is far more risk in failure to act."

Within two days, the House committee that had been debating the Marshall Plan reported the bill out to the full House and recommended its passage to "reverse the trend of Communism in Europe." The bill went through the House with ease.

In the final roll-call vote, as a reporter for the *Washington Post* put it, "in a seething and excited House shouts of 'aye' came from one Republican after another who had seldom, if ever, voted for any international legislation." The United States was committed at last to being a great international power.

26
THE MARSHALL PLAN
INACTION

THE INK WAS not dry on the words of gratitude from Bevin and Bidault before the first ships set sail from the port of Galveston, Texas, with 19,000 tons of wheat - followed by the SS *Godrun Maersk* out of Baltimore with tractors, synthetic resin, and cellulose acetate; the SS *Gibbes Lykes* with 3,500 tons of sulfur; the SS *Rhondda* with farm machines, chemicals, and oil; the SS *Geirulo,* the SS *Delmundo,* and the SS *Lapland* with cotton. Soon, at any given moment, 150 ships would be on the high seas, carrying Marshall Plan cargoes of wheat, flour, cotton, tires, borax, drilling equipment, aircraft parts, tobacco, and $20 million worth of horsemeat.

When shipments of carbon black began to reach Birmingham, England, Europe's largest tire plant was put back into production and 10,000 workers returned to their jobs. One of the workers at the Birmingham plant told a reporter: "If there was a boat crossing the Atlantic with black aboard, we'd follow its progress across the Atlantic, and wait for it to dock. If we heard it was at Liverpool, some of us went out to meet the trucks on the way from the docks. We begged the drivers not to stop even for a meal on the road." "This Marshall aid," said another of the workers, "has got my thanks."

Indeed, the gratitude and new hope were so emphatic that, as George Kennan was to say, "The psychological success at the outset was so amazing that we felt that the psychological effect was four-fifths accomplished before the first supplies arrived."

To oversee the vast program of gathering up American goods and credits and dollars and transmitting them to Europe, Truman chose, as the Economic Cooperation Administrator, Paul G. Hoffman. In truth, Truman first suggested that he wanted to appoint his loyal friend Dean Acheson to the job, but Senator Vandenberg, with a keen sense of the impression that Acheson made up on the Hill, said to Truman, "Mr. President, he can never be confirmed."

Besides, Vandenberg wanted a Republican to be made administrator. Lists of possible candidates had been drawn up. Hoffman's name appeared at or near the top of all of them. He was a Republican but not a professional partisan politician. He had been a member of Harriman's committee of businessmen. Vandenberg thought there was general agreement on Hoffman. Or, as Hoffman himself said with buoyant good humor, "It seems that I was the least obnoxious of the Republicans."

A first-rate automobile salesman (selling, he said, is "the process of transferring a conviction from the mind of the seller to that of the buyer"), Hoffman had been born just outside Chicago fifty-six years before, one of five children whose father, an inventor, bumped from inspiration to inspiration and financial windfall to financial disaster. Hoffman did well in school and went off to the University of Chicago for a year, until his father's financial reverses forced the young man to get a job. He took a position as a salesman for the Halladay motorcar company and set about his work with a unique sales technique. He would take one of the new cars and drive out into a suburb, where he would invite the local banker for a ride. Cars were novel enough that a banker would rarely refuse. Hoffman would not try to make a sale; instead he would ask the banker which of his neighbors had the cash and the wish to have a car. In this way, in only a few years, he became the Halladay company's top salesman and, soon after, was pulled in as manager of the Studebaker Corporation's retail and wholesale division in Los Angeles. In another dozen years - after taking time out for a stint of service in World War I - he founded the Paul G. Hoffman Company, pumped sales up to $7 million a year, and became, at the age of thirty-four, a millionaire. When Studebaker Corporation itself fell on hard times in the early thirties and went into receivership, Hoffman was called on to rescue the corporation. Within two years, by 1935, Hoffman had guided Studebaker out of receivership, and himself into the presidency of the company. During World War II, Studebaker landed some hefty war contracts for airplane engines and heavy-duty trucks - and not until years later, after Hoffman had drifted away from the company, did Studebaker fade, and die, as an automobile maker.

Hoffman was a man of irrepressible energy, booming self-confidence, and inexhaustible good cheer. He loved poker, bridge, gin rummy, and golf (and talked to himself on the golf course: "Now, Hoffman, you damned fool, hit the ball!"), and loved his six children. He was the sort of man, his friends said, who could play an intricate bridge hand - something on the order of a grand slam redoubled, with a young Hoffman on his knee and a dogfight going on under the table - and win. He was the sort of fellow who, in spite of his fortune, liked to grab a cheeseburger at the local drugstore, and who, when he sat in on a meeting, would toss a leg over the arm of his chair and sprinkle his sentences with modest Midwestern disclaimers of omniscience: "as I see it," "in my opinion," "from our point of view." He did, however, expect to win. He was never importunate. He was low-key, soft-sell all the way. He simply believed that a calm, orderly presentation of reasons for buying his product would persuade anyone that he was right.

What Hoffman knew he was right about was productivity: growth, raising output by 30 percent, 50 percent, and more and more. He staffed his Washington office with fellow businessmen, investment bankers, corporation lawyers, automobile salesmen, soft-drinks men, and pep-talked them into a froth. America, with a population of 150 million, turned out $300 billion worth of goods a year. Europe, with a population of 260 million, turned out only $150 billion worth of goods. If the Europeans could be made as productive as the Americans, Europe would turn out three times as much as it did. Productivity was the key. And then where would the Communists be? As Georges Villiers, the president of the French businessmen's council, said, "Instead of giving over to class hatred about the division of our wealth, let us double or triple the quantity of this wealth." The trick was multiplication, not division. Rather than talking of a new way of dividing the pie, make a bigger pie, and there would be plenty to go around.

In pursuit of higher productivity, the Americans would badger, wheedle, scold, and humor the Europeans to a frazzle.

The man appointed to stand between Hoffman's ebullient enthusiasm and the *amour propre* of the Europeans - to set up headquarters in Paris as the ambassador from America's organization, the ECA, or Economic Cooperation Administration, to Europe's organization, the OEEC, or Organization for European Economic Cooperation - was none other than Averell Harriman, who set up offices at the Hotel de Talleyrand on the place de la Concorde. "A labyrinthine maze," as a member of the American press corps was to say, "of cubicles, pens, partitions and old corridors," the hotel had served - briefly - the aristocrats of the eighteenth century who watched the workings of the guillotine from its windows. Napoleon gave the four-story, high-walled palace to his shrewd Foreign Minister, Talleyrand, who conducted his love affairs there and, in his spare time, drew to him ("as a spider to its web," Victor Hugo said) the princes and diplomats of Europe, and destroyed them one by one - and for a time brought unity, of a kind, to Europe.

Harriman ensconced himself in a gilt and green inner office, under a bust of Benjamin Franklin (Harriman's great predecessor as friendly, well-loved American emissary to Europe), and from there communicated with his senior chiefs of mission: for France, David K. E. Bruce, Virginia gentleman, former son-in-law of Andrew Mellon, Princeton graduate, son of a United States Senator, brother of an ambassador, former associate of the W. A. Harriman Company, tall, distinguished, firm, and inexhaustibly good humored; in England, Thomas Finletter, a Wall Street lawyer, born in Philadelphia, a man with a quick mind and a caustic sense of humor, known to some as "the little acid drop"; in Germany, Norman Collisson, a stocky former industrial engineer, whose principal job seemed to be fighting off General Clay, who was still firmly entrenched in Germany when the Marshall Plan first got under way; in Italy, James Zellerbach, a slight, balding man, former paper and pulp man (Crown Zellerbach) from the Pacific Coast, a man who managed to antagonize all political factions in Italy equally (such as the time the Italian government ministers first tried to explain their notions of land redistribution to him and he had cut them off: "I'm not interested in politics. . . . It's strictly a business proposition").

Harriman's own sensitivity to the delicacies of European relations was completely refined. When a Frenchwoman wrote to him that the fluorescent lights burning late in the Hotel de Talleyrand were an unfortunate intrusion on the somber beauty of the place de la Concorde after dark, the ambassador ordered black curtains and had them drawn over the windows of the Talleyrand every night.

To be young, to be American, were wonderful things in the late forties; to be one of Averell Harriman's aides - or an aide to one of his aides - was transcendental. By 1952, 2,500 people would come to work for the American Embassy in Paris; with their wives and children they would form an American community of some 7,500. Of them all, only 129 were Foreign Service officers. The rest were experts, or would-be experts, bright young men, young fellows on their way up who had managed to land a plum appointment to Paris, young men with a connection, young men with a future. Their clerks and stenographers would transmit 4 million words of reports back to Washington every month (and get back about half as many in reply). They filled the Hotel Talleyrand, and seven large office buildings, and seven grand residences for special dignitaries, and stored $15 million worth of desks and teletype machines and radio equipment and stationery in a warehouse.

Their habits were noted: their Thanksgiving celebrations with turkey and cranberry sauce; their Fourth of July garden parties with thin sandwiches; their casual, free, friendly manner. Their pleasures began to seep into French society: their hamburgers, their Kleenex, their magazines with pictures of negligeed women and spaceships, the *New York Herald Tribune, Time* and *Newsweek* (available on the same day that they were back in the States), *True Detective, Real Western,* Alfred Hitchcock movies, X-ray equipment, "Way Down Upon the Swanee River," jukeboxes, hot dogs, Mickey Spillane, Scotch tape, Hemingway, slot machines, Coca-Cola, Humphrey Bogart.

In the late forties, the place to be was the snack bar downstairs at the Talleyrand, or across the place de la Concorde at the bar of the Hotel Crillon, where the Americans gathered to chat over dry martinis. There, the talk might turn to the problems of transporting millions of tons of wheat from one hemisphere to another or solving the centuries-old problems of drought in some arid climate. They were a happy, confident lot, all of them strictly can-do. One day, when the talk over lunch turned to the specter of famine in India, a professor of economics pulled his pipe from his mouth just long enough to solve the problem: "Now, if there's a big famine, we'll have to buck it through to Congress and let Congress handle it, but if it's a small famine, we'll handle it out of our own funds without any trouble."

The American "expert," as Theodore White wrote from France, "has become in the outer world as much a stock character as was the British traveler of the nineteenth century, as 2,000 years ago the Roman centurion must have been in conquered

Greece." They ate at the best restaurants, drove the best cars, talked the brightest talk, these experts in malleable iron ore and insecticides, in coal mining and garment cutting, in tax law and oil drilling, in microbiology and public health, fishing, sheet steel, balance of payments, labor relations, government security, and agronomy.

In pursuit of ever higher productivity, the Americans reasoned that the Europeans needed to break up their cartels, that they needed to eliminate their tariffs, smash national barriers to trade, integrate their economies, lift quotas, liberalize trade, apply the latest techniques of scientific management in order to maximize labor resources, introduce new labor-saving technologies. In every way, the Americans showed the Europeans how it could be done better, and when the Europeans commenced to show some recalcitrance, the Americans did not hesitate to fall silent and let the tacit understanding well up in the consciousness of all who sat around a dinner table or a conference room that the Americans could, if they chose (though in fact they couldn't quite), with the turn of a credit or the twist of a loan, break any government they chose. The Europeans, wrote Theodore White, "submitted to incessant prying, pushing and prodding by Americans." The Europeans tried desperately to placate the Americans. "But every minute they do so they sense a smoldering, unexpressed indignity working within them, because America still keeps asking for more and remains forever unsatisfied."

The achievements, however, could be touched. At the Doboelmann Soap Works, one of the oldest soap factories in Holland, American experts showed the Dutch how to cut processing time from five days to two hours with a new American machine. In Norway, fishermen used new nets made from yarn spun in Italy out of cotton from the United States. In Offenbach, Germany, Marshall Plan leather revived the handbag industry. In Denmark, a Philadelphia knitting machine raised production at Hanson Brothers Knitting Works by 10 percent. In Vienna, children received 1,000 baby chicks from American 4-H Club members, financed by the Marshall Plan. In Greece, American experts informed dairymen that the reason their cows licked the whitewashed stone walls was that they suffered from a calcium deficiency. In Turkey, American public health officials predicted they could wipe out malaria in three years. On Moroccan farms, camels were replaced by American tractors. In Nigeria, American scientists studied ways to eliminate the tsetse fly.

In Lille, Marshall Plan coal kept a steel factory in business. In Roubaix, Marshall Plan wool kept one of the world's largest textile mills in operation. French harbors, 70 percent destroyed during the war, were completely restored after two years of

Marshall Plan aid. Jeanne Vidal, stricken with polio, received an iron lung from Denver. French shoemakers, brought to America to learn efficiency, discovered how to cut 20 percent from the cost of production by altering their patterns. Whereas, in 1945, only 25,000 tractors could be found working French fields, within two years, Marshall Plan aid put another 100,000 tractors into the fields. By 1949, food ration tickets had been eliminated in France. In Paris, meals prepared - as the official *Marshall Plan News* boasted - "by France's great chefs" were quick-frozen and exported by air.

The political effects of Marshall Plan aid were felt at once, too - even, as George Kennan said, before the first supplies arrived. Within days of the dispatch of the first ships to Europe, the Italians held an election. Premier Alcide de Gasperi had based the campaign of the anti-Communist Christian Democrat Party on the Marshall Plan. He called it, as *The New York Times* said, "Italy's hope." Palmiro Togliatti, the Communist leader, based his campaign, as the *Times* said, "largely on opposition" to the Marshall Plan, calling it "a danger to Italy's independence and a threat to peace." The Vatican, the *Times* noted, "threw its support behind the Christian Democrats." Posters were put up on walls linking the bread supply to American aid. Gas and light bills bore the legend that the utilities were dependent on American coal supplies. American officials greeted cargo ships at Italian docks. Radio commentators made it clear that American aid would cease if Italy went Communist. The Christian Democrats took almost 50 percent of the vote, the Communists, and other left-wing parties who joined them in the Popular Front took 30 percent. Other minority parties divided the rest.

During the next several years, Italy made a shaky, but in the end remarkable, recovery. Never a highly developed industrial country, its output before the Second World War had been only a third of Germany's. At the end of the war, Italy's industrial production was at a mere 20 percent of prewar levels; agricultural production had been cut in half. Postwar inflation was ferocious. A married civil servant made thirty to fifty dollars a month - not enough to buy meat or even oranges, except on rare occasions. Prices had become so bizarre that some items on the black market were cheaper than on the officially rationed market. And while working people - and vast, milling crowds of unemployed - walked the streets in search of bargains on bread and olive oil, the elegant rich, though few in number, were provocative as they cruised past in their noiseless luxury cars, driven by liveried chauffeurs.

The Italian government imposed stringent anti-inflation measures, tightened bank credit, stiffened reserve requirements, and seemed largely indifferent to unemployment. Despite the predictable resentment that grew among the lower classes, the left wing was kept successfully at bay for the next several decades, and although, as Luigi Barzini would write, Italian governments would rise and fall with startling rapidity, the same people would continue to rule Italy from year to year.

After 1950, as general economic conditions in Europe improved, Italy was buoyed up along with the rest of the Continent. Although Italy lacks raw materials, by the early 1960s, the Italians had established themselves as among the most interesting designers and manufacturers of cars, office equipment, and electrical machinery. Olivetti typewriters and Italian sports cars found large markets. (Low wages kept prices down.) Between 1961 and 1963, productivity rose by 30 percent. And, by the middle and late 1960s, prosperity had begun to reach even the lower middle classes. In 1960, one out of twenty-one Italians owned a car; by 1968, one out of seven owned a car. By the end of the 1960s, Italians had as many telephones and television sets per thousand inhabitants as the French.

In England, editorial writers speculated on what would have happened had there been no Marshall Plan: "Bread, cake, and pastry supplies cut to half of what they are now. Butter, cheese, and sugar rations down by one-third. No cotton goods in the shops. . . . New housing programs down by half." Still, Great Britain was barely bumping along, beset by constant balance-of-payments crises, credit shortages, fluctuations in the economy. The British economy did not come to a halt, but it lurched alarmingly, and even when it did advance, it went more slowly than its Continental neighbors, so that its share in world trade dropped steadily over the years. It was said that the state took up too large a chunk of British wealth for welfare spending, but the French government took an even larger share. It was said that taxes were too high in Britain, but taxes were higher in both France and Germany. It was said that the British did not spend enough on research and development, but they spent more than any other country in Europe.

True enough, wages rose faster than productivity (though, even so, wages were not high). Management was not adventurous; it was, rather, still bound by class and privilege; few could work their way up; hard work had no rewards. Wildcat strikes occurred over whether the tea break should come at ten or eleven. Still, Britain's irreducible economic problem was that it had lost its colonies and its favorable trading relationships. No government could solve that problem. From time to time, it seemed that the Conservatives were luckier at it than Labour, but there was no solution. Under the circumstances, a scapegoat was needed, and the welfare state took the blame. "Europe," as

Jean-Jacques Servan-Schreiber wrote from Paris, "now seems ripe for a return to the *status quo ante* . . . . The Europe that emerged from the war was a Europe of the *'lendemains qui chantent,'* of a joyful march towards Socialism. But one by one, all the features of this Europe are rapidly disappearing. What is coming is a Liberal . . . Europe." Or, as Paul Henri Spaak was saying in private, "You see that the Labor experiment in England is well down the drain."

Nonetheless, for seeming to have halted or reversed this inevitable decline, by grabbing hold of the Marshall Plan with both hands, the Labourites were sustained in office for several years, and Ernest Bevin spoke for England until, in March 1951, ill health finally forced him to accept the merely decorative position of Lord Privy Seal. Five weeks later, while he was at a football match, the "old ticker," as he called it, gave out.

In France, the country that had been, in Walter Laqueur's memorable phrase, "the museum of Europe" - in which nothing ever changed, in which the number of deaths consistently surpassed the number of births from 1934 onward - the postwar period brought about a boom of astounding suddenness and magnitude. Plagued in the beginning by lack of raw materials, inflation, a flight of capital abroad, and by the fact that 60 percent of its industries and 90 percent of its retail trade were family enterprises, plagued by a resistance to accept new techniques (peasants had no use for their new tractors), the French nonetheless had a long-standing tradition of centralized planning. With the help of the Marshall Plan and Jean Monnet, with the nationalization of industries, the manipulation of investment credits and tax rebates, and the (finally) energetic entry into a pan-European market, the French modernized their steel industry, doubled their electricity output by 1954, raised industrial production by 50 percent above prewar levels, developed the best railway system in Europe, and turned in a steady 5 percent annual growth in gross national product. French integration into a European market was a great boon. By 1958, sales to European Economic Community countries accounted for 22 percent of all French foreign sales; by 1968, the EEC accounted for 41 percent of French exports. In 1958, the falling French agricultural economy exported 18 percent of its output to EEC countries; by 1968, French agriculture had been revived by exporting 50 percent of its products to the EEC.

As for politics, according to Theodore White, the departure of the Communists from the government changed the whole tone of things in France. The projects of reform and revolution that the left wing had proposed, and that had gained the support of such large numbers of voters, "lay half finished on the statute books in illogical confusion. . . . The voters of France, perplexed and embittered, knew they had been cheated, but did not know precisely whom to blame." During the five years from 1947 to 1952, having lost the Communists from their governments, the remaining left-liberal factions had to move farther and farther right to be able to construct majority coalition governments. Such new coalitions, as White reported from France, "now no longer had common aspirations, for some wanted to continue the reforms of Liberation and the others wanted to undo them." As the governing parties compromised and regrouped, rearranged coalitions and cabinets, policies that one party or another had just recently stigmatized as evil had to be incorporated into a new coalition, until French voters were utterly confused and entirely disgusted. By 1952, hit with a fresh gust of inflation, the French were ready to turn for the first time in twelve years to the far right and give the government to Antoine Pinay, a frail little man who had once been a supporter of the collaborationist Vichy government.

Georges Bidault lasted for a surprisingly long time through these upsetting times. Altogether, through the late forties and early fifties, he served as Foreign Minister, Deputy Prime Minister, and Prime Minister, ever the astute negotiator, ever the hard bargainer. As the turmoil of the postwar world developed, Bidault, the old Resistance leader, resolute enemy of fascism, was revealed at last to be something of a right-winger himself. When it appeared that France would lose Algeria to an independence movement, Bidault joined, in 1956, an organization called the Union for the Safety and Resurrection of French Algeria. Two years later, he formed an organization that went so far as to countenance terrorist activities in order to block Algerian independence. With that, his old ally in the Resistance, General de Gaulle, then President of France, issued a warrant for Bidault's arrest. Bidault fled the country and spent six years in exile, moving from country to country around the borders of France until, in 1968, de Gaulle issued a general amnesty and Bidault returned to his native country to live in obscurity.

In Germany, meanwhile, the four zones of occupation had hardened into a nation divided between the Soviet Union and the West, with General Clay continuing to take the lead in the administration of the western zones. Clay's job had by this time altered, however, into one of transferring authority from the military occupation forces to a civilian government. From the autumn of 1948 to the spring of 1949, West German representatives gathered in Bonn to frame a new, democratic constitution for themselves. They were not yet allowed, quite, to rule themselves. General Clay and the other occupation authorities watched over the constitution-making; and, once the constitution was framed, and Clay and the others went home, the new republic of Germany was attended by three high commissioners, one each from Britain, France, and the United States. Every few weeks, the Chancellor of the new republic - Konrad Adenauer, seventy-three years old, tall, grave, stiff, and starched - would make the long trek from the parliament building on the west bank of the Rhine, across the river, and up a forested hill to a vast white mansion, the Petersberger Hof, where Adolf Hitler had received Neville Chamberlain before the war, and present the acts of parliament to the high commissioners, who would look through them, advise, consent, and instruct.

The U.S. High Commissioner was John J. McCloy, a Philadelphia Republican who had attended Amherst College and Harvard Law School and worked for Cadwalader, Wickersham & Taft, and later on for Cravath, De Gersdorff, Swaine & Wood as a specialist in corporate law. His Wall Street connections drew him into the government in 1941 as Assistant Secretary of War to Henry Stimson. McCloy, a tennis player and fisherman, short and balding, with a compact, athlete's frame and high energy, had a devoted amateur interest in military history, and was known as a man with vast resources of discretion, an insider's insider. Harriman thought McCloy ought eventually to become the Secretary of State for a Republican president. C. L. Sulzberger, reporting for the *Times* from Europe, was not so sure; Adenauer, he said, was "a shrewd, patient and determined man, autocratic and arrogant. . . . Of course he pulled plenty of wool over McCloy's eyes, but that is not a very difficult task because McCloy is not as bright as he thinks he is." McCloy was, in any case, well on his way to becoming, as he would eventually be known, the chairman (if there were one) of the American establishment (if it existed), and during the latter half of 1949, and on into 1950, the ambiguous ritual of obeisance occurred with punctilious regularity: Adenauer, flanked by two briefcase-carrying aides, would pay his call on the high commissioners at Petersberger Hof.

General Clay, and subsequently the three commissioners and the new democratic government of Germany, oversaw a revival that was soon called, with a shrug of amazement, the economic miracle (*Wirtschaftswunder*). In a country whose eastern agricultural lands had been lopped off and taken over by the Soviet Union, between 1949 and 1950, the volume of foreign trade doubled. The next year, foreign trade rose by 75 percent. Between 1954 and 1964, it tripled. Between 1948 and 1964, industrial production increased sixfold. Unemployment fell during the same period from 8 or 9 percent to 0.4 percent. In 1946, 2.5 million tons of steel were poured in Germany. By 1949, 9 million tons were poured. By 1953, 14.5 million tons were poured. Coal production doubled. The manufacture of radios doubled. Between 1948 and 1964, 8 million new dwelling units were constructed. New bridges went up, new highways were laid down. By 1953, Germany was producing twice the number of automobiles as it had in 1936: Opels, Volkswagens, Porsches, Mercedes-Benzes went on the export market.

In part, this economic revival could be attributed to the austere administration of Germany at the hands of the occupation forces and the high commissioners. It was far easier for General Clay to keep people on starvation diets of 1,000 calories a day and to shake up the old German cartels (not to destroy them, but to bring in new men to run them) than it would have been for a German democratic government, which would need to be more responsive to domestic political demands. But the occupation forces discovered, too, somewhat to their surprise, that the damage the war had inflicted on Germany was not as extensive as everyone had supposed. To be sure, as one toured German cities and farmlands, the destruction looked dreadful. Piles of brick and stone, bomb craters, twisted steel girders rising from the rubble, children in rags: All presented a vision of desolation. And yet, once the ruins were cleared away, it turned out that much of the industrial capacity of Germany was intact. Indeed, in some industries, it had actually increased during the war. Whereas the inventory of machine tools had stood at 1,281,000 in 1938, by the end of the war, the number of machine tools had been almost doubled. Trade relationships had been destroyed, financial structures and markets wrecked, but many of the tools and all the skills remained. Under the disciplined guidance of the high commissioners, Germany revived with alacrity. Luxury shops opened in Düsseldorf. Stores were stocked with tropical pineapples and bananas, Burgundy champagnes, Scandinavian hams. In West Berlin, not only were the shop windows filled with consumer goods, but little kiosks set out at intervals along the sidewalks were stuffed with shoes, silk scarves, watches, and gloves, and the soldiers of the Allied occupation forces began to wonder, as they said, "who had won and who had lost the war."

Altogether, the Marshall Plan contributed $13,015,000,000 to European recovery - and it was not uniformly appreciated. At first, objections came from the left. In London, in the spring of 1948, in Finsbury Town Hall, the center of a drab working-class district, 300 Britons gave a rousing ovation to John Platts-Mills, a left-wing member of Parliament who insisted that the European Recovery Program was nothing but a political bridgehead "for the Yankee businessman's invasion of Europe." (For these and similar views, Platts-Mills was soon driven out of the Labour Party.) In Italy, left-wing politicians complained that Marshall aid "has filled our shops with luxuries and our streets with unemployed." The standards of upper-class consumption had been raised; Marshall Plan funds had buttressed such monopolies as Fiat, Pirelli, and Montecatini, whose small number of shareholders split large profits; but the new wealth was not reaching Italian workers, whose wages were not rising, but whose cost of living, fed by inflation, had risen to 51 times the level of just before the war. In France, the journal *Combat* surveyed the postwar scene and pronounced that the Marshall Plan had produced a "banker's Europe." Even Theodore White, as he looked around him in France, began to worry about what the Americans were calling a "logistical" approach to reviving Europe: "The logistical approach had relied on technical features - if so much new steel capacity was put in, then so many new tractors or automobiles might be built. . . . Some of the opponents of the logistical approach called it the "trickle theory," or the theory which held that if enough is poured in at the top, something will trickle down to the bottom. The trickle theory had, thus far, resulted in a brilliant recovery of European production. But it had yielded no love for America and little diminution of Communist loyalty where it was entrenched in the misery of the continental workers. The rich and well-to-do rolled about once more in automobiles. . . . But the workers had barely held their own; they lived in stinking, festering slums, dressed in shabby second-hand clothes."

In time, others joined the left in their complaints. Even the imperialist *Daily Express* and the Tory *Daily Telegraph* in London thought that American planners were imposing "shameful" and "humiliating" limitations on British sovereignty. Still others felt invaded by the businessmen who followed the Marshall Plan administrators, and the Europeans could not help noticing that the book value of United States companies' direct foreign investments in British and European industries - which had risen by only 1.5 percent between 1929 and 1940 - suddenly took off: Immediately after the war, American investments rose by 38 percent in mining, by 58 percent in manufacturing, and by 143 percent in petroleum. And as time went on, such investments rose even more startlingly.

Between 1950 and 1970, investments in overseas mining rose by 770 percent, in manufacturing by 1300 percent, and in petroleum by 1600 percent. The base on which America built its overseas interest was from the beginning, and remained, Europe. While investments increased in Asia by 556 percent between 1950 and 1970, and in Latin America by 320 percent, investments in Europe increased by 1400 percent. Branches of American banks increased in the United Kingdom and Ireland from eleven to forty-four between 1955 and 1970, and in Europe, in the same period, from six to seventy-two.

By the mid-1960s, American-controlled companies in Britain accounted for 80 percent or more of the production of boot and shoe machinery, canned baby food, carbon black, color film, custard powder and starch, sewing machines, typewriters; 60-79 percent of boilers, breakfast cereals, calculating machines, cigarette lighters, potato chips, razor blades, spark plugs; 50-59 percent of automobiles, cake mixes, canned milk, cosmetics and toilet preparations, electric shavers, electric switches, drugs, foundation garments, pens and pencils, pet foods, petroleum-refining construction equipment, tractors, vacuum cleaners; 40-49 percent of computers, locks and keys, photographic equipment, printing and typesetting machinery, rubber tires, soaps and detergents, watches and clocks.

In France, by the early 1960s, American companies controlled 80 percent of computers and 95 percent of the market for integrated circuits, 65 percent of farm machinery, 65 percent of the production of films and photographic paper, 65 percent of telecommunications equipment, 50 percent of semiconductors, 45 percent of synthetic rubber, 40 percent of the petroleum market.

In the appalled view of Jean-Jacques Servan-Schreiber, Europe had become "a new Far West for American businessmen. Their investments do not so much involve a transfer of capital, as an actual *seizure of power* within the European economy."

Europeans found they were no longer easily amused by American movies, nor quite so enamored of Coca-Cola and hot dogs. In truth, the Americans had come to seem somewhat rude and vulgar, and their constant efforts to prod the Europeans into doing things in the American way had become exasperating. And more and more Europeans began to worry about the rhetoric of the Cold War and the possibility that the United States and the Soviet Union might engage in a nuclear exchange, for which Europe would once again, provide the battlefield. The American presence in Europe had become a burden and even, some thought, a mortal danger. Nor was the American conviction about productivity an idea that stayed firmly implanted in every European mind. Every time inflation wiped out or diminished the gains of productivity, and the promise of "multiplication" became elusive, the Socialist demands for "division" would reassert themselves.

But then, before all these contrary forces had quite sorted themselves, out, on June 25, 1950, the North Koreans invaded South Korea, and the United States government and economy were turned toward planning for war. The Marshall Plan ended - or was "swallowed up," as Kennan said - amidst requests by the United

States for Europe to make some contribution toward defense. Soon, 80 percent of American aid to Europe went for defense. What had been a passionate debate, in Europe and America and in Germany, as well, over the question whether or not Germany ought to be rearmed was settled at once: Germany was rearmed. The Marshall Plan for economic recovery was subsumed under plans for a military alliance in Western Europe.

The planning for such an alliance had, in truth, begun as early as December 1947, while the Marshall Plan legislation was still making its way through Congress. Just after a meeting of foreign ministers in London, Bevin had taken Secretary Marshall aside and suggested that the British and Americans ought to get together on "some Western democratic system comprising the Americans, ourselves, France, Italy, etc.," that would stop "further Communist inroads" by way of a mutual defense arrangement. Marshall agreed at once that "there was no choice in the matter," but the Americans, he said, would prefer to have the Europeans take the lead in forming such an alliance, just as they had taken the lead in putting together the Marshall Plan. In March 1948, at a meeting in Brussels, the English and French signed a pact with the Benelux countries, pledging a commitment to mutual defense for a period of fifty years. In April 1949, the United States joined with the Brussels pact countries and other Western European nations to form the North Atlantic Treaty Organization. And NATO took over where the Marshall Plan had left off.

Having tried to assert himself at first with the Truman Doctrine - and having been rebuffed for its bellicosity - the President now succeeded by following his peaceful, generous plan with a military plan. And where the Truman Doctrine had failed, the Marshall Plan and NATO succeeded: America broke out of its historic, self-imposed isolation in the Western Hemisphere and engaged the rest of the world - economically, politically, and militarily - as a global power.

The makers of the Marshall Plan can hardly take all the credit, or blame, for the formation of the entire postwar world. The Russians deserve some credit and blame, too. Larger historical forces outside the control of any of the major powers played their part. The dissolution of empires in the twentieth century had, by the end of the Second World War, become entirely inevitable. Technologies had acquired their own momentum. Liberation movements in the Third World, which would shape so much of the latter half of the century, could not be held back by any nation. And in economic terms alone, the Marshall Plan cannot be solely credited even with the astonishing resurgence of the European economy.

In retrospect, it is clear that an enormously complex set of factors operated on the economy of Europe. First of all, the disastrous agricultural harvest of 1947 was followed by a superb harvest in 1948. Second, the German monetary reform in June 1948 was reckoned one of the great feats of economic engineering in all history. Labor, in general, throughout Europe, understanding the seriousness of the postwar economic situation, did not push for wage gains but held off, and so let capital flow into the building of new plants. Monetary stabilization programs were enforced throughout Europe with particular strictness. A whole generation of government planners had become accustomed to accepting the notions of Keynesian deficit financing, and applied such notions with fearlessness and sophistication. A new generation of entrepreneurs was ready to take risks across national boundaries and so organized vigorous new multinational corporations. Tariff barriers were reduced to assist international trade. Measures of assistance often seemed to have twofold effects: New tractors and fertilizers, for instance, not only aided agriculture, but also liberated workers to rebuild industry. Established industries came under better-trained, efficiency-oriented managements that had a fashionable interest in rational planning and investment in research. Europe had always been the world's greatest market; with a more integrated economy (leading, eventually, to the Common Market), its potentials could be more fully realized. The capitalist economies became - at least in such areas as coal, energy, and transport - more subject to central government planning, and a new confidence among business and government planners led to more aggressive, expansionist planning. In time, military spending fueled expansion.

No single factor can be withdrawn from such a combination of forces and made to explain the entire phenomenon of postwar growth. But the achievement of the Marshall Plan emerges from all these complexities with real clarity: The plan contributed, more than dollars or credits or goods, the crucial element of confidence - for governments to reach across borders, for entrepreneurs to take new risks, for banks to extend credit, for workers to set aside immediate gains. The most important effect of the plan was, as George Kennan had foreseen from the very beginning, essentially "psychological." It was a piece of planning about finances and trade, wheat and machine tools, oil and carbon black, radio components and rubber tires, but one whose ultimate goods were intangible.

Nor were its intangible benefits limited to economic matters alone. Without doubt, the Marshall Plan seriously damaged the Communist parties of Western Europe - and gave prodigious support to the liberal and conservative political forces of Europe. Moreover, it is difficult to see how, without the Marshall Plan, Europe could have been drawn together as quickly as it was after the war, or how it could otherwise have been (however imperfectly) "integrated." Nor is it possible to see how, without the Marshall Plan, the United States could have been placed so firmly at the center of Europe. Indeed, so successful was the plan in this respect that it could be said to redefine geography by confirming the existence of the Atlantic Community and metaphorically shifting the very center of Europe to the middle of the Atlantic Ocean.

Nor is it clear how it would have been otherwise possible for the United States to take its place as the leading member of this Atlantic Community, to draw Europe together as the base for its new role as a world power, to direct what some bright young English journalists soon began to call the Pax Americana. For, with the Marshall Plan and NATO, there could no longer be any doubt that the United States had at last embarked upon a venture that would finally extend its power and influence to nearly every province of the world, and join America to ancient Greece and Rome, to Holland and Spain and Portugal - and most especially, as the men in the State Department recognized back on February 21, 1947, when Lord Inverchapel's secretary called to say that he had a blue piece of paper to deliver, to Great Britain - in the long history of the world's most renowned and reviled empires.

APPENDIX I
PRESIDENT TRUMAN'S ADDRESS TO CONGRESS PROGLAIMING THE TRUMAN DOCTRINE

President Harry S Truman's Address Before a Joint Session of Congress, March 12, 1947

MR. PRESIDENT, MR. SPEAKER,

MEMBERS OF THE CONGRESS OF THE UNITED STATES

The gravity of the situation which confronts the world today necessitates my appearance before a joint session of the Congress.

The foreign policy and the national security of this country are involved.

One aspect of the present situation, which I wish to present to you at this time for your consideration and decision, concerns Greece and Turkey.

The United States has received from the Greek Government an urgent appeal for financial and economic assistance. Preliminary reports from the American Economic Mission now in Greece and reports from the American Ambassador in Greece corroborate the statement of the Greek Government that assistance is imperative if Greece is to survive as a free nation.

I do not believe that the American people and the Congress wish to turn a deaf ear to the appeal of the Greek Government.

Greece is not a rich country. Lack of sufficient natural resources has always forced the Greek people to work hard to make both ends meet. Since 1940, this industrious and peace loving country has suffered invasion, four years of cruel enemy occupation, and bitter internal strife.

When forces of liberation entered Greece they found that the retreating Germans had destroyed virtually all the railways, roads, port facilities, communications, and merchant marine. More than a thousand villages had been burned. Eighty-five percent of the children were tubercular. Livestock, poultry, and draft animals had almost disappeared. Inflation had wiped out practically all savings.

As a result of these tragic conditions, a militant minority, exploiting human want and misery, was able to create political chaos which, until now, has made economic recovery impossible.

Greece is today without funds to finance the importation of these goods which are essential to bare subsistence. Under these circumstances the people of Greece cannot make progress in solving their problems of reconstruction. Greece is in desperate need of financial and economic assistance to enable it to resume purchases of food, clothing, fuel, and seeds. These are indispensable for the subsistence of its people and are obtainable only from abroad. Greece must have help to import the goods necessary to restore internal order and security so essential for economic and political recovery.

The Greek Government has also asked for the assistance of experienced American administrators, economists and technicians to ensure that the financial and other aid given to Greece shall be used effectively in creating a stable and self-sustaining economy and in improving its public administration.

The very existence of the Greek state is today threatened by the terrorist activities of several thousand armed men, led by Communists, who defy the government's authority at a number of points, particularly along the northern boundaries. A Commission appointed by the United Nations Security Council is at present investigating disturbed conditions in northern Greece and alleged border violations along the frontier between Greece on the one hand and Albania, Bulgaria, and Yugoslavia on the other.

Meanwhile, the Greek Government is unable to cope with the situation. The Greek army is small and poorly equipped. It needs supplies and equipment if it is to restore the authority of the government throughout Greek territory.

Greece must have assistance if it is to become a self-supporting and self-respecting democracy.

The United States must supply that assistance. We have already extended to Greece certain types of relief and economic aid but these are inadequate.

There is no other country to which democratic Greece can turn.

No other nation is willing and able to provide the necessary support for a democratic Greek government.

The British Government, which has been helping Greece, can give no further financial or economic aid after March 31. Great Britain finds itself under the necessity of reducing or liquidating its commitments in several parts of the world, including Greece.

We have considered how the United Nations might assist in this crisis. But the situation is an urgent one requiring immediate action, and the United Nations and its related organizations are not in a position to extend help of the kind that is required.

It is important to note that the Greek Government has asked for our aid in utilizing effectively the financial and other assistance we may give to Greece, and in improving its public administration. It is of the utmost importance that we supervise the use of any funds made available to Greece; in such a manner that each dollar spent will count toward making Greece self-supporting, and will help to build an economy in which a healthy democracy can flourish.

No government is perfect. One of the chief virtues of a democracy, however, is that its defects are always visible and under democratic processes can be pointed out and corrected. The government of Greece is not perfect. Nevertheless it represents eighty-five percent of the members of the Greek Parliament who were chosen in an election last year. Foreign observers, including 692 Americans, considered this election to be a fair expression of the views of the Greek people.

The Greek Government has been operating in an atmosphere of chaos and extremism. It has made mistakes. The extension of aid by this country does not mean that the United States condones everything that the Greek Government has done or will do. We have condemned in the past, and we condemn now, extremist measures of the right or the left. We have in the past advised tolerance, and we advise tolerance now.

Greece's neighbor, Turkey, also deserves our attention.

The future of Turkey as an independent and economically sound state is clearly no less important to the freedom-loving peoples of the world than the future of Greece. The circumstances in which Turkey finds itself today are considerably different from those of Greece. Turkey has been spared the disasters that have beset Greece. And during the war, the United States and Great Britain furnished Turkey with material aid.

Nevertheless, Turkey now needs our support.

Since the war Turkey has sought financial assistance from Great Britain and the United States for the purpose of effecting that modernization necessary for the maintenance of its national integrity.

That integrity is essential to the preservation of order in the Middle East.

The British Government has informed us that, owing to its own difficulties, it can no longer extend financial or economic aid to Turkey.

As in the case of Greece, if Turkey is to have the assistance it needs, the United States must supply it. We are the only country able to provide that help.

I am fully aware of the broad implications involved if the United States extends assistance to Greece and Turkey, and I shall discuss these implications with you at this time.

One of the primary objectives of the foreign policy of the United States is the creation of conditions in which we and other nations will be able to work out a way of life free from coercion. This was a fundamental issue in the war with Germany and Japan. Our victory was won over countries which sought to impose their will, and their way of life, upon other nations.

To ensure the peaceful development of nations, free from coercion, the United States has taken a leading part in establishing the United Nations. The United Nations is designed to make possible lasting freedom and independence for all its members. We shall not realize our objectives, however, unless we are willing to help free peoples to maintain their free institutions and their national integrity against aggressive movements that seek to impose upon them totalitarian regimes. This is no more than a frank recognition that totalitarian regimes imposed on free peoples, by direct or indirect aggression, undermine the foundations of international peace and hence the security of the United States.

The peoples of a number of countries of the world have recently had totalitarian regimes forced upon them against their will. The Government of the

United States has made frequent protests against coercion and intimidation, in violation of the Yalta agreement, in Poland, Rumania, and Bulgaria. I must also state that in a number of other countries there have been similar developments.

At the present moment in world history nearly every nation must choose between alternative ways of life. The choice is too often not a free one.

One way of life is based upon the will of the majority, and is distinguished by free institutions, representative government, free elections, guarantees of individual liberty, freedom of speech and religion, and freedom from political oppression.

The second way of life is based upon the will of a minority forcibly imposed upon the majority. It relies upon terror and oppression, a controlled press and radio, fixed elections, and the suppression of personal freedoms.

I believe that it must be the policy of the United States to support free peoples who are resisting attempted subjugation by armed minorities or by outside pressures.

I believe that we must assist free peoples to work out their own destinies in their own way.

I believe that our help should be primarily through economic and financial aid which is essential to economic stability and orderly political processes.

The world is not static, and the *status quo* is not sacred. But we cannot allow changes in the *status quo* in violation of the Charter of the United Nations by such methods as coercion, or by such subterfuges as political infiltration. In helping free and independent nations to maintain their freedom, the United States will be giving effect to the principles of the Charter of the United Nations.

It is necessary only to glance at a map to realize that the survival and integrity of the Greek nation are of grave importance in a much wider situation. If Greece should fall under the control of an armed minority, the effect upon its neighbor, Turkey, would be immediate and serious. Confusion and disorder might well spread throughout the entire Middle East.

Moreover, the disappearance of Greece as an independent state would have a profound effect upon those countries in Europe whose peoples are struggling against great difficulties to maintain their freedoms and their independence while they repair the damages of war.

It would be an unspeakable tragedy if these countries, which have struggled so long against overwhelming odds, should lose that victory for which they sacrificed so much. Collapse of free institutions and loss of independence would be disastrous not only for them but for the world. Discouragement and possibly failure would quickly be the lot of neighboring peoples striving to maintain their freedom and independence.

Should we fail to aid Greece and Turkey in this fateful hour, the effect will be far reaching to the West as well as to the East.

We must take immediate and resolute action.

I therefore ask the Congress to provide authority for assistance to Greece and Turkey in the amount of $400 million for the period ending June 30, 1948. In requesting these funds, I have taken into consideration the maximum amount of relief assistance which would be furnished to Greece out of the $350 million which I recently requested that the Congress authorize for the prevention of starvation and suffering in countries devastated by the war.

In addition to funds, I ask the Congress to authorize the detail of American civilian and military personnel to Greece and Turkey, at the request of those countries, to assist in the tasks of reconstruction, and for the purpose of supervising the use of such financial and material assistance as may be furnished. I recommend that authority also be provided for the instruction and training of selected Greek and Turkish personnel.

Finally, I ask that the Congress provide authority which will permit the speediest and most effective use, in terms of needed commodities, supplies, and equipment, of such funds as may be authorized.

If further funds, or further authority, should be needed for purposes indicated in this message, I shall not hesitate to bring the situation before the Congress. On this subject the Executive and Legislative branches of the Government must work together.

This is a serious course upon which we embark.

I would not recommend it except that the alternative is much more serious.

The United States contributed $341 million toward winning World War II. This is an investment in world freedom and world peace.

The assistance that I am recommending for Greece and Turkey amounts to little more than 1 tenth of 1 percent of this investment. It is only common sense that we should safeguard this investment and make sure that it was not in vain.

The seeds of totalitarian regimes are nurtured by misery and want. They spread and grow in the evil soil of poverty and strife. They reach their full growth when the hope of a people for a better life has died.

We must keep the hope alive.

The free peoples of the world look to us for support in maintaining their freedoms.

If we falter in our leadership, we may endanger the peace of the world - and we shall surely endanger the welfare of our own nation.

Great responsibilities have been placed upon us by the swift movement of events.

I am confident that the Congress will face these responsibilities squarely.

APPENDIX II
GENERAL MARSHALL'S SPEECH AT HARVARD UNIVERSITY ANNOUNCING THE MARSHALL PLAN

Secretary of State George C. Marshall's Address at the Commencement Exercises of Harvard University, Cambridge, Massachusetts, June 5, 1947

I need not tell you, gentlemen, that the world situation is very serious. That must be apparent to all intelligent people. I think one difficulty is that the problem is one of such enormous complexity that the very mass of facts presented to the public by press and radio make it exceedingly difficult for the man in the street to reach a clear appraisement of the situation. Furthermore, the people of this country are distant from the troubled areas of the earth and it is hard for them to comprehend the plight and consequent reactions of the long-suffering peoples, and the effect of those reactions on their governments in connection with our efforts to promote peace in the world.

In considering the requirements for the rehabilitation of Europe, the physical loss of life, the visible destruction of cities, factories, mines, and railroads was correctly estimated, but it has become obvious during recent months that this visible destruction was probably less serious than the dislocation of the entire fabric of European economy. For the past 10 years conditions have been highly abnormal. The feverish preparation for war and the more feverish maintenance of the war effort engulfed all aspects of national economies. Machinery has fallen into disrepair or is entirely obsolete. Under the arbitrary and destructive Nazi rule, virtually every possible enterprise was geared into the German war machine. Long-standing commercial ties, private institutions, banks, insurance companies, and shipping companies disappeared, through loss of capital, absorption through nationalization, or by simple destruction. In many countries, confidence in the local currency has been severely shaken. The breakdown of the business structure of Europe during the war was complete. Recovery has been seriously retarded by the fact that two years after the close of hostilities a peace settlement with Germany and Austria has not been agreed upon. But even given a more prompt solution of these difficult problems, the rehabilitation of the economic structure of Europe quite evidently will require a much longer time and greater effort than had been foreseen.

There is a phase of this matter which is both interesting and serious. The farmer has always produced the foodstuffs to exchange with the city dweller for the other necessities of life. This division of labor is the basis of modern civilization. At the present time it is threatened with breakdown. The town and city industries are not producing adequate goods to exchange with the food-producing farmer. Raw materials and fuel are in short supply. Machinery is lacking or worn out. The farmer or the peasant cannot find the goods for sale which he desires to purchase. So the sale of his farm produce for money which he cannot use seems to him an unprofitable transaction. He, therefore, has withdrawn many fields from crop cultivation and is using them for grazing. He feeds more grain to stock and finds for himself and his family an ample supply of food, however short he may be on clothing and the other ordinary gadgets of civilization. Meanwhile people in the cities are short of food and fuel. So the governments are forced to use their foreign money and credits to procure these necessities abroad. This process exhausts funds which are urgently needed for reconstruction. Thus a very serious situation is rapidly developing which bodes no good for the world. The modern system of the division of labor upon which the exchange of products is based is in danger of breaking down.

The truth of the matter is that Europe's requirements for the next three or four years of foreign food and other essential products - principally from America - are so much greater than her present ability to pay that she must have substantial additional help or face economic, social, and political deterioration of a very grave character.

The remedy lies in breaking the vicious circle and restoring the confidence of the European people in the economic future of their own countries and of Europe as a whole. The manufacturer and the farmer throughout wide areas must be able and willing to exchange their product for currencies the continuing value of which is not open to question.

Aside from the demoralizing effect on the world at large and the possibilities of disturbances arising as a result of the desperation of the people concerned, the consequences to the economy of the United States should be apparent to all. It is logical that the United States should do whatever it is able to do to assist in the return of normal economic health in the world, without which there can be no political stability and no assured peace. Our policy is directed not against any country or doctrine but against hunger, poverty, desperation, and chaos. Its purpose should be the revival of a working economy in the world so as to permit the emergence of political and social conditions in which free institutions can exist. Such assistance, I am convinced, must not be on a piecemeal basis as various crises develop. Any assistance that this Government may render in the future should provide a cure rather than a mere palliative. Any government that is willing to assist in the task of recovery will find full cooperation, I am sure, on the part of the United States Government. Any government which maneuvers to block the recovery of other countries cannot expect help from us. Furthermore, governments, political parties, or groups which seek to perpetuate human misery in order to profit therefrom politically or otherwise will encounter the opposition of the United States.

It is already evident that, before the United States Government can proceed much further in its efforts to alleviate the situation and help start the European world on its way to recovery, there must be some agreement among the countries of Europe as to the requirements of the situation and the part those countries themselves will take in order to give proper effect to whatever action might be undertaken by this Government. It would be neither fitting nor efficacious for this Government to undertake to draw up unilaterally a program designed to place Europe on its feet economically. This is the business of the Europeans. The initiative, I think, must come from Europe. The role of this country should consist of friendly aid in the drafting of a European program and of later support of such a program so far as it may be practical for us to do so. The program should be a joint one, agreed to by a number, if not all, European nations.

An essential part of any successful action on the part of the United States is an understanding on the part of the people of America of the character of the problem and the remedies to be applied. Political passion and prejudice should have no part. With foresight, and a willingness on the part of our people to face up to the vast responsibility which history has clearly placed upon our country, the difficulties I have outlined can and will be overcome.

NOTES

A NOTE ON SOURCES

The essential sources for this book were the memoranda, cables, and minutes of meetings that reside in the archives of the United States, British, and French governments. The American documents are to be found, for the most part, in the State Department's Decimal Files, particularly the 840 Recovery Files. Many of the most important of these documents have been published in the *Foreign Relations of the United States* (cited below as FRUS), in particular in volumes II, III, and V for 1947. The British documents, not published, are in the Public Record Office in London, and are referred to in the notes below by their Foreign Office (abbreviated FO) document numbers.

French documents are quoted here from the *French Yellow Book.*

Many of the participants in the framing of the Marshall Plan have been interviewed, beginning in the early 1950s, and these interviews, which can be found in the Truman and Marshall libraries, have been extremely helpful.

In addition to these principal sources, I have made frequent recourse to records of congressional hearings, to the memoirs of Truman, Acheson, and Kennan, to Joseph Jones's *Fifteen Weeks,* and, among secondary sources, I am especially indebted - for matters of broad interpretation as well as for specific information - to Daniel Yergin's *Shattered Peace,* Richard Freeland's *The Truman Doctrine and the Origins of McCarthyism,* and to the essays that Charles Maier has published recently in journals.

1. THE OPPORTUNITY

For an account of the Greek situation, see Yergin, 287-296; for the quote of Subhi Sadi, see Yergin, 291; for the American diplomatic reports on food prices, see FRUS III, 40; for the report of Richard Windle, see the State Department Decimal Files 501.BC Greece/2-2147: Telegram, in FRUS V, 38; for there being "no state" in Greece, see 868.50/2-1747, in FRUS V, 20; for general observations on the state of Europe at the end of the war, see Yergin, 304-311, Roberts, 308-309, Freeland, 13-22 and 28-68 *passim*, Maier, 7 ff., *Life* magazine of 4/28/48, 105 ff.; for the observations on membership of the State Department, see *Life* magazine of 6/23/47, 93 ff.; for the reference to the "blue piece of paper," see Jones, 3-4; for Acheson's understanding of the meaning of the piece of paper, see Acheson's *Present at the Creation*, 217 ff.; for Acheson's background, see Yergin, 276-281, and Gardner, 202-205, and for the quotations about the places of Acheson's childhood, see Acheson, *Morning and Noon*, 1 ff.; for Acheson's quotation about the pilgrimage to choose what is good, see Gardner, 204; for his remark about always being conservative, see his biographical sketch in *Current Biography*; for his remark on the judgment of nature upon error, see *Morning and Noon*, 219; for the need for alertness, Yergin, 279; for the monstrous evil in the world, Gardner, 205; for the task to create half a world, Acheson's prefatory note to *Present*; for his gathering of his staff, *Present*, 218-219.

2. THE PRESIDENT

For Truman in general, I have relied on Donovan; for the story about Truman's middle initial, see Donovan, 9; much of the subsequent material can be found in many sources, including Jonathan Daniels, Margaret Truman's book about her father, *Current Biography*, and my own book *Meeting at Potsdam;* the quotation about the "lunatic fringe" comes from Donovan, 27, about Truman thinking he was not big enough for the presidency from Donovan, 15, the story about making the appointment "just now" from Donovan, 15; for observations on Harriman and the Molotov meeting, see Yergin, 75 ff.; I have kept the quote from Truman about "carry out your agreements" because it seems to capture the gist of the encounter (and Truman, in his memoirs, says he said it), although Donovan says that Bohlen (who was there taking notes) told him that Truman said no such thing. Donovan is probably reliable as usual. Acheson says (*Present,* 136), "On most occasions Mr. Truman's report of his bark vastly exaggerated it." For the quote about Truman liking to make up his mind in advance of thinking, see Donovan, 24; for the solution of fourteen problems, Donovan, 20; for Rayburn's advice, Donovan, 20; for the unusual number of military men appointed to traditionally civilian jobs, Murphy, 305; for Acheson going to the station to meet Truman, Yergin, 278; for the Forrestal-Clifford meeting, Forrestal, 335 ff.

3. THE OVAL ROOM

For Acheson's account of the meeting, see *Present,* 219 ff.; for Truman's account, see his memoirs, II, 103 ff.; for observations on Marshall, see Yergin, 261-263; for Marshall's remark that he has no feelings except those for Mrs. Marshall, see Acheson's *Sketches from Life,* 154; for Marshall's early childhood, see *Education of a General,* 20 ff.; for his later life, see *Education,* 80 ff.; for his life in Quarters Number 1, see *Annals of an Army Wife,* 58 ff., and *End of an Era,* 22 ff; for Marshall on sentiment, *Annals,* 110; for Marshall's failure to impress the congressmen, Jones, 138-139; Acheson resumes the narrative on 219 ff.; see also Jones, 140-142, and Yergin, 281-283, for subsequent quotations; for Vandenberg, see *Current Biography;* for the Vandenberg Amendment, see Acheson's *Sketches,* 123 ff., and for Vandenberg's remark ("if you will say that to the Congress . . ."), see Acheson's *Present,* 219; for Acheson's remark about briefing the press, see Jones, 144; for Baldwin's quote, see Gardner, 219.

4. THE DOCTRINE

For Acheson's briefing of his aides, see Jones, 145 ff; see also Freeland, 97-100; for the meeting on March 4, see Acheson's *Present,* 221; for Truman's comment on the speech, see his memoirs, II, 105; for the Clifford and Acheson quotations, see Jones, 156 and 159; for the controversy over the harshness of the speech, see Donovan, 282; for Vandenberg, the *Times,* and the Eaton quotes that follow, see Jones, 163, 164, and 169; for a description of the President's appearance in Congress, see Jones, 17, 168-170, Acheson's

Present, 221-223, and *Life* magazine of 3/24/47, 40 ff.; for the reactions to the speech, see Gardner, 221, and Freeland, 100.

5. THE COMPETITION

For general observations on the Marshall-Stalin meeting, see Yergin, 297 ff., Sulzberger, 347, and *Life* magazine of 3/31/47, 29 ff.; for the situation in Russia after the war, see Yergin, 228 ff., and Gimbel, 179 ff.; for the Russian-French relationship, see Werth, 360 ff.; for the details of the limousine arriving at the Kremlin, see Smith, 48-49 and 210-212; for Stalin in general, I have relied on Ulam; for Stalin's postwar military position, see Evangelista's "Stalin's Postwar Army Reappraised"; for Laqueur's observations, see Laqueur, 67 ff.; for the conversations between Marshall and Stalin, see FRUS II, 337 ff., and Smith, 51; for the party at the end, see Smith, 227 ff.; for the *Pravda* quotation, see Yergin, 300; for Marshall's speech, see Jones, 223; for the conclusions of one of Marshall's advisers, see Yergin, 301; for Bidault's observations, see Bidault, 145.

6. THE HOME FRONT

For Wallace, see Blum, *The Price of Vision, passim,* and Donovan, 219 ff.; for Taft, see *Prophets on the Right,* 153 ff.; for HUAC, see Freeland, 117 ff.; for Truman on parlor pinks, see Donovan, 293; for Clark's activities, see Freeland, 146 ff.; for Herbert

Hoover's quote, see LaFeber's *Origins of the Cold War,* 164.

7. A CHANGE OF TACTICS

For Churchill's appeal to America, see *Life* magazine of 4/14/47, 106 ff.; for Luce on the American Century, see LaFeber, 27 ff.; for congressional resentment, see Gardner, 220 ff., Ambrose, 151-152, Jones, 171, Acheson, 223-225, Freeland, 100; and for Francis Case, see Freeland, 87; for the Kindleberger memo, see 840.50 Recovery/7-2248, in FRUS III, 242-243; for the men at State looking over other area studies, see Jones, 130 ff., as well as FRUS III, 198; for the Ad Hoc Committee, see especially SWNCC Files, series 360, in FRUS III, 204 ff.; for the understanding of Roosevelt's economic advisers, see Freeland, 17 ff.; for Clayton, see Gardner, 113 ff., and *Current Biography;* for Clayton's remark "let us admit right off," see Freeland, 17.

8. THE POLICY

For Kennan's childhood, see Kennan's memoirs, 5 ff.; for his troubles with ulcers, see Yergin, 27; for the long cable, see Kennan's memoirs, 293 and 550; versions of "The Sources of Soviet Conduct" appeared in several places, including *Life* of 7/28/47, 53, from which this passage is quoted. Kennan's letter to Forrestal (of 9/29/47) is in the Marshall Library; Kennan's remark about the impact of the Moscow cable on his life is in his memoirs, 295, and the quotation of Marshall's advice to avoid trivia, 325-326; Savage's remarks are from his interview in the Marshall Library; Kennan's manner of speaking and correcting himself comes from the interview of Weir Adams in the Marshall Library; the Planning Staff summary is from a Planning Staff paper, PPS/ 4 of 7/23/47 in the Marshall Library; the subsequent quotation is from a PPS paper of 5/23/47; Kennan's observation about the psychological value of the Marshall Plan is contained in a letter to Marshall of 6/6/47, in Lot 64D563, Box 70042, at the Marshall Library; the conclusion of the Ad Hoc Committee is in FRUS III, 217, and Kennan's observations about Britain are in FRUS III, 404; the note about Russian satellites is in the PPS paper of 5/23/47; the concluding quotation is from Caesar's *Conquest of Gaul,* translated by S. A. Handford, published in 1980 in London, p. 260.

9. THE SPEECH

For Strout, see TRB, 50; for Acheson's speech, see Jones, 274 ff., and Acheson, *Present,* 227; for Acheson's conversation with Truman, see Acheson's Princeton Seminars in the Truman Library; for Acheson's speech, see Jones, 274 ff.; for Acheson's remarks to Reston, see Miall, 4, in the Truman Library; for Acheson's remarks about Barkley, see his Princeton Seminars; for the instruction to Jones to work up a speech that would "hit the same line," see Jones, 244; for Clayton's lunch at the

Metropolitan Club, see the Price interview of Nitze; for Clayton's memo, see 840.50 Recovery/5-2747; for the Hummelsine anecdote, see Jones, 246-255; for Marshall and Bohlen, see Acheson's *Present,* 232, and the Price interview of Bohlen; for reaction to Acheson's speech, see Freeland, 183 ff., the Price interview of Marshall, and Jones, 255; for Marshall's remarks about McCormick, see the Price interview and also the Pogue interview; for the Reston *Times* story, see Price's interview of Reston; for Bohlen's remark, see Price's interview; for the observation that Truman called a press conference to deflect attention from Marshall, see Freeland, 183; for the Acheson lunch, see the Miall interview; for Acheson's remarks at the lunch, see his Princeton Seminars; for his taking credit, see *Present,* 228-229; for the Wigan-Miall conversation, see the Miall transcript; for Marshall's speech, see the text in LaFeber, 157 ff.

10. LONDON

For Bevin's reminiscence, see Nicholls, 572; for Strang, see Strang, 288 ff; for Diana Cooper's observations on Bevin, see her memoirs, 206; for Bevin's youth, see Don Cook, 5, and Acheson's *Sketches,* 2 ff.; for the court scene, see Acheson's *Sketches,* 5 ff.; about Bevin's penmanship, see Strang, 294, and for the subsequent observations on Bevin, Duff Cooper, 360 ff.; for Bevin saying "look 'ere" to Strang, see Acheson's *Sketches,* 2-3;

for Bevin's relationship with Attlee, see Cadogan's diaries, 776-778, Cook, 18-19, and Attlee's *Prime Minister Remembers,* 149 ff.; for Bevin's cable to Inverchapel, see 840.00/6-1447 in FRUS III, 253; for Bidault's reaction, see 840.00/6-1647: Telegram, in FRUS III, 255.

11. PARIS

For the quote at the end of the first paragraph, see the Price interview of Denny Marris; for the account of Bevin's meeting with his aides, see FO 371/62402; for Clayton on Ramadier, see Garwood, 29; for the quote on de Gaulle, see Sulzberger, 356; for the influence of Communists within the French government, see 851.50/7-1147, in FRUS III, 719; for the anecdote about correcting the present situation, see Yergin, 312, and FRUS III, 894; for McCloy's announcement of a loan, see Yergin, 312; for Bidault, see *Current Biography* and Sulzberger, 347; for the Bevin-Ramadier-Bidault conversation, see FO 371/62400; for newspaper reactions, see 840.00 Recovery/6-1847; for the concerns about how the French would handle an invitation to Russia, see FO 371/62402; for Bevin's comments on the invitation, see FO 371/62400-9816; for Bevin talking at the end, see Duff Cooper, 375.

12. FRIENDLY AID

For the Kennan-Bohlen call on the British Embassy, see FO 371/62401-9936; for Clayton's London conversations, see 840.50 Recovery/7-147, in FRUS III, 284 ff.; for Bevin's thoughts on being considered on a special basis, see FRUS III, 270; on the Ruhr, see FO 371/62405-10091; for Wood's remarks, see FRUS III, 274; for the British concluding memo, see FRUS III, 288.

13. EXIT MOLOTOV

In general, see the *French Yellow Book* for the meetings with Molotov and, especially, for the French proposals put to Molotov; see also FRUS III, 296-308, and for the British records of conversations, see FO 371/62403-10304, 62404-10311 and 62405-10091; Harriman's remarks on Molotov's dullness occurred in the Price interview of 10/1/52; Kennan's remarks occurred in the Price interview of 2/19/53; the concluding Marshall cable is 840.50 Recovery/7-347: Telegram, and the marginal notation by the President is remarked in a footnote in FRUS III, 308.

14. THE FRENCH THREAT

Bidault's conversations with Clayton are in 840.50 Recovery, a cable from Paris of 7/11/47.

15. THE DIPLOMATS

For Sir Oliver Franks, see *Current Biography* and a profile in *The Times* of London of 7/6/82; for Duff Cooper, see *Dictionary of National Biography*, in which, in particular, Nicholson's quote is found; for Douglas, see *Current Biography,* and for Clayton's remarks about Douglas's habits, see Clayton's interview with Garwood; for Caffery, see *Current Biography,* and for Caffery's style, too, see the Garwood interview of Clayton; on the question of inviting foreign ministers, see FO 371/62406 and 62407; for Spaak, see *Current Biography;* for the Count Sforza story, see FO 371/62406, 62409, and 62413; for the telegrams going out to Eastern European countries, see FO 371/62407; for the Budapest story, see cable #1171 from Budapest in 840.50 Recovery, 7/11/47; for Czechoslovakia, see cable #905 from Prague in 840.50 Recovery, 7/15/47; for Stalin's encounter with Gottwald, see Werth, 267-268; for the conclusion of the Czechoslovakia story, see FO 371/62410, 62411, and 840.50 Recovery/7-1547; for the protocol of the opening meeting, see FO 371/ 62411 and 62568; for Inverchapel's remark on Alphand, see FO 371/68869.

16. DIPLOMACY

For the opening paragraphs, see FO 371/62563 and 62414, and FRUS III, 335-340 *passim;* for the Greek agreement with the Turkish remark and the following exchange, see FO 371/62568; for Caffery's cable home, see 840.50 Recovery/7-2047: Telegram; for Balfour's note to Marshall, see 840.50 Recovery/7-1647; for the letter from Sir Roger

Stevens, I am indebted to Mrs. Stevens for showing it to me from her personal correspondence; for the Board of Trade meeting with other officials, see FO 371/62563; for van der Beugel's remarks, see his interview in the Truman Library; for the British statement that their interests are against direct comparison of consumption levels, see FO 371/62414; for the material on the "spending spree," see 840.50 Recovery/7-2047: Telegram; for Léon Blum, see the report in 840.50 Recovery/7-2047; for the stingy lunch, see the Ivan White interview in the Truman Library Oral History Collections; for the story about Ramadier in the waiting room, see Werth, *France,* 364; for Monnet's dinner with Clayton, see cable #3026 in 840.50 Recovery/7-3047; for Harriman's background, see *Current Biography* and my own book *Meeting at Potsdam;* for Harriman's conversation with Bidault, see 840.50 Recovery/7-2147; for Spaak's remark about the French, see cable #1133 in 840.50 Recovery/7-1847; for Hirschfeld, see FO 371/62568 and 62598; for the story about Monsignor Montini, see cable #1996 in 840.50 Recovery/7-1847 and FO 371/62415.

17. MORE FRIENDLY AID

Kennan's memo is in FRUS III, 335 ff.; for the meeting at Old State offices, see minutes of Committee on ERP for 7/31/47 in the Marshall Library; for Nitze's mission to Paris, see FRUS III, 345-360.

18. THE WAR AGAINST THE ARMY

For the opening paragraphs, see Sapp's dissertation, 211 ff.; for Lovett, see *Current Biography;* for Lovett's memo to Marshall, see FRUS II, 1014 ff.; for Marshall's remarks to Royall, see the footnote on p. 1025 of FRUS II; for Murphy on Clay, see 862.60/8-947: Telegram; for Clay, see *Current Biography* and Yergin, 373 ff.; Marshall's response to Clay's threatened resignation is in a footnote on p. 1027 of FRUS II; the Lovett cable to Caffery and Clayton is in 840.50 Recovery/8-1447: Telegram.

19. SKIRMISH IN THE FOREIGN SERVICE

In general, see FRUS III, 364 ff.; for Franks' exchanges with the Americans, see 840.50 Recovery/8-2047: Telegram; for the Lovett cabled reprimand, see 840.50 Recovery/8-1847: Telegram; for the Douglas cable, 840.50 Recovery/8-2147: Telegram; for Kennan's meeting, 840.50 Recovery/8-2247. For Lovett's cable to Marshall, see 840.50 Recovery/8-2447: Telegram; for Marshall's reply, 840.50 Recovery/8-2547; for Lovett's cable to Europe, 840.50 Recovery/8-2247: Telegram; for Caffery's reply, 840.50 Recovery/8-2647: Telegram; for Clayton, 840.50 Recovery/8-2547: Telegram. For Lovett's cable to Marshall, see 840.50 Recovery/8-2447: Telegram; for Marshall's reply, 840.50 Recovery/8-2547; for Lovett's cable to Europe, 840.50 Recovery/8-2247: Telegram; for Caffery's reply, 840.50 Recovery/8-2647: Telegram; for Clayton, 840.50 Recovery/8-2547: Telegram.

20. AMERICANS IN PARIS

For the observation that many American groups went to Paris, see the Ivan White interview; for the Herter committee, see Price's interview of Philip Watts of 3/11/53; for the sense of having loosed a boulder from a cliff, see Kennan's memoirs, 356; for the meetings of Kennan and Bonesteel in Paris, see 840.50 Recovery/8-3147: Telegram; for Kennan at the dinner parties, see FO 371/62570-11702; for Kennan's conclusions, see his report from the PPS files in FRUS III, 397 ff.

21. HARDBALL

For Caffery's cable, see 840.50 Recovery/9-547: Telegram; for Lovett's cable to "certain American diplomatic officers," see 840.50 Recovery/9-747: Circular Telegram; for Bevin's complaints, see 840.50 Recovery/9-947: Telegram; for the Americans pointing out "weaknesses" in the report, see 840.50 Recovery/9-1147: Telegram; for Hall-Patch's reaction, see FO 371/62570-11702; for the Executive Committee members' replies to the Americans, see 840.50 Recovery/9-1147: Telegram; for the cable from Marshall to Douglas, see 840.50 Recovery/9-947: Telegram; for Clayton, Caffery, and Douglas asking earlier for interim aid, see FRUS III, 428-433 *passim;* for the Europeans' change of heart, see FO 371/62597 and 62569; for Bevin's being "disturbed," see 840.50 Recovery/9-1247: Telegram; for Caffery's cable of 9/17/47, see 840.50 Recovery/9-1747: Telegram; for the opinion "held by a few," see 840.50 Recovery/9-1547: Telegram; for the Douglas cable to Marshall and Lovett, see 840.50 Recovery/9-1747: Telegram; for the Hammarskjold story, see Caffery's cable of 9/17, cited above; see the same cable for Caffery's remarks to the assembled Europeans; for Lovett's cable "for your info," see 840.50 Recovery/9-2247: Telegram.

22. THE MOLOTOV PLAN

In general, see Ulam's *Stalin,* 660 ff., Halle, 150 ff., Yergin, 325 ff., Djilas, 129 ff., and Fontaine, 333 ff.; for Zhdanov's speech, see Ulam's *Titoism,* 50 ff.; for Kardelj, see Ulam's *Titoism,* 53 ff.; for Duclos, see Yergin, 326 ff.; for the Czech minister's bitterness over the grain deal, see Yergin, 345 ff.

23. WASHINGTON

For knowledge of the plan, see Yergin, 326-328, and Donovan, 136-137; for congressmen's reactions to Truman, see Yergin, 328-329; for Acheson's committee work, see Freeland, 252-259; for the Krug committee, see FRUS III, 457; for Attorney General Clark, see Yergin, 204-224, Donovan, 293 ff., Forrestal, 229-240; for the Office of Education, see Freeland, 230 ff.; for the Freedom Train, see Monaghan, *passim,* and Freeland, 233 ff.; for the Security Advisory Board, see Freeland, 236 ff.; for the CIA, see Donovan, 305-311; for the quote about the Attorney General's list, see Freeland, 237; for HUAC, see Bentley, 139-180 *passim,* and Goodman, 207 ff.

24. SELLING CONGRESS

For Inverchapel's cable, see FO 371/62671 XC/A 13016; for his later cable, see the same file; for the British negotiators' response, see the same file; for Franks stepping in, see FO 371/62673 XC/A 13016; for the story of the Kansas farmer, see Franks' report of 12/22/47 in FO 371/62749 XC/A 013255; for the first plenary meeting of delegates, see FO 371/62672 XC/A 13016; for Franks' conversation with Lovett, see FRUS III, 446 ff.; for Franks' remark about a "startling effect," see his report of 12/22 cited above; for Franks' notes about a "difficult first three weeks," see FO 371/62567-11702; for the Bidault conversations, see FRUS III, 786 ff.; for the cables from Caffery and Douglas, see 800.48 FAA/12-247; for Caffery's cable from France, see 851.00/12-347: Telegram; for the plight of Italy, see 865.51/9-1147 and 840.50 Recovery/9-1647; for Tarchiani's talk with Lovett's aides, see 865.51/9-1647; for Kennan's memo on Italy, see the Executive Secretariat Files in FRUS III, 976 ff; for other observations on the Communists in Europe, see Westerfield, 262-263;

for the Mendès-France quote, see Werth, *France,* 351; for the Allen Dulles story, see FO 371/62674 XC/A 13016; for what to expect from congressional debate, see FO 371/62747 XC/A 013255; for Busby's remark, see Freeland, 196; for Vandenberg's remark, see Vandenberg, 380; for the last sentence, see FO 371/62672, Inverchapel's cable #5458.

25. *PASSAGE*

Vandenberg's diary entries are on pp. 380-389; the remark that things were one dimension too big comes from the Price interview of Stein; the Acheson committee ghost-writing chores are mentioned in Acheson, *Present,* 241; the note about the Cotton Council and other testimony is in Freeland, 246-292 *passim;* Dean Rusk's remark is quoted in Yergin, 278; Acheson's abrupt remark to a congressman is in the Stein interview; Calvin Hoover's testimony is quoted in Gimbel, 272; for Clayton's quote about Europe being overrun by communism, see Gardner, 136; for "Doctrinaire Willy," see Yergin, 321; for the letter to Chan Gurney, see Forrestal, 349 ff.; for Marshall's words to Congress, see Freeland, 255; for the administration moving from argument to argument, see Gimbel, 278-279; for Vandenberg's instructions to "leave those words in," see Vandenberg, 389; for public opinion polls, see Freeland, 262; for the fall of the Czechoslovakian government, see Yergin, 346-357, and Donovan, 358-359; for the Clay cable, see Forrestal, 387; for Forrestal's eagerness to capitalize on the fall of Czechoslovakia, see Forrestal, 385; for Truman's letter to his daughter, see Yergin, 350; for "whispers of war," see Freeland, 269 ff.; for the Clifford election strategy, see Yergin, 351-353, and Freeland, 192; for Marshall's concern about playing with fire, see Forrestal, 373; for Truman's speech, see Freeland, 271, and Yergin, 354; for the final quote from the *Washington Post,* see Freeland, 275.

26. THE MARSHALL PLAN IN ACTION

For the first shipments, see White, 58-59, and *The New York Times,* 4/14/48, a page-one story; for the workers in Birmingham, see *Time* magazine of 4/11/49; for Kennan's remark about the psychological effect, see Price's Kennan interview of 2/19/53; for the remark that Acheson could not be confirmed, see Price's Hoffman interview of 1/28/53; for Hoffman's remark about being the least obnoxious Republican, see the same interview; for Hoffman's background, see *Current Biography* and his *New York Times* obituary of 10/9/74; for the Georges Villiers quote, see *Time,* cited above; for the Hotel Talleyrand, see White, 60; for Zellerbach's impolite remark, see *Time,* cited above; for the young Americans helping Harriman, see White, 359; for the American customs abroad, see White, 364 ff.; for the remark about the way to handle a famine,

White, 62; for the American expert, White, 359; for the unexpressed indignity, White, 372; for the achievements of the Marshall Plan, White, *passim,* and, more especially, the *Marshall Plan News,* the first five issues, *passim;* for specifics of French recovery, see *American Federationist* magazine of March 1949, 10 ff.; for the note on French tractors, see the speech by Barry Bingham to the American Society of Newspaper Editors on 4/22/50; for the impact of the Marshall Plan on the Italian elections, see *Current History* of November 1948 (275), and *The New York Times,* 4/25/48; for general statistics on the Italian economy, see Laqueur, 220 ff.; for notes about luxury cars and tightened bank credit, see *Current History,* cited above; for the impact on England, see *Time,* cited above; for the remarks by Servan-Schreiber and Spaak, see Werth, *France,* 429; for statistics on France, see Laqueur, 212 ff.; White's remarks about French politics are on p. 90 of his book; for Bidault, see his *New York Times* obituary of 1/28/83; for Adenauer and his appearances before the high commissioners, see White, 149 ff.; for the remark about Adenauer and McCloy, see Sulzberger, 893; for the statistics on Germany, see Laqueur, 216 ff.; for the question of who had won and who had lost the war, see White, 154; for the John Platts-Mills story, see *The New York Times,* 5/14/48; for the complaints of left-wing politicians in Italy, see the *New Statesman* of 10/28/50; for the "logistical approach" to recovery, see White, 69; for others joining the protests against American aid, see *The Nation* of 8/7/48; Servan-Schreiber's remark about the new West is quoted in Gardner, 137; the outbreak of the Korean War and its implications for the Marshall Plan are in Freeland, 320; the conversation between Bevin and Marshall is noted in Donovan, 359 ff.

BIBLIOGRAPHY

PRINCIPAL ARCHIVES

Churchill College, Cambridge, England

Clement Attlee papers

Columbia University, Oral History Collection

Ellen Garwood interview of her father, Will Clayton

Council on Foreign Relations, New York

Council on Foreign Relations papers

Marshall Library, Lexington, Va.

Interviews, of September 1970, with

Ware Adams

Charles Bohlen

Benjamin Cohen

Elbridge Durbrow

H. Freeman Matthews

Paul H. Nitze

Carleton Savage

Interview of General Marshall by Forrest C. Pogue

Policy Planning Staff papers and minutes of meetings

National Archives, Washington, D.C.

State Department Decimal Files

Princeton University, Princeton, N.J.

James Forrestal diary

George F. Kennan papers

Public Record Office, London, England

Foreign Office and cabinet papers

Harry S Truman Library, Independence, Mo.

Dean Acheson papers

William Clayton papers

Clark Clifford files and papers

Jonathan Daniels papers

George Elsey files and papers

Ellen Clayton Garwood papers

Joseph M. Jones papers

Charles Murphy papers

Edwin G. Nourse papers

President's Committee on Foreign Aid papers

Harry B. Price notes and interviews of

Dean Acheson

Richard Birnberg

Charles E. Bohlen

General Lucius D. Clay

Thomas K. Finletter

W. Averell Harriman

Dr. H. M. Hirschfeld

Paul G. Hoffman

Sam van Hyning

George F. Kennan

Denny Marris

George C. Marshall

Sol Ozer

James Reston

Harold Stein

Philip Watts

Samuel Rosenman papers

Charles Ross papers

Walter S. Salant papers

John W. Snyder papers

Steven Spingarn papers

John Steelman papers

Harry S Truman papers:

Confidential files

Official file

President's secretary's file

Truman Library Oral History Collections:

Dean Acheson (Princeton Seminars)

Charles E. Bohlen

David K. E. Bruce

General Lucius D. Clay

Clark M. Clifford

Matthew J. Connelly

Thomas Finletter

Sir Edmund Hall-Patch

W. Averell Harriman

Loy Henderson

John D. Hickerson

Charles Kindleberger

George C. Marshall

H. Freeman Matthews

Leonard Miall

Charles Murphy

Edwin G. Nourse

James Reston

James Riddleberger

Samuel I. Rosenman

John W. Snyder

Willard L. Thorp

E. H. van der Beugel

Ivan B. White

University College, Oxford, England

Clement Attlee papers

DOCUMENTS

Committee of European Economic Development, *Report: July-September, 1947*. London, 1947.

French Government, *French Yellow Book,* Meetings of June 27-July 3, 1947. London, 1947.

Office of Information, ECA, *Marshall Plan News.* Washington, D.C., 1948.

United Nations, Department of Economic Affairs, *Economic Report: Salient Features of the World Economic Situation 1945-47.* New York, 1948.

United Nations, Economic Commission for Europe, A *Survey of the Economic Situation and Prospects of Europe.* Geneva, 1948.

U.S. Congress, *Congressional Record.*

U.S. Congress, Senate, *Foreign Relief Aid: 1947, Hearings Held in Executive Session before the Senate Committee on Foreign Relations on S. 1774.* 80th Congress, 1st session, 1947.

U.S. Congress, Senate, *Foreign Relief Assistance Act of 1948, Hearings Held in Executive Session.* 80th Congress, 2nd Session, 1948.

U.S. Department of State, *Foreign Relations of the United States.*

ESSAYS AND DISSERTATIONS

Evangelista, Matthew A., "Stalin's Postwar Army Reappraised." *International Security,* VII, 3 (Winter 1982/83).

Maier, Charles S. "Revisionism and the Interpretation of Cold War Origins," in *Perspectives in American History,* Vol. IV. Cambridge, Mass., 1970.

Miscomble, Wilson Douglas. *George F. Kennan, The Policy Planning Staff.* Ph.D. dissertation, University of Notre Dame, 1980.

Pritchard, Ross J. *Will Clayton: A Study of Business-Statesmanship in the Formulation of United States Economic Foreign Policy.* Ph.D. dissertation, Fletcher School of Law and Diplomacy, 1956.

Sapp, Steven Paul. *The United States, France, and the Cold War.* Ph.D. dissertation, Kent State University, 1978.

BOOKS

Acheson, Dean. *Morning and Noon.* Boston, 1965.

_____. *Present at the Creation.* New York, 1970.

_____. *Sketches from Life.* New York, 1960.

Adenauer, Konrad. *Memoirs 1945-1953.* Trans, by Beate Ruhm von Oppen. Chicago, 1965.

Ambrose, Stephen E. *Rise to Globalism.* London, 1971.

Arkes, Hadley. *Bureaucracy, the Marshall Plan and the National Interest.* Princeton, 1972.

Bentley, Eric. *Thirty Years of Treason.* New York, 1971.

Bidault, Georges. *Resistance: The Political Autobiography.* Trans, by Marianne Sinclair. New York, 1965.

Blum, John Morton, ed. *The Price of Vision: The Diary of Henry A. Wallace.* Boston, 1973.

Bohlen, Charles. *Witness to History, 1929-69.* New York, 1973.

Bullock, Alan. *Life and Times of Ernest Bevin.* London, 1960.

Byrnes, James F. *Speaking Frankly.* New York, 1947.

Caute, David. *The Great Fear.* New York, 1978.

Clay, Lucius D. *Decision in Germany.* Garden City, N.Y., 1950.

Cochran, Bert. *Harry Truman and the Crisis Presidency.* New York, 1973.

Cook, Don. *Ten Men and History.* Garden City, N.Y., 1981.

Cooper, A. Duff. *Old Men Forget.* London, 1953.

Cooper, Diana. *Trumpets from the Steep.* London, 1956.

Deutscher, Isaac. *Stalin: A Political Biography.* Rev. ed. London, 1966.

Divine, Robert. *Foreign Policy and U.S. Presidential Elections.* New York, 1974.

Dobney, Frederick J., ed. *Selected Papers of Will Clayton.* Baltimore, 1971.

Elliott, William Y., ed. *The Political Economy of American Foreign Policy.* New York, 1955.

Evans, Trevor. *Bevin.* London, 1946.

Fleming, D. W. *The Cold War and Its Origins, 1917-1960.* 2 vols. Garden City, N.Y., 1961.

Fontaine, André. *History of the Cold War.* Trans, by D. D. Paige. New York, 1968.

Freeland, Richard M. *The Truman Doctrine and the Origins of McCarthy ism.* New York, 1972.

Frye, William. *Marshall, Citizen Soldier.* New York, 1947.

Gallup, George. *The Gallup Poll: Public Opinion 1935-1971.* Vol. 1. New York, 1972.

Gardner, Lloyd C. *Architects of Illusion.* Chicago, 1972.

Gardner, Richard N. *Sterling Dollar Diplomacy.* Rev. ed. New York, 1969.

Garwood, Ellen Clayton. *Will Clayton: A Short Biography.* Austin, 1958.

Gimbel, John. *The American Occupation of Germany.* Stanford, 1968.

———. *The Origins of the Marshall Plan.* Stanford, 1976.

Goldman, Eric F. *The Crucial Decade-and After: America 1945-1960.* New York, 1960.

Goodman, Walter. *The Committee.* New York, 1968.

Goulden, Joseph C. *The Best Years, 1945-1950.* New York, 1976.

Halle, Louis J. *The Cold War as History.* New York, 1967.

Hansen, Alvin H. *The Postwar American Economy.* New York, 1964.

Hartmann, Susan. *The Marshall Plan.* Columbus Ohio, 1968.

———. *Truman and the 80th Congress.* New York, 1971.

Hickman, Warren. *Genesis of the European Recovery Program.* Geneva, 1949.

Hughes, H. Stuart. *The United States and Italy.* Cambridge, Mass. 1965.

Jones, Joseph M. *The Fifteen Weeks.* New York, 1964.

Kennan, George. *Memoirs 1925-50.* Boston, 1967.

_____. *Russia and the West Under Lenin and Stalin.* New York, 1961.

Kolko, Gabriel. *The Politics of War.* London, 1968.

_____. *The Roots of American Foreign Policy.* Boston, 1969.

Kolko, Joyce, and Gabriel Kolko. *The Limits of Power.* New York, 1972.

Kousoulas, D. George. *Revolution and Defeat: The Story of the Greek Communist Party.* London, 1965.

Krock, Arthur. *Memoirs: Sixty Years on the Firing Line.* New York, 1968.

Kuklick, Bruce. *American Foreign Policy and the Division of Germany.* Ithaca, N.Y., 1972.

LaFeber, Walter. *The New Empire.* Ithaca, N.Y., 1963.

_____. *The Origins of the Cold War, 1941-1947.* New York, 1971.

Latham, Earl. *The Communist Controversy in Washington.* Cambridge, Mass., 1966.

Lippmann, Walter. *The Cold War.* Ronald Steele, ed. New York, 1972.

MacColl, René. *Deadline and Dateline.* London, 1956.

Markel, Lester. *Public Opinion and Foreign Policy.* New York, 1949.

Marshall, Katherine Tupper. *Together.* New York, 1946.

Mayer, Herbert Carleton. *German Recovery and the Marshall Plan.* New York, 1969.

Mayne Richard. *The Recovery of Europe 1945-73.* Rev. ed. New York, 1973.

McLellan, David S. *Dean Acheson: The State Department Years.* New York, 1976.

Miller, Merle. *Plain Speaking.* New York, 1973.

Millis, Walter, ed. *The Forrestal Diaries.* New York, 1951.

Monaghan, Frank. *Heritage of Freedom.* Princeton, 1948.

Monnet, Jean. *Memoirs.* New York, 1977.

Murphy, Robert. *Diplomat Among Warriors.* New York, 1965.

Nixon, Richard. *Six Crises.* New York, 1962.

Nourse, Edwin G. *Economics in the Public Service.* New York, 1953.

O'Ballance, Edgar. *The Greek Civil War, 1944-49.* New York, 1966.

Osgood, Robert E. *NATO: The Entangling Alliance.* Chicago, 1962.

Patterson, James T. *Mr. Republican: A Biography of Robert A. Taft.* Boston, 1972.

Penrose, E. F. *Economic Planning for Peace.* Princeton, 1953.

Phillips, Cabell. *The Truman Presidency.* New York, 1966.

Pogue, Forrest C. *Education of a General.* New York, 1963.

Ponomaryov, B., A. Gromyko, and V. Khvostov, eds. *History of Soviet Foreign Policy 1945-70.* Moscow, 1974.

Price, Harry Bayard. *The Marshall Plan and Its Meaning.* Ithaca, N.Y., 1955.

Roberts, Henry. *Eastern Europe: Politics, Revolution and Diplomacy.* New York, 1970.

Salera, Virgil. *Multinational Business.* Boston, 1969.

Schurmann, Franz. *The Logic of World Power.* New York, 1974.

Sherwin, Martin. *A World Destroyed.* New York, 1975.

Smith, Gaddis. *Dean Acheson,* Vol. 16, *The American Secretaries of State and Their Diplomacy,* ed. Robert Ferrell. New York, 1972.

Smith, Jean Edward, ed. *The Papers of General Lucius D. Clay, Germany 1945-49.* 2 vols. Bloomington, Ind., 1974.

Smith, Walter Bedell. *My Three Years in Moscow.* Philadelphia, 1950.

Spaak, Paul Henri. *The Continuing Battle.* Trans, by Henry Fox. Boston, 1972.

Spanier, John W. *American Foreign Policy Since World War II.* 3rd ed. New York, 1968.

Steele, Ronald. *Imperialists and Other Heroes: A Chronicle of the American Empire.* New York, 1971.

Strang, Lord. *Home and Abroad.* London, 1956.

Strout, Richard L. *TRB.* New York, 1978.

Sulzberger, C. L. A *Long Row of Candles.* New York, 1969.

Truman, Harry S. *Memoirs: Year of Decisions.* Garden City, N.Y., 1955.

_____. *Memoirs: Years of Trial and Hope.* Garden City, N.Y., 1956.

Truman, Margaret. *Harry S. Truman.* New York, 1973.

Ulam, Adam B. *Stalin: The Man and His Era.* New York, 1973.

_____. *Titoism and the Cominform.* Cambridge, Mass., 1952.

Vandenberg, Arthur, Jr., ed. *The Private Papers of Senator Vandenberg.* Boston, 1972.

van der Beugel, Ernst. *From Marshall Aid to Atlantic Partnership.* New York, 1966.

Walton, Richard J. *Henry Wallace, Harry Truman, and the Cold War.* New York, 1976.

Werth, Alexander. *France, 1940-1955.* New York, 1956.

Westerfield, H. Bradford. *Foreign Policy and Party Politics.* New Haven, 1955.

Wheeler-Bennett, Sir John, and Anthony Nicholls. *The Semblance of Peace.* New York, 1972.

White, Theodore H. *Fire in the Ashes.* New York, 1953.

Wilkins, Mira. *The Maturing of the Multinational Enterprise.* Cambridge, Mass., 1974.

Williams, Francis. A *Prime Minister Remembers: The War and Post-War Memoirs of the Rt. Hon. Earl Attlee.* London, 1961.

_____. *Ernest Bevin: Portrait of a Great Englishman.* London, 1952.

Williams, William A. *The Tragedy of American Diplomacy.* 2nd ed. New York, 1962.

Winks, Robert W. *The Marshall Plan and the American Economy.* New York, 1960.

Yergin, Daniel. *Shattered Peace.* Boston, 1977.

Made in United States
North Haven, CT
19 May 2022

19356729R00313